Great Recession-Proof?

Shattering the Myth of Canadian Exceptionalism

ALTERNATE
ROUTES

2013

Edited by:
Carlo Fanelli & Bryan Evans

RED QUILL BOOKS

© Red Quill Books Ltd. 2013
Ottawa

www.redquillbooks.com

ISBN 978-1-926958-24-8

∞ ♻

Printed on acid-free paper. The paper used in this book incorporates post-consumer waste and has not been sourced from endangered old growth forests, forests of exceptional conservation value or the Amazon Basin. Red Quill Books subscribes to a one-book-at-a-time manufacturing process that substantially lessens supply chain waste, reduces greenhouse emissions, and conserves valuable natural resources.

Includes bibliographical references.

ISBN 978-1-926958-24-8
Also published as a serial:

"Alternate Routes"
ISSN 1923-7081 (online)

ISSN 0702-8865 (print)

Red Quill Books is an alternative publishing house. Proceeds from the sale of this book will support future critical scholarship.

alternate routes

published since 1977 · a journal of critical social research

Alternate Routes: A Journal of Critical Social Research
Volume 24, 2013

EDITORS: Carlo Fanelli and Bryan Evans
BOOK REVIEW EDITORS: Priscillia Lefebvre and Nicolas Carrier
EDITORIAL BOARD: Nahla Abdo, Pat Armstrong, David Camfield, Nicolas Carrier, Wallace Clement, Simten Cosar, Simon Dalby, Aaron Doyle, Ann Duffy, Bryan Mitchell Evans, Luis Fernandez, Randall Germain, Peter Gose, Alan Hunt, Paul Kellogg, Jacqueline Kennelly, Mark Neocleous, Mi Park, Georgios Papanicolaou, Justin Paulson, Garry Potter, Stephanie Ross, Herman Rosenfeld, George S. Rigakos, Heidi Rimke, Arne Christoph Ruckert, Alan Sears, Mitu Sengupta, Donald Swartz, Ingo Schmidt, Toby Sanger, Janet Lee Siltanen, Susan Jane Spronk, Mark P. Thomas, Rosemary Warskett.

JOURNAL MANDATE

Established in 1977 at the Department of Sociology and Anthropology, Carleton University, Alternate Routes' central mandate has been to create outlets for critical social research and interdisciplinary inquiry. A scholarly peer-reviewed annual, AR works closely with labour and social justice activists to promote the publication of non-traditional, provocative and radical analyses that may not find a forum in conventional academic venues. AR seeks to be a public academic journal and encourages submissions that advance or challenge theoretical, historical and contemporary socio-political, economic and cultural issues. In addition to full-length articles, we welcome review essays sparked by previously published material, interviews, short commentaries, as well as poetry, drawings and photos. AR publishes primarily special-themed issues and therefore requests that submissions be related to the current call for papers. Submissions must be free of racist and sexist language, have limited technical or specialized terms and be written in a style that is accessible to our diverse readership.

4 | Great Recession-Proof?:
Shattering the Myth of Canadian Exceptionalism

Table of Contents

Editorial Introduction

From Great Recession to Great Deception: Reimagining the Roots of the Crisis

—*Carlo Fanelli and Bryan Evans*

On March 23, 2012, *Alternate Routes* in conjunction with Carleton University and Ryerson University's Centre for Labour-Management Relations hosted the conference: *The Global Economic Crisis and Canada: Perception Versus Reality*. The original call for papers which inspired the event and later this issue, stated:

"It is now broadly recognized that the global economic crisis that struck in late 2007 is by far the most significant and wide-ranging since the Depression years of the 1930s. While there have been signs of tepid recovery over the last five years, the International Monetary Fund (2011, p.xv) has recently warned that "[t]he global economy is in a dangerous new phase. Global activity has weakened and become more uneven, confidence has fallen sharply recently, and downside risks are growing...Thus, the structural problems facing recession-hit economies have proven more intractable than expected, and the process of devising and implementing reforms more complicated." Given fears of an ongoing recession, particularly as a result of Europe's sovereign debt crisis and a record level U.S. budget deficit, the global recession that struck in 2007 is by no means over.

"In Canada, however, the economic downturn has been shorter and milder than many of its G7 counterparts. In fact, according to Statistics Canada, while the Canadian economy began contracting in the fourth quarter of 2008 by the third quarter of 2009 the recession had already passed. Indeed, the Great Recession is allegedly no greater than previous slumps such as those in the early 1980s and 1990s as measured by job losses, home sales, bankruptcies, credit availability and consumer spending (Cross, 2011). But numbers rarely, if ever, tell the whole story. Federal, provincial and local governments across the country, regardless of political stripes, are turning to a range of austerity measures that will erode public services and the quality of public sector employment. It is also being demanded that private sector workers take pay and benefit cuts."

Despite official pronouncements suggesting a recovery is well underway, the articles and interviews collected here problematize prevailing characterizations of recession and recovery. Rather than focusing on narrowly economistic measures, contributors challenge standard explanations of the Great Recession drawing attention to the multifaceted socio-political, ethno-racial and gendered dimensions of austerity and retrenchment. Furthermore, instead of glossing over or ignoring the capitalist context that leaves workers dependent on the imperatives of capital, the analyses collected here take seriously the inherently antagonistic class relations that structure our daily lives. The challenge, as we saw it, was to bring together contributors who considered the uneven and often contradictory impacts of recession that stretch across the Canadian political economic landscape. We are confident that the voices presented in this edition of *AR* have made a serious contribution to that objective.

As the 2008 global economic slump made its way to Canada, the initial response by the federal Conservatives to a deteriorating economic climate was one of confusion and denial. In the midst of the 2008 general election P.M. Harper suggested that there were some great buying opportunities in the stock market, while his Finance Minister, Jim Flaherty, insisted that Canada would not run a deficit. Six months later the deficit was estimated to be roughly $50 billion (Laxer, 2009). Despite dubious financial advice and eyebrow-raising budgetary forecasting, the Conservatives have since gone on to win a majority government in 2011. Like their counterparts across the provinces, most notably in Ontario, Alberta, and Nova Scotia —each province having elected a different political party —austerity and attacks against public services and unionized workers has been established as the orthodox policy response. Needless to say, the shape taken by struggles over austerity and the protection of public services may well determine whether (neoliberal) capitalism continues uninterrupted or, alternatively, whether something new and historically unique can capture the public's imagination.

Before introducing the articles presented here, however, we found it necessary to bring attention to what we are calling the Great Deception. It is plain to see that the assault on trade union rights and freedoms, the public provision of social services and working class standards of living are currently under attack and will remain so indefinitely.[1] While austerity has been the buzzword of the last five years, when considered in historical perspective it is clear that

---

1 Parts of this section are drawn from Fanelli, 2012

Canadians have been living with varying degrees of austerity for at least the last three decades (McBride and Shields, 1997; Panitch and Swartz, 2003). In this sense, public services and collective bargaining have been gradually eroded over an otherwise "permanent era of austerity" (Evans and Albo, 2010). The severity of the Great Recession has merely intensified and given impetus to long-term efforts to undermine the public production and delivery of public services and reduce workers' ability to chart a path independent from the vagaries of capital. Indeed, democracy in the workplace, understood as the ability of workers to have a say over how and what gets made, under what conditions and what rewards, are proving increasingly incompatible with the logic of capitalist development. Since the 1980s, there has been a slow but steady downward convergence in working conditions and wages, backed by employer and state efforts to lower working class expectations. These efforts have been in combination with unprecedented amounts of personal affluence among certain groups in the midst of public sector austerity. .

As the Great Recession recedes from public scrutiny in Canada, its aftereffects continue to frame political debate and strain public finances. Despite the public treasury bailing-out corporations, supplying new subsidies, lowering corporate taxes, and increasing state spending in order to counter the recession, the banks and capitalist classes continue to demand public sector austerity. Emphasis has increasingly moved away from a critical investigation into the historical origins and root causes of the recession, excessive executive compensation, and even inquiries into the nature of capitalism to an emphasis on cutting public services and attacking those who produce, deliver and use those services, the poor, the elderly, and beyond. In our view, the redefinition of the crisis as stemming from a bloated and inefficient public sector and unionized workers' wages more broadly, can be understood as nothing less than a Great Deception.

This is not to imply that those who believe that the public sector is wasteful and unproductive are duped or foolish, nor to suggest that the public sector is uniformly a beacon of efficiency (since efficiency itself is a politically loaded phrase that often obscures more than it reveals), but to draw attention to the purposeful attempt to obfuscate, confuse, muddy, mislead and deflect critical inquiry away from a social and economic system —capitalism —that not only caused the crisis but constrains the scope for change. The essays collected here ensure that such a deception does not go unnoticed.

While greater detail is beyond the purview of this short editorial introduction and issue in its entirety, it is our contention that a new historical project that seeks to transcend (neoliberal) capitalism is urgently needed. A strong starting point for such a project — counter to the prevailing orthodoxy — is to expand the scope of the public sector. While the capitalist class bathed in excess in the midst of the crisis, politicians, the media and leading business pundits dogmatically asserted that workers must do more with less, that pensions, healthcare, unemployment insurance and social services were in need of modernization to better fit the new normal of declining working class incomes, increasingly ineffective collective bargaining, and global competition for investment. Honest explanations as to why such social protections were no longer possible were few and far between. The fact that decades of cuts to high-income earners and corporations' taxes had utterly failed to produce any real benefits for the majority of working people continued to elude the economic and political officialdom. Quite paradoxically, decades of neoliberal reforms almost disappeared from the historical record as collective dementia (or deception) shifted the debate away from the origins and causes of the private sector-led Great Recession to a one-sided emphasis on the public sector.

In our view, making the case for an expanded public sector necessarily entails the conversion of spaces formerly understood to be the sacrosanct domain of the private sector. Nationalizing some parts of the economy, from the banking and finance sectors which sustain the institutional power of capital to the goods-producing sectors which create tangible outputs, may open up the possibility for escaping from the cycle of austerity and retrenchment which has long since characterized the body politic. Democracy is never a fast-frozen state of being. Rather democratic rights and freedoms are always a work in progress. Expanding the terrain of the public sector via the democratization of finance and industry, carries the potential to deepen and extend such popular capacities, rights and freedoms.

As Marx (1875, n.p.) once put it, freedom consists in converting the state from being an organ of despotism superimposed upon society to one completely subordinate to it. Thus an alternative class project from below must seek to extend the application of democratic forms out of the limited political sphere and into the organization of society as a whole. In a similar vein, Marx also suggested that social reforms are never carried out by the weakness of the strong, but always by the strength of the weak (Marx, 1847, n.p.). Despite the setbacks to trade unionists and social justice activists over the period of neoliberalism, new political forms and organizational experiments are necessary in order to turn defeats into victory. All things considered, contrary to claims that the Great Recession is a thing of the past —as P.M. Harper and Finance Minister Flaherty are keen to remind —the articles assembled here collectively shatter the myth of Canadian exceptionalism by showing that the aftershocks of the recession continue to have grave implications.

Starting us off, Jim Stanford debunks the notion that Canada stands as a bastion of economic stability and superior economic management. Rather, he demonstrates the shortcomings of conventional economic indicators arguing, contrary to mainstream analyses, that Canada's so-called recovery has been incomplete and relatively weak when compared with similar Organization for Economic Cooperation and Development countries. Stoney and Krawchencko follow with an overview of the transition from rescue strategies to exit strategies, that is, the shift from stimulus to austerity. They analyze where and how large changes in spending and restraint have taken place within the narrative of 'crisis' and the political opportunism that this has afforded. Their analysis shows that rather than abandoning the neoliberal project, recent budgets, policies and priorities indicate a more intense and comprehensive neoliberal agenda is emerging in Canada.

Moving forward, Toby Sanger argues that the acceleration of neoliberal-inspired austerity budgets will accomplish the same thing as previous recessions: lowering wage growth and shrinking the share of labour's national income. Focusing on the 2011 and 2012 federal Conservative budgets, he makes the case that conventional economic approaches are incapable of adequately addressing contemporary needs, thus an alternative framework is gravely needed. The following article by Heather Whiteside explores the troubled track record of public-private-partnerships (P3s) in Canada when delivering public infrastructure and services. Her chapter investigates how recent projects in British Columbia and Ontario —"P3 enthusiasts" —have enabled privatization measures while disabling public oversight.

The fifth article in this issue by Joel Harden details the Canadian Labour Congress' (CLC) "Retirement Security for Everyone" campaign. Harden discusses how the CLC grappled with the complexities of Canada's pension plan and the concrete challenges encountered along the way. Despite some important shortcomings in the CLC's campaign, Harden stresses the importance of expanding Canada's public pension plan in accordance with rebuilding the political capacities of organized labour. The final article by David Camfield problematizes the uncritical treatment of 'trade union bureaucracy' by academics and labour activists asking what do we mean when we talk about the trade union bureaucracy? In short, he argues that the sources of bureaucracy in unions lie in wage-labour contracts, the separation of conception from execution in human practical activity, the political administration of unions by state power, and the trade union officialdom.

This year's *Interventions* section, which continues *AR's* long-held emphasis on pushing the boundaries of academic orthodoxy, brings together some of the most original and innovative thinkers in a variety of sub-fields. In her wide-ranging and insightful interview, Ellen Meiksins Wood discusses the similarities and differences of the current phase of austerity with past policy objectives; what is meant by "Political Marxism"; ongoing debates about the value of the term "imperialism"; the significance of the Occupy movements and horizontalism; and the importance of freedom as a politically animating principle. The following interview with Michael Lebowitz explores the current crisis of world capitalism and its relation to Canadian exceptionalism; the present state of the anti-capitalist Left and its relation to party politics; the contradictions of 'really-existing socialism' and what socialistic responses to the recession might look like.

In "Neoliberalization and the Matrix of Action", Neil Brenner, Jamie Peck and Nick Theodore take us through an examination of the different forms that neoliberalism has taken over the years; the urban dimensions of the crisis and the specific ways in which cities reproduce capital accumulation yet create openings for organized resistance to the ongoing encroachments of capital; the significance of the Right to the City and Occupy movements; and the importance of counter-hegemonic strategies and alternatives to capitalism. In the following commentary, Shelia Block considers the gender and distributional impacts of the 2012 Ontario budget. She argues that reductions to services will have disproportionate impacts on low-income Ontarians, and racialized and immigrant communities. Furthermore, Block shows how cutbacks in public sector employment will increase inequality and unemployment, in addition to expanding the share of unpaid caregiving work done primarily by women.

An interview with David Newhouse follows where he discusses the impacts of austerity on Aboriginal communities. Newhouse discusses issues related to housing and poverty reduction; health and education; mandatory minimum sentences and their impact on rehabilitative services; the relationship between First Nations communities and social justice; and the continuing importance of First

Nations studies. In his valuable study of the Electro-Motive Lockout, Herman Rosenfeld addresses the shortcomings and limitations of union tactics and strategy in fighting against concessionary demands from the Caterpillar-owned plant. He asks why unions' responses to concessionary demands have been so tepid and unwilling to demonstrate some of the confrontational tactics of the past? While Rosenfeld is critical of the union's non-occupation, he concludes that unions themselves are incapable of posing alternative industrial strategies that reject corporatism and dependence on progressive-sounding schemes for competitive private sector projects. Instead, he argues that this requires a larger socialist and anti-capitalist movement —left of social democracy —that could research, debate and place a range of alternatives onto the larger political arena.

The final article by Sam Gindin argues that the 'crisis' that desperately needs addressing is not just the economic crisis but the crisis inside the labour movement. He argues that working people have now been under concerted attack for some three decades, culminating in the austerity agenda presented as the 'solution' to the latest crisis. Gindin reminds that the last time an economic and social crisis this deep occurred —the Great Depression of the 1930s —working people responded by reinventing forms of labour organization: placing industrial unionism firmly on the map and introducing dramatic new tactics like sit-downs and plant occupations. He asks: What comparable institutional and strategic changes might emerge from the present moment? Rounding off *AR's* thirty-sixth year of publication and twenty-fourth issue are ten book reviews which explore issues ranging from social movements and progressive activism to indigenous resistance, revolutionary health care and political theory. In including a broad survey of recently published material we hope that readers will find our reviews section useful.

This issue of *Alternate Routes* would not have been possible without the tremendous support of Carleton University's Departments of: Sociology and Anthropology; Political Science; Law; Geography and Environmental Studies; as well as, the Institute of Interdisciplinary Studies; Institute of Political Economy; and the Faculty of Graduate and Postdoctoral Affairs. We would also like to thank Ryerson University's Department of Politics and Public Administration and, in particular, the very generous support —financial, administrative and otherwise —of the Centre for Labour-Management Relations at the Ted Rogers School of Management, and its Director Maurice Mazerolle. Thanks are also due to Eric Leclerc and Hillary Ryde Collins for their valuable assistance. Without the above-mentioned sources of support, this issue of *AR* would not have been possible. We look forward to what we hope is a long and fruitful relationship in the promotion of critical social research.

Last but certainly not least, a sincere thank you to all contributors and referees who took time out of their schedules to write, review, revise and re-evaluate the articles assembled here. Your commitment to the most pressing issues of the day is a constant reminder of the importance of dissenting voices. For that we are grateful. In the year since the publication of *AR's* 2011 issue, we are pleased to have added an online photo and video section which contains a series of presentations from past *AR* conferences.[2] Thanks are due to Pance Stojkovski for his tremendous assistance in editing 2012's online conference presentations. We hope that readers and viewers will find them useful for stimulating class and other discussions.

As a final note, all previously published material from 1977 to 2012 are now fully available on our website — www.alternateroutes. ca — free of charge.

REFERENCES

Cross, P. (2011). How Did the 2008-10 Recession and Recovery Compare to Previous Cycles. *Statistics Canada*. http://www.statcan.gc.ca/pub/11-010-x/2011001/part- partie3-eng.htm

Evans, B. and G. Albo. (2010). Permanent Austerity: The Politics of the Canadian Exit Strategy From Fiscal Stimulus. In Fanelli, C. , C. Hurl, P. Lefebvre and G. Ozcan (Eds.), *saving Global Capitalism: Interrogating Austerity and Working Class Responses to Crises* (pp.7-28). Ottawa: Red Quill Books.

Fanelli, C. (forthcoming, 2012). *Fragile Future. Public Services and Collective Bargaining in an Era of Austerity*. Unpublished doctoral dissertation. Carleton University, Ottawa, ON.

International Monetary Fund. (2011, September). *World Economic Outlook: Slowing Growth, Rising Risks*. http://www.imf.org/external/pubs/ft/weo/2011/02/pdf/text.pdf

Laxer, J. (2009). *Beyond the Bubble: Imagining a New Canadian Economy*. Toronto: Between the Lines.

Marx, K. (1847). *The Poverty of Philosophy*. http://www.marxists.org/archive/marx/works/subject/hist-mat/pov-phil/ch02.htm

---

2   See http://www.alternateroutes.ca/index.php/ar/pages/view/Video

———(1875). *Critique of the Gotha Programme.* http://www.marxists.org/archive/marx/works/1875/gotha/

McBride, S. and J. Shields. (1997). *Dismantling a Nation: The Transition to Corporate Rule in Canada,* second edition. Halifax: Fernwood Publishing.

Panitch, L. & D. Swartz. (2003). *From Consent to Coercion: The Assault on Trade Union Freedoms.* Aurora, ON: Garamond Press.

16 | Great Recession-Proof?:
    Shattering the Myth of Canadian Exceptionalism

Articles

18 | Great Recession-Proof?:
   Shattering the Myth of Canadian Exceptionalism

The Myth of Canadian Exceptionalism: Crisis, Non-Recovery, and Austerity

—Jim Stanford[1]

Since the onset of the global financial crisis and resulting worldwide recession in 2008, Canadian political leaders have consistently boasted (to both domestic and international audiences) about Canada's supposedly superior record in avoiding the worst effects of that crisis, and then quickly repairing the damage and getting back to previous trajectories of growth and prosperity.[2] Indeed, at first federal leaders (led by Finance Minister Jim Flaherty) even denied that Canada would be caught in the global conflagration at all – illustrated most strikingly by Mr. Flaherty's ill-fated fiscal update of October 2008, which denied the existence of a recession which in fact had already hit the country (Department of Finance, 2008).[3] Once it became obvious that this could not be true, the government changed tack, and – in cooperation with other countries, as agreed at the G20's emergency summit meeting in Washington in November 2008 – launched a powerful but temporary series of emergency fiscal, monetary, and financial measures.

The recession that then hit Canada was quick and sharp, but short-lived (by technical economic definitions, anyway): real gross domestic product (GDP) bottomed out in July 2009 and began to grow again. By the autumn of 2010 real GDP had regained its pre-recession peak (reached two years earlier). A few months later (by January 2011), total employment also regained its pre-recession peak, and the government crowed that the damage from the recession had thus been fully repaired. Political

---

1 Jim Stanford is an economist with the Canadian Auto Workers. He can be reached at stanford@caw.ca. The author acknowledges very helpful comments on an earlier draft from Stephen McBride.
2 This work extends and updates previous research by the author. See Stanford, 2012; 2012b.
3 The glaring sense of denial which infused that document sparked the subsequent political crisis during which the opposition parties united to vote non-confidence in the minority Conservative government, followed by the prorogation of Parliament by the Governor-General.

figures naturally credited their own economic management for this purported recovery – including, variously, tax cuts (implemented before and during the recession), Canada's relatively lower public debt, the emergency fiscal and financial measures taken during the crisis, and Canada's more stringent banking regulations. Economic conditions may be suboptimal, it was acknowledged, but Canadians should be grateful that the country survived the crisis so much better than the rest of the world. This argument was a potent weapon in the Conservatives' successful campaign to win a majority mandate in the election of spring 2011.

The traditional "rule of thumb" of economists in Canada is that a recession occurs when real GDP declines for two consecutive quarters, and a "recovery" commences when real GDP begins to expand again. By this definition, the recession lasted for three quarters beginning in the autumn of 2008, and recovery began in the summer of 2009. Real GDP has continued to edge ahead (albeit unspectacularly and unsteadily), employment has increased (also fitfully), and the economy seems headed in a forward direction. So has the Canadian economy indeed been "exceptional" in how the crisis was experienced and managed here?

It turns out that both components of the government's dual boast – that Canada fared much better than other countries, and that the damage from the recession has already been repaired – are false. And both claims founder on the same underlying empirical fact: Canada's population grows over time, and relatively quickly. Trends in absolute levels of output and employment need to be considered in the context of that population growth. On average over the last five years, Canada's total population has increased by about 1.2 percent per year. The working age population (aged 15 years and over, by Canadian statistical definitions) has been growing slightly faster than that: about 1.3 percent per year. With a growing population, therefore, the economy must continuously generate new employment opportunities, and new output and income, simply to support a constant standard of living and a steady degree of labour market utilization. Comparisons of the total number of jobs, or the total volume of output, over time require adjustments for this ongoing expansion in the Canadian population.

In fact, Canada's population growth is among the fastest in the industrialized world. Canada's population growth rate is faster than any other G7 economy (including the U.S.), faster than Mexico's, and nearly twice the Organization for Economic Cooperation and Development (OECD) average. Strong population growth generates a certain underlying economic momentum (since growing population naturally stimulates underlying growth in consumer spending and other variables). But it also sets a higher "bar" in order to maintain a steady-state economic standard: the Canadian economy must generate hundreds of thousands of new jobs each year, and tens of billions of dollars in new GDP, just to maintain existing economic and labour market conditions. When Canadian officials boast that the pace of job-creation or GDP growth is relatively high compared to other countries, they neglect to mention that Canada's economy *must* generate more growth and jobs, just to stand still. Other industrialized countries (like Japan or Germany), where population is stagnant or even declining, do not need to generate such significant annual expansion in order to protect existing benchmarks. Similarly, when political leaders claim that the absolute level of employment or production has regained and surpassed pre-recession peaks, they neglect to consider the impact of ongoing population growth in the several years since those pre-recession peaks were reached.

Any comparisons of economic and employment performance, therefore, whether over time or across countries, must take account of the impact of population growth on measures of utilization or prosperity. Once those adjustments are made, then the tone of self-congratulation which typifies so many official pronouncements on Canada's recent economic performance is shown to be thoroughly unjustified. This paper will consider in turn the twin claims made by Canadian political leaders: namely, that the damage done by the recession to the Canadian economy and labour market has now been repaired, and that Canada did much better than other industrialized countries in traversing the difficult economic conditions of the last few years. Section I indicates that after adjusting for population growth, the recovery in neither GDP nor employment since the recession has yet to recoup the ground lost during the 2008-09 downturn. In the labour market, in particular, the pace of employment-creation has lagged far behind the pace of population growth. After adjusting for population growth, just one-fifth of the damage done by the recession had been repaired by mid-2012 – fully three years after the official onset of the recovery. Moreover, this key labour market indicator has not improved since the spring of 2010, highlighting the stalling of the Canadian recovery since that time.

As discussed in Section II, Canada's international economic reputation similarly loses considerable lustre when the data are adjusted for Canada's faster-than-average population growth. In per capita terms, the change in Canada's real GDP since 2007 ranks an uninspiring 16th among the 34 countries of the OECD. Similarly, after adjusting for growth in the working age population, Canada's employment performance has been equally middling: once again ranking 17th (out of 33 reporting countries) in terms of the change in the employment rate since 2007. If there is one word to summarize Canada's economic standing among its industrialized peers, it should be "mediocre."

Section III provides further comment on another factor that has been suggested as contributing to Canada's economic performance during and after the global financial crisis: the relative stability of the Canadian banking system. While Canadian financial markets experienced significant stress during the worst moments of the global crisis, no Canadian banks failed, and credit conditions did not experience the same degree of contraction as in U.S. and European markets. This relative stability certainly constituted a Canadian "advantage" in recent years. The reasons for this stability are considered, with special emphasis on the role of powerful stabilizing state interventions – both long-standing policies and regulations, and emergency measures implemented during the crisis. The exceptionalist claim that Canadian banks were somehow inherently immune from the global meltdown is refuted; the success of the Canadian financial system in traversing the global meltdown reflects state policy, not any embedded advantages of Canadian banks.

PART I: HISTORICAL COMPARISONS

Canada's economy (measured by real output) began to shrink in the third quarter of 2008, and declined close to 4 percent by summer 2009, when the official recession ended and real GDP began to recover. In per capita terms, however, the downturn began somewhat earlier: at the beginning of 2008, when slowing economic expansion began to lag behind ongoing population growth. Real per capita GDP then fell by over 5 percent by summer 2009. The decline in the per capita measure was worse than the fall in total GDP, because of the impact of ongoing population growth that continued even as the economy was in recession.

As indicated in Figure 1, real per capita GDP has improved fairly steadily but slowly since mid-2009, with the exception of the second quarter of 2011 when total GDP (and, of course, per capita GDP) declined. However, those 9 quarters (over two years) of economic progress have repaired only about 70 percent of the reduction in real per capita GDP that occurred during the downturn. Real per capita GDP remains 1.4 percent lower as of the third quarter of 2011, than it was at the beginning of 2008. In fact, real per capita GDP is still lower in Canada than it was at the beginning of 2006 (when the Harper Conservative government first took power); during almost six years of Conservative "stewardship," therefore, Canadians have experienced no economic progress (by this measure) whatsoever.

Put differently, real GDP declined by some $2,100 per Canadian (measured in 2002 dollar terms) during the 9 months of the official recession. The subsequent 27 months of recovery recouped some $1,500 of that loss, leaving GDP per person $600 lower than before the recession. Of course, trends in average real GDP per capita are not an adequate portrayal of actual living standards of the majority of Canadians anyway, for several well-known reasons. Average GDP per capita takes no account of the distribution of income, so at a time of growing income polarization, the average measure is an increasingly misleading indicator of the actual material standards experienced by the growing share of marginalized Canadians. And many components of GDP (including corporate profits, depreciation, and others) are never fully reflected in individual incomes or living standards. For this reason, the decline in average real per capita personal incomes has been slightly worse than the decline in real per capita GDP.

In fact, the lasting damage from the recession is considerably worse than that. It is normal for an economy to demonstrate *rising* real per capita output over time, as a result of technological improvements and productivity growth. The pre-recession trend in Canada was for real per capita GDP to increase by around 1.5 percent per year (reflecting capital accumulation, productivity growth, and innovation). Trend *potential* output has continued to grow during the years of recession and subsequent slow recovery (as indicated in Figure 1). Relative to that potential,[4] current real per capita GDP (of about $39,400 per person, in 2002 dollar terms) is at least 6 percent (or $3,000) below the level it *would* have reached if the pre-recession trend had been sustained. In this regard, the fact that Canada's economy continues to operate well below its productive potential costs each Canadian thousands of dollars in foregone income each year. And the modest rebound in real per capita GDP experienced since summer 2009 has not been strong enough to begin to close that gap with potential output that was opened up during the recession. This is different from most previous recoveries, which featured periods of above-trend growth which allowed the economy to catch up to potential output.[5]

---

4 The Canadian economy was not fully-employed even before the crisis and recession hit in 2008, so even that pre-recession trend does not capture the true full-employment potential of the economy.

5 For example, as Canada exited the painful recession of 1981-82, real GDP began to grow at an annual average rate of 5.6 percent during the first three years after the trough of the recession –more than twice as fast as the average GDP growth experienced in the first three years of the present recovery (author's calculations from Statistics Canada CANSIM Table 380-0002). The recovery after the 1990s recession, however, was also initially halting and uncertain; only by the last five years of that decade was the economy growing at a fast enough clip (almost 5 percent on an average annual basis) to absorb excess capacity still being carried from the 1990-91 recession.

Adjusting employment statistics for population growth results in an even starker comparison to pre-recession benchmarks. Because the potential labour force (represented by the working age population) grows by some 1.3 percent (or around 350,000 Canadians) each year, it is not enough for the Canadian economy to simply create new jobs. It *must* produce enough new jobs to keep up with ongoing population growth; in fact, during a recovery job creation must be even faster, in order to repair the damage done by the recession (as well as offsetting ongoing population growth). The best statistic for comparing the pace of job creation with ongoing population growth is the employment rate, which is the ratio of total employment to the working age population. Especially during periods of sustained labour market slackness, the employment rate is a more appropriate indicator of labour market well-being than the unemployment rate; in particular, it is unaffected by factors such as the decline in formal labour force participation which results when discouraged workers simply give up looking for work.[6] Falling labour force participation reduces the unemployment rate, making it seem like the labour market is strengthening, when in fact discouraged workers are simply throwing in the towel. In this context, the employment rate provides a more accurate reading on labour market conditions than the unemployment rate.

Like real per capita GDP, Canada's employment rate peaked some months before the official onset of recession. The employment rate peaked at 63.8 percent of the working age population in February 2008, after which point the decelerating pace of job creation no longer kept up with ongoing population growth. During the next 17 frightening months, the employment rate plunged by 2.5 percentage points, reaching a trough of 61.3 percent of the working age population in July 2009. That represented the fastest decline in the employment rate of any recession since the 1930s.

The subsequent bottoming and recovery of real output in Canada has hardly recouped any of this sharp downturn. From July 2009 through mid-2010, the employment rate recovered by about one-half of a percentage point, representing one-fifth of the damage that was done to Canadian labour markets by the recession. After summer 2010, however, further labour market progress ground to a halt, as governments shifted from stimulus to austerity and private business investment stagnated.

---

6   As will be discussed, even the employment rate does not capture the deterioration in the quality of work (represented by trends such as increased part-time, contract, and precarious work) that is another feature of a chronically depressed labour market.

During the two years from mid-2010 through mid-2012, the employ-ment rate stagnated at an average of 61.8 percent. The employment rate remains 2 full percentage points below the pre-recession peak. Regaining that pre-recession peak would require the creation of an incremental 570,000 jobs, doubling the number of actual net jobs created in Canada between fall 2008 and mid-2012.

This analysis is rooted solely in the quantity of employment in Canada's labour market, not its quality. But since 2008 there has also been a significant deterioration in the quality of employment in Canada, measured by the incidence of part-time, temporary, and low-wage work. From October 2008 (the pre-recession peak in Canadian employment) through summer 2012, over one third of net new jobs created in Canada were part-time. The share of part-time employ-ment has declined slightly since the recovery formally began in July 2009, but is nevertheless considerably higher than before the reces-sion began.

Similarly, there has been a net reallocation of employment toward lower-wage industries since the recession began. Employment in those sectors of the economy (defined at the two-digit level) which pay higher-than-average wages was still lower in mid-2012 than in October 2008 (mostly due to the net loss of over 200,000 jobs during this time in manufacturing). That means that new jobs in lower-wage sectors account for more than 100 percent of all net new jobs cre-ated since the pre-recession peak. This has reinforced the continuing longer-run decline in the average quality of jobs in the Canadian labour market. This decline in employment quality means that the quantitative data on the employment rate described above (properly adjusted for population growth) understates the true extent of weak-ness in the Canadian labour market.

Whether measured by output or employment, therefore, it is clear that Canada is still grappling with the after-effects of the 2008-09 downturn. In an interesting public opinion poll conducted in late 2011 by the Pollara (2011) firm for the Economic Club of Canada, a full 70 percent of Canadians believed the country was still in an economic recession – even though, according to economists, the recession had officially ended two-and-a-half years earlier. From the perspective of a labour market that was hammered by the recession, and has barely recouped any of that damage since, it is quite understandable why average Canadians could be forgiven for concluding that the reces-sion is still with us. In terms of the employment rate, it clearly still is.

PART II: INTERNATIONAL COMPARISONS

Failing to take account of population growth also distorts international comparisons of economic and employment performance, just as it distorts comparisons over time. For example, Canada experienced the 9th fastest rate of GDP expansion in the OECD, on average, since 2007. However, Canada has a higher-than-average rate of population growth, and hence must generate faster GDP growth simply to "stand still" in terms of per capita standards. If we adjust for differential population growth rates, then Canada's GDP performance is only mediocre within the sample of industrialized countries.

Table 1 reports the cumulative evolution of real per capita GDP across the OECD from 2007 through 2011. Of the 34 countries in the OECD, Canada ranks only 16th – almost exactly in the middle. Real per capita GDP for 2011 was still 1.4 percent lower than in 2007. Twelve OECD countries have regained and surpassed their pre-recession levels of real per capita GDP (including Germany, Korea, Australia, and several others). These countries might more honestly be able to claim to have repaired the economic damage from their recessions.[7] Canada, in contrast, can make no such claim. Other countries (including Sweden, the Netherlands, Belgium, and New Zealand) have yet to regain their pre-recession real per capita GDP benchmarks, but have experienced smaller declines in that measure than Canada has.

Of the countries which have experienced a worse decline in real per capita GDP since 2007 than Canada, several experienced full-blown financial crises, complete with bank failures and large losses of apparent wealth. This group includes Ireland, Greece, and Iceland (the worst-hit countries), along with the U.K. and the U.S. The fact that Canada's more strongly regulated banking system avoided these worst-case manifestations of the global crisis clearly contributed to Canada's avoidance of those very large declines in living standards (and the reasons for this outcome are discussed below). However, among the sub-set of countries which did *not* experience bank failures and associated consequences, Canada's GDP performance has been relatively poor. Of course, there are many factors affecting each country's performance during and after the crisis (in addition to the stability of their respective financial institutions).

Canada's international standing is similarly mediocre in terms of our labour market recovery. Canada's economy must generate some-

---

7   As noted in Section I, however, simply regaining a pre-recession peak in per capita GDP does not take into account the problem that real output, in the intervening years, has continued to lag far behind potential output.

thing like 225,000 new jobs per year just to keep pace with the ongoing expansion of the working age population.[8] It is not sufficient, then, for politicians to point out that the total number of jobs now exceeds the pre-recession peak. In the nearly four years since that time, the working age population has grown by 1.3 million. A much faster pace of job creation would have been needed in order to create opportunity for new labour force entrants, as well as re-employ those who were displaced by the downturn. Many other industrialized countries, in contrast, do not face that same challenge. Population in some OECD countries (like Japan, Germany, much of eastern Europe, and several others) is stagnant or growing very slowly. In that context, total employment might not grow much at all – yet a given employment rate could still be sustained.

Table 2 reports the change in each OECD country's employment rate from 2007 (the last full year before the recession) to 2011.[9] Canada's average employment rate for 2011 was 0.8 points below its average level for 2007.[10] That ranks Canada 17th out of the 33 reporting OECD countries included in Table 2. Eleven countries (including Germany, Korea, and Australia) achieved a higher employment rate by 2011 than was experienced before the recession. These countries, then, can more genuinely claim to have fully repaired the labour market damage of the recession. In France and Japan, the employment rate is still lower than in 2007, but the decline was not as steep as in Canada.

As with Table 1, the hardest-hit countries in terms of the decline in the employment rate include those (such as Greece, Ireland, Iceland, and the U.S.) where banks collapsed and vast amounts of credit were destroyed. Among a peer group of OECD economies which did not experience such extreme financial shocks, however, Canada's employment performance (like the evolution of GDP) has been relatively poor.

PART III: UNDERSTANDING CANADIAN FINANCIAL STABILITY

An influential stream within the broader ideology of Canadian exceptionalism is the myth that Canadian banks were blameless in the events of the 2008-09 financial crisis and the resulting recession. Canadian banks are strong and safe, the argument goes; they were prudent,

---

8 This estimate represents the product of the annual absolute growth in the working age population times the pre-recession employment rate.

9 Chile does not report this data and hence is excluded from Table 2.

10 Table 2 reports the decline in Canada's employment rate between 2007 and 2011 as 0.8 percentage points, compared to the full 2-point decline in that rate illustrated above in Figure 2. The reason for the difference is because Table 2 reports the difference in full-year averages (in order to facilitate international comparisons), whereas Figure 2 illustrates the more dramatic evolution in the monthly series.

and above all they (unlike U.S. banks) were not bailed out.[11] This argument is invoked in order to deflect critical attention away from Canadian financial players, even as other countries (like the U.K. and U.S.) debate how to strengthen financial regulation, and indeed challenge the general political and cultural legitimacy of financial elites.

In actuality, Canadian banks were bailed out – and powerfully so. At the end of 2008, and the beginning of 2009, federal Finance Minister Flaherty and other federal officials implemented a new program called the Extraordinary Financing Framework (EFF). This package of measures consisted of several different ways to assist Canadian banks, enhancing their liquidity and shifting risks off their balance sheets, during their hour of need.

The major components of the EFF included:

- Using the public mortgage insurance company (Canadian Mortgage and Housing Corporation) to buy securitized mortgages from the banks in order to inject cash into the banks' coffers.
- Providing large loans, at near-zero interest rates, from the Bank of Canada, when commercial lenders would not do so.
- Providing other lines of credit from the Bank of Canada and other agencies, including in U.S. dollars.
- Even the U.S. Federal Reserve Bank supported the Canadian banks with major assistance offered through its emergency liquidity program.

These loans and other liquidity injections were backed up with very unusual forms of collateral – or sometimes with no collateral at all. For example, the Bank of Canada was willing to accept asset-backed commercial paper (ABCP) from the banks to back up some of these emergency loans. This was just a year after the entire ABCP market froze up in Canada, even before the global meltdown, as a result of growing investor concern regarding the true nature and value of some of the securitized assets contained in ABCP products. Individual ABCP owners were left

---

11   Federal government officials boasted about the relative stability of Canadian banks right through the crisis – even as they were channeling unprecedented sums of emergency assistance to those institutions. For example, the government claimed in 2009 that "Canada's financial system has shown exceptional stability throughout the crisis and has become a globally noted leader in best banking practices." (Government of Canada, 2009, p.165). The President of the Canadian Bankers' Association (CBA) stated baldly that "not one bank in Canada …required a cent in taxpayer-funded bailouts" (Anthony, 2010, p.11). Some of the debate hinges on a matter of semantics: when is a bail-out not a bail-out? As another CBA spokesperson put it, bank critics "seem to be implying that liquidity support is the same as a bank bailout and this is not the case" (Tencer, 2012). Whether it is called a "bailout" or "liquidity support," it is a matter of record that over $100 billion of public funds were injected into the private banks in their moment of need.

holding illiquid paper. But banks with ABCP were able to convert it into liquid cash, courtesy of the Bank of Canada, when they needed it.

In total, various federal agencies offered the banks a maximum of up to $200 billion in cash and short term low-interest loans, at a point in time when the banks could not attain this financing from normal commercial sources because of the global crisis. At peak, it is estimated that Canadian banks tapped $114 billion of this potential line of credit (Macdonald, 2012). Incredibly, Canadian banks remained profitable right through the dramatic events of 2008 and 2009. Every one of the five largest banks declared an annual profit, and only one of them (the CIBC) declared even a quarterly loss during the darkest days of the crisis. As credit and economic conditions stabilized, profits strengthened further, and the banks were able to quickly repay the government assistance, with interest in some cases. Nevertheless, there is no denying that Canadian banks received unprecedented financial support from government in order to survive the crisis, and that without that support there is considerable likelihood that one or more major Canadian banks would have failed.[12] In this regard, Canadian banks were clearly "saved" (or "bailed out") by powerful public intervention.

Moreover, quite distinct from the emergency support offered up during the moment of crisis in 2008-09, the Canadian financial system has benefited in a longer-term sense from a public policy regime which is accommodating, supportive, and protective. These long-standing protections and subsidies have served to create a domestic financial industry that is more stable and profitable than those in other countries. It was this policy context (not the good judgment or "prudence" of Canadian bank executives) which explains why Canada's financial system withstood the storms of 2008-09 more safely than banks in the U.S., the U.K., or Europe did.[13]

Deposits up to $100,000 per person per bank are fully guaranteed by the Canadian Deposit Insurance Corporation. This eliminates the incentive for a "run" on the bank, and stabilizes the whole system.

Most home mortgages are insured by the Canadian Mortgage and Housing Corporation. This eliminates most of the risk for banks in

---

12 Macdonald's (2012) study notes that at various times the estimated extent of public lending to three of the big five Canadian banks exceeded the market value of the banks; without government support, then, those banks would have been fully "under water."

13 A very useful summary of the history and nature of Canadian bank regulation, and the continuing risks associated with leveraged private banking even in that more stable context, is provided by Russell, 2012.

writing new mortgages, and also makes it easier for them to "collateralize" their mortgages (packaging them into bonds which are sold to financial investors).[14] By attaching conditions to the mortgages it ensures (such as requiring minimum down payment ratios or maximum amortization timetables), the CMHC contributes to higher quality in mortgage loans, further reducing risk.

The federal government prohibits foreign takeovers of Canadian banks. This prevented any major bank from being swallowed up in the mid-2000s when U.S. banks (riding high on the bubble) were scouring the world for acquisitions. Earlier in the 200s, the previous Liberal federal government also vetoed mergers between the major Canadian banks, which also likely contributed to their relatively lower leverage ratios as they headed into the crisis.

Canadian bank services are heavily subsidized by the Canadian tax system, including through the partial taxation of capital gains and dividends, the deductibility of carrying charges, and a plethora of tax shelters for financial investments (such as Registered Retirement Savings Plans, Registered Education Savings Plans, Tax-Free Savings Accounts, and now Pooled Registered Pension Plans.

Both during the global financial crisis, and in a longer-term perspective, the Canadian financial industry benefits from a multidimensional framework of government support, subsidy, and stabilization. It is certainly true that the relative stability of Canadian banks has been a positive feature of Canada's economic experience since 2008. But that relative stability can be ascribed neither to the judgment or acumen of Canadian bankers (who were heavily engaged in leveraged, speculative activities like their counterparts around the world), nor to the specific policy actions of the current Canadian government (which inherited the structure of Canadian bank regulation from much-earlier predecessors).

CONCLUSION

Since the onset of the global financial crisis and subsequent recession, Canadian political leaders have stressed that while things may be difficult for Canadians, they are getting better, and the ground lost in the recession has been quickly recovered. Moreover, Canada is said to have escaped the worst effects of the recession, which hit home

---

14 This practice also meant that the incremental risk shifted to government by the purchase of mortgages from the banks during the crisis was modest, since those mortgages were already insured by the public agency.

more painfully in other industrialized countries. Many Canadians accepted this argument (perhaps due more to the power of sheer repetition, rather than empirical validity), and this contributed to the Conservative Party's successful campaign for a majority mandate in May 2011.

This mantra of Canadian exceptionalism is refuted by an analysis of appropriate measures of economic performance. The damage of the recession is still very much with Canadians – and is especially visible in the labour market. Real per capita GDP is still below its pre-recession peak, and several thousand dollars per person below its potential level (given pre-recession trends). And the labour market is still much weaker (measured by the employment rate) than before the recession. Indeed, measured by the employment rate, only one-fifth of the damage has been repaired, and no further progress has been made on this measure in the last two years.

Internationally, Canada's performance according to both standards is at best mediocre. Certainly, Canada has done better than those countries which experienced major banking and financial crises during the 2008-09 downturn (such as the U.S., the U.K., Ireland, Iceland, Greece, and Italy). But among the broader set of industrialized countries, Canadian performance in terms of output and employment ranks exactly at the mid-point of the sample. Instead of allowing politicians to claim credit for doing better than America or Italy, they should be challenged to explain why Canada's performance during this time has lagged so far behind many other industrial countries (including Germany, Korea, Australia, and others).

In short, the self-congratulatory and triumphalist tone of so many official economic pronouncements in Canada is clearly unjustified. In terms of its implications for economic and fiscal policy, the incomplete and relatively weak state of Canada's economic recovery should give considerable pause to policy-makers before embarking on a campaign of fiscal austerity – a campaign which will clearly further undermine output and employment which are still weak. Instead, top priority needs to be placed on expansionary measures to strengthen a recovery that has been slow, incomplete, and unsteady.

REFERENCES

Anthony, N.H. (2010, June 30). The Facts on Banks. *Winnipeg Free Press*, p.11.

Department of Finance Canada. (2008, November 21). *Protecting Canada's Future: Economic and Fiscal Statement*. Ottawa: Department of Finance.

Government of Canada. (2009). *Canada's Economic Action Plan: A Fourth Report to Canadians.* Ottawa: Government of Canada.

Macdonald, D. (2012). *The Big Banks' Big Secret: Estimating Government Support for Canadian Banks During the Financial Crisis.* Ottawa: Canadian Centre for Policy Alternatives.

Pollara. (2011). *The Economic Club of Canada.* http://www.pollara.com/eclub2012/report.pdf

Russell, E. (2012). *No More Swimming Naked: The Need for Modesty in Canadian* Banking. Ottawa: Canadian Centre for Policy Alternatives.

Stanford, J. (2012). *Canada's Incomplete, Mediocre Recovery.* Ottawa: Canadian Centre for Policy Alternatives.

— — — (2012). *A Budget for the Rest of Us: Alternative Federal Budget 2012.* Ottawa: Canadian Centre for Policy Alternatives.

Tencer, D. (2012, April 30). Canada Bank Bailout Cost $114 Billion at Peak. *Huffington Post.* http://www.huffingtonpost.ca/2012/04/30/canada-bank-bailout-cost- ccpa_n_1464398.html

Crisis and Opportunism: Public Finance Trends from Stimulus to Austerity in Canada

— Christopher Stoney and Tamara Krawchenko[1]

With crisis comes uncertainly and with it, opportunity. This has certainly characterized responses to the 2007 economic crises and its aftermath. In the early days of the crisis, economists and the neoclassical model alike were battered with contempt from internal and external criticism (Nadeau, 2008). Even the staunchly neoliberal magazine, *The Economist*, briefly declared the death of neoclassical economics—only to rectify and defend it in its subsequent issue. Leading up to the 2007 economic crisis, there had been a movement within economics to question market fundamentalist logic and the increasingly divorced-from-reality mathematical models that had come to define the profession (Williams & McNeill, 2005, p.3).

Neoclassical economics and its bedfellow, neoliberalism, has dominated public policy for so long that its widespread critique since the most recent economic crisis has led to speculation that we are witnessing a paradigm shift.

Our review of Canadian federal public policy and expenditures finds that there has been no such significant or sustained shift and the economic crisis and resulting federal stimulus expenditures have done little to reorient the dominance of neoliberal policy in Canada. Indeed by 2012 talk of a paradigm shift or significant realignment in the neoliberal consensus had largely evaporated.

---

1   Christopher Stoney is Associate Professor in the School of Public Policy and Administration, Director of the Centre for Urban Research and Education at Carleton University, and co-editor of *How Ottawa Spends*. His research interests include infrastructure funding, municipal government and urban sustainability. Tamara Krawchenko is Assistant Professor in Political Science at Dalhousie University. Her current research focuses on rural community and economic development in the Atlantic provinces.

Using powerful imagery, Harvie and Milburn (2011) epitomize the sense of despair felt by many towards neoliberalism's seemingly inexorable march:

> "Neoliberalism no longer "makes sense", but its logic keeps stumbling on, without conscious direction, like a zombie: ugly, persistent and dangerous. Such is the "unlife" of a zombie, a body stripped of its goals, unable to adjust itself to the future, unable to make plans. It can only act habitually as it pursues a monomaniacal hunger" (Harvie and Milburn, 2011).

In order to illuminate aspects of the return to 'business as usual,' the paper focuses on telling the story of stimulus and austerity in Canada by examining federal government expenditures from 2006 onwards using public accounts data (fiscal years 2005-2011). We highlight how the crisis (and the way it was presented) provided opportunities for the Harper government to deliver strategic shifts in priorities and spending. In particular, we focus in on the two biggest ministerial portfolio 'winners' over this period –the Ministries of Transport (namely, the Department of Infrastructure Canada) and Natural Resources. Rather than initiating a change in thinking amongst the policy elites we see a continuation, if not a heightening of existing 'growth-first' priorities. For Canada, this has included a focus on supporting a natural resource driven export economy in support of a political commitment to economic expansion, wealth creation and employment.

Canada's stimulus response to the economic crisis can be seen to have been consistent with the Harper government's overall approach of "open federalism," the two major tenets of which are: smaller government ("keeping the federal government's spending power within bounds") and adherence to the constitutional divisions of powers ("respecting areas of provincial jurisdiction" (PM of Canada, 2006). Significantly, compared to many other countries, the size of Canada's stimulus measures were relatively small (CCPA, 2009, p.2) and much of it focused on tax cuts and some infrastructure spending in which funding contributions from other levels of government were required.

Harmes argues that 'open federalism' is consistent with a "broader neoliberal approach to federalism which, among other aims, seeks to use institutional reforms to lock in more market-oriented public policies" (2007, p.418). Of interest in the areas of natural resources and trade is how public policy has promoted an energy-based export agenda—a continuation and yet, new manifestation of Harold Innis' staples theory of Canadian development (Innis, 1956). Here, open federalism's tenets are somewhat relaxed, as the federal government takes a strong interest in resource extraction and the development of infrastructure to support Canada's export markets – areas of major government expenditure and intervention in provincial affairs. In this area the Prime Minister has been eager to exploit opportunities to sell Canada's oil, gas and other natural resources abroad with particular attention focused on the giant US and emerging Chinese markets. Consequently, despite a commitment to smaller government and respect for provincial jurisdiction, the federal government finds itself involved in major interventions that favor some regions over others and appears to contradict the basic principles of open federalism. Given the political and calculated nature of these interventions we contend that 'strategic federalism' provides a better description of the government's approach than 'open federalism'.

Because our focus is on federal spending in Canada, we engage mainly with the literature seeking to dissect how neoliberal policies are adopted across time and place. This includes the literature on 'varieties of neoliberalism' (Cerny, 2004) and that which seeks to understand the distinctive ways in which it is practiced at different scales (e.g., Varro, 2010; MacKinnon & Shaw, 2010). However we are also influenced by ongoing debates concerning broader manifestations of neoliberalism and the impact of particular types of state intervention. In this wider context the paper's conception of neoliberalization draws on the so called neoliberal commandments (Harvey, 2003) predicated on the Washington Consensus (Williamson, 1990). In particular we emphasize the focus these approaches place on fiscal and monetary austerity, the lowering of inflation rates, trade and financial liberalization, deregulation, and reorientation of public expenditure, the freeing of interest rates, and emergence of independent central banks. We also share Harvey's view that neo-liberalism must be understood as a comprehensive theory of political as well as economic practices as this firmly acknowledges that the state has a key and selective role to play in advancing the neo-liberal project including the creation of "free markets" and "free trade". (Harvey, 2003)

State interventions into the economy during the neoliberal era have shifted drastically from protecting individuals from the perils of the market and limiting corporate power during the Keynesian era to subsidizing corporations, promoting competitiveness of national economies, and undermining the power of labor (Ruckert, 2006). Significant in this shift has been the growing power of increasingly global capital, in contrast to largely immobile labour (Ruckert, 2009). This has been facilitated and reflected by the 'internationalization of the state' whereby nation states increasingly prioritize the interests of transnational (financial) capital over domestic (industrial) capital and social groupings (Ruckert, 2010; Baker, 1999). This has helped fashion the deregulation of financial markets and the opening up of national economies to international competition. Importantly Ruckert (2010) connects this process to institutional changes, in particular the growing influence of the state agencies that are linked to (and often directly represent) the interests of transnational capital, such as ministries of finance and central banks.

The ascendency of financial institutions and the deregulation that has accompanied it has been highly significant in the emergence of neoliberalism and the resulting crisis. As Harvie and Milburn (2011) argue, while the postwar Keynesian settlement contained an explicit deal linking rising real wages to rising productivity, neoliberalism contained an implicit deal based on access to cheap credit. While real wages have stagnated since the late 1970s, the mechanisms of debt have maintained most people's living standards. The financial crisis shattered the central component of this deal by restricting access to cheap credit and undermining confidence in financial markets and continued growth.

Faced with a severe financial crisis, governments initially intervened to stimulate spending, subsidize corporations and shore up markets leading to suggestions of a return to Keynesian style government and the demise of neoliberal hegemony. However, the hasty return to austerity measures combined with attacks on public services and the public servants that provide them have reaffirmed that any shift in policy will be short-lived and should not be conflated with paradigmatic or fundamental reforms. Our analysis of spending trends combined with the government's stated priorities suggests that Canadians face an intensification of neoliberal policies rather than a shift or decline. As such we are likely to see continued and growing inequality within Canadian society on a scale greater than before the crisis.

Warning of the dangers of growing inequality, Stiglitz (2012) identifies this trend in the US, with America's current level of income inequality at historic levels not seen before the Great Depression. In the boom years before the financial crisis in 2008, the top 1 percent seized more than 65 percent of the gain in national income. In 2010, as the US struggled to emerge from a deep recession, the 1 percent gained 93 percent of the additional income created in the so-called recovery (Stiglitz, 2012). With respect to neoliberalism, Stiglitz points out that inequality does not arise in a vacuum but from the interplay of market forces and political machinations. Over time, he argues, politics has shaped the market in ways that advantage those at the top at the expense of the rest of society. With an economic system that seems to fail most citizens and a political system that appears captive to moneyed interests, he warns of the price of growing inequality in terms of slower growth, lower GDP, greater instability and a variety of social and democratic threats. It is in this context that we examine the policy response of the Harper government following the financial crisis and consider the implications for Canada

The paper is organized into four parts. First, we examine the 'big picture' of federal revenue and expenses in Canada over the last decade with a focus on stimulus and austerity measures. Second, we turn to the Ministries of Trade and Natural Resources—two of the biggest 'winners' in revenue terms over recent years. We examine just how these Ministries have expanded and consider the meaning of this within the broader context of fiscal federalism and the economy. From this high level analysis of public accounts we consider the federal government's policy priorities and policy focus. Third, we reflect on the most recent budget (2012) and what this means for the direction of change. The final section offers conclusions.

FROM STIMULUS TO AUSTERITY

The onset of the global economic crisis led to a common refrain amongst commentators that "we are all Keynesians now". Interestingly, governments that were ideologically opposed to such spending would now need to adopt stimulus policies in order to strengthen investment, consumer and business confidence (and capital liquidity). Canada's response was launched through its *2007 Economic Statement*. The stimulus budget proposed $60 billion in broad-based tax relief over five years. This was followed by a two-year commitment to financial stimulus measures focused on taxation, Employment Insurance benefits, and infrastructure investments, as outlined in the 2009-10 Budget, entitled *Canada's Economic Action Plan*. Similar to other countries, the stimulus measures adopted through Canada's 2009-2010 Budget focused on encouraging economic growth.

That Budget stated stimulus measures were guided by three principles—that they be "timely, targeted and temporary" (Government of Canada 2009, p.4). The Budget further stated that measures would begin within 120 days of the budget being passed; that the measures would focus on targeting businesses and families in the greatest need in order to trigger increases in jobs and output and; finally, that the plan would be phased out "when the economy recovers [in order] to avoid long-term structural deficits" (ibid). While some aspects of the plan would be phased out (i.e., infrastructure spending) the stimulus measures clearly stated that one objective would be to "reduce taxes permanently" (Department of Finance, 2010).

We can see in Chart 1 below the recession reflected in the government's public accounts. Program expenses increased as a percent of GDP while revenues decreased. It is important to note that part of this revenue decline comes from the decision to reduce taxation in a number of areas. For example the decision to drop two percentage points off of the Goods and Services Tax(GST) and to reduce the corporate tax rate. This figure is further compounded by a contraction of economic growth over these years. While federal Government revenues as a percentage of GDP have steadily decreased over the past decade (from 18.1 per cent in 2000-01 to 14.6 per cent in 2010-11), program expenses as a percentage of GDP saw increases in the 2009-10 and 2010-11 periods (at 16.0 and 14.7 per cent respectively). This is a slight increase from the previous three years where program expenditures as a percentage of GDP were steady at 13 per cent. In the past two years there has been an operating deficit (2009-10 and 2010-11) and over the past three year period there has been a budgetary deficit (between 2008-09 and 2010-11). The increasing size of the deficit (both budgetary and operational) has been instrumental in the *narrative of austerity*.

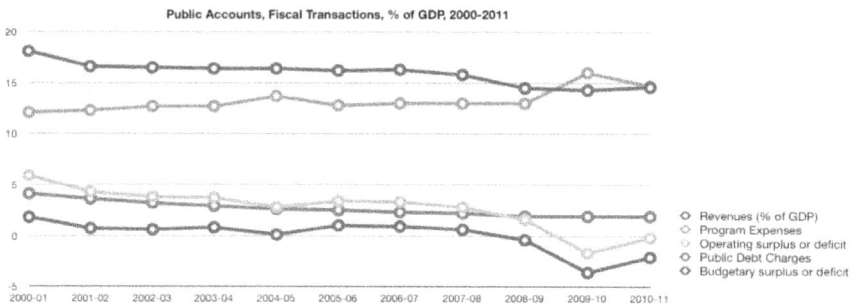

Chart 1. Public Accounts, Fiscal Transactions, per cent of GDP, 2000-2011

The Government posted a budgetary deficit of $55.6 billion for the fiscal year ending March 31, 2010 (Department of Finance, 2010). Finance Minister Flaherty blamed the 2010 fiscal year record deficit on the $5.6 billion payout to British Columbia and Ontario to assist with the transition to the harmonized sales tax, and the decision to limit increases in Employment Insurance premiums (ibid.). While these obviously contributed to the overall size of the deficit, they are only part of the fiscal equation with the government also responsible for cuts in direct and indirect taxation over this period in addition to its spending on stimulus measures. Clearly the policy preference for tax cuts has helped to diminish government revenues and in doing so has also contributed to the narrative of 'belt tightening' for the public sector. Having helped manufacture a sizeable deficit, Minister Flaherty has made it the deficit into as a major public issue and used it to justify austerity measures, warning Canadians to brace themselves against significant cutbacks in budget 2012 (ibid.).

The chart below illustrates these trends. Personal income tax, expressed as a percentage of GDP, has consistently declined over that past decade, with the exception of the 2010-11 period, when there was a slight increase (from 6.8 percent to 7.0 per cent of GDP). Total tax revenue as a percentage of GDP has declined and flattened, hitting an all time low over the past three years. Corporate income tax as a percentage of GDP has been lower in the past three years than in the previous five. Overall, revenues as a percentage of GDP show a declining trend over the past decade. Economically, this shift is consistent with the political shift to 'open federalism's' commitment to smaller government.

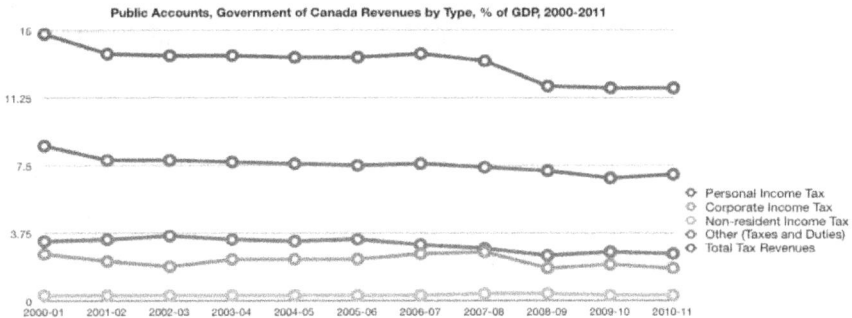

Chart 2. Public Accounts, Government of Canada Revenue by Type, percent of GDP, 2000-2011

A high level analysis of public accounts from the past decade shows evidence of 'roll-back neoliberalism' (Peck and Tickell, 2002). Government revenues have slowly declined and the public sector is urged to do less with less. The Conservative Government has expressed a commitment to leave as much as possible to the private sector. The economic crisis has brought with it opportunism – it has led to a wide swath of tax cuts (some of them, permanent) and has reoriented spending in a number of areas. The size of the deficit is however part of a fiscal *choice* to reduce taxation.

While the Conservative Government expresses preference for smaller government and limited spending, there are inconsistencies in the expression of these preferences across portfolios—some Ministries and Departments have grown considerably, while others have diminished in revenue and policy importance. While we have seen evidence of 'roll-back neo-liberalism' there is also evidence of 'roll-out neoliberalism' as certain Ministries become the focus of government policies and spending.

The chart below provides an analysis of the changes in public accounts since 2006. It shows the percentage change of total net expenditures by Ministry between the years 2006 and 2001 (in constant 2002 dollars). The red line denotes the average percentage change for all – a 14.30 percentage increase. Those Ministries above the red line gained more than the average in revenue terms over those years, and those below it lost more than the average. Hence, this gives some indications of relative spending priorities. By this analysis, the Ministries of Transport and Natural Resources have seen the greatest percentage increases.

This percentage change figure should be read with caution in the case of some Ministries – the Privy Council, the Governor General, Parliament, Finance and Justice can see major fluctuations in funding for a variety of reasons. For example, Parliament and the Governor General may have large capital expenditure due to renovations. The Privy Council (PCO) may have special Royal Commission expenditures (or see fluctuations because it includes the Office of the Chief Electoral Officer), and Finance can have highly fluctuating transfer payments. From this overall analysis, two federal priorities clearly emerge – infrastructure and natural resources.

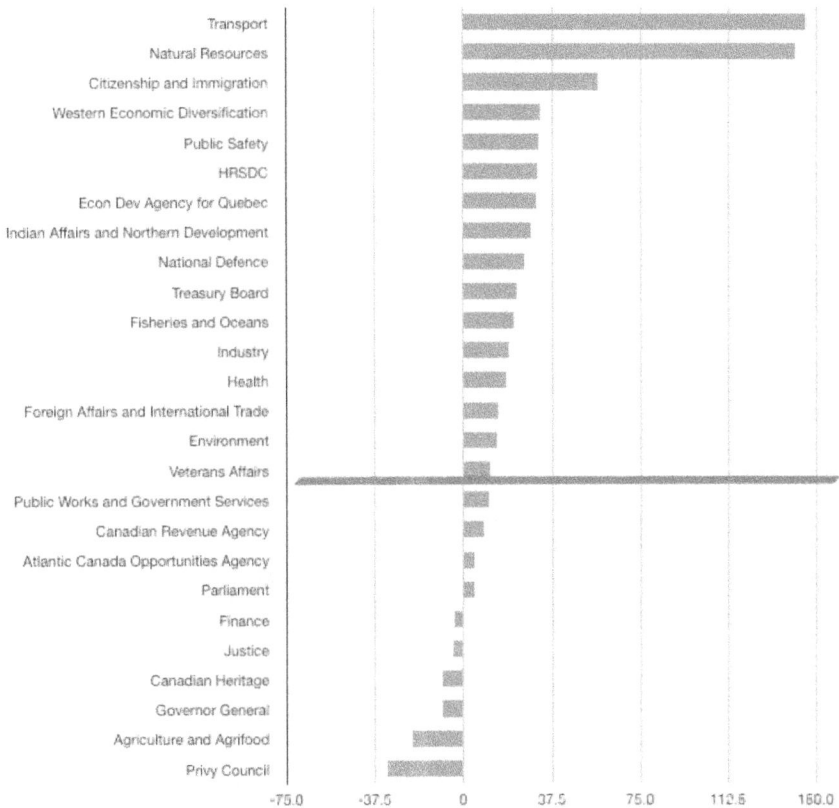

Transport		
Natural Resources		
Citizenship and Immigration		
Western Economic Diversification		
Public Safety		
HRSDC		
Econ Dev Agency for Quebec		
Indian Affairs and Northern Development		
National Defence		
Treasury Board		
Fisheries and Oceans		
Industry		
Health		
Foreign Affairs and International Trade		
Environment		
Veterans Affairs		
Public Works and Government Services		
Canadian Revenue Agency		
Atlantic Canada Opportunities Agency		
Parliament		
Finance		
Justice		
Canadian Heritage		
Governor General		
Agriculture and Agrifood		
Privy Council		

-75.0   -37.5   0   37.5   75.0   112.5   150.0

Chart 3. Public Accounts, Percentage change total net ministerial expenditure, 2006-2011, constant dollars

FEDERAL PRIORITIES: INFRASTRUCTURE AND NATURAL RESOURCES TRANSPORT AND INFRASTRUCTURE

The Ministry of Transport has grown in importance over the years, with numerous agencies and authorities being added to it.[2] The chart below shows the total budget by authority within the Transport Ministry for the fiscal years 2006-2011 (in millions, 2002 constant dollars). It is clear from this analysis why the revenues of the Ministry have increased

---

2   In 2004, the Ministry was composed of Transport Canada, the Canadian Transportation Agency (a regulatory agency) and the Transportation Appeal Tribunal of Canada. In 2005, this portfolio was expanded to include the Office of Infrastructure of Canada, the National Capital Commission, the Canada Post Corporation and the Royal Canadian Mint two years later, it would include the Canadian Air Transport Security Authority, the Federal Bridge Corporation Limited, the Jacques Cartier and Champlain Bridges Incorporated, VIA Rail Canada Inc., Marine Atlantic Inc. and Old Port of Montreal Corporation Inc. The Old Port of Montreal Corporation existed under this portfolio from 2006-2009.

so considerably in the past several years – Infrastructure Canada has seen massive budgetary increases over this period. The remainder of this section will focus on the gains of this Department.

Transport Ministry - total budget authorities used, by year (2002 constant dollars)

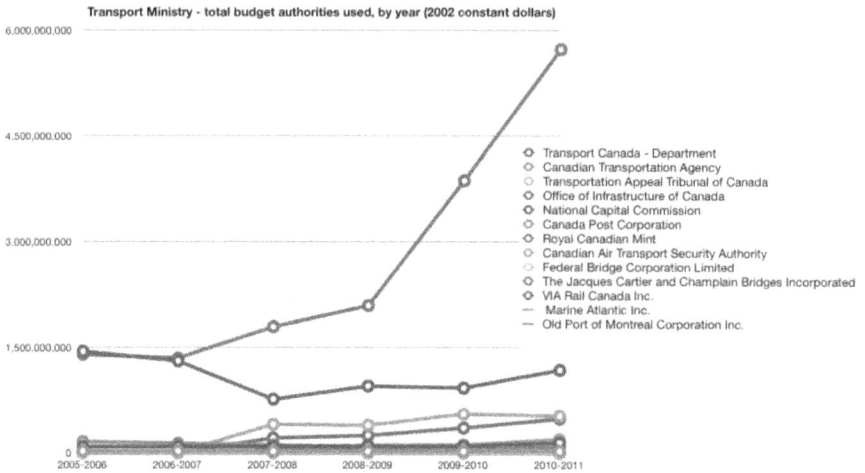

Chart 4. Transport Ministry—total budget of authorities used by fiscal year, millions of dollars, 2002 constant dollars

Stimulus responses in the wake of the late 2007 financial crisis focused on short-term growth (raising aggregate demand) as well as long-term growth by aiming to create favorable conditions for investment and innovation. These measures entailed both revenue side policies (cuts to direct and indirect taxes and social insurance contributions) and spending side policies of which there are many possibilities. One of the most popular choices made by governments on the spending side has been the ramping up of public investment in infrastructure. The infrastructure components of the stimulus measures in Canada were approximately $40 billion (CAD) over two years.[3] The largest portions of the infrastructure measures were tax credits for households – e.g., home renovation and energy efficiency tax credits administered through the Canada Revenue Agency.[4] These tax incentives to households accounted for approximately 28 per cent of all

---

3   This figure is the sum of total reported stimulus measures for 2009 and 2010. This figure does not include funds leveraged by other orders of government - e.g., through the creation of stimulus programs requiring matching grants, which, in the Canadian case are a significant amount (Department of Finance Canada, 2009).

4   Knowledge infrastructure has been excluded (Department of Finance Canada, 2009).

infrastructure related stimulus spending.[5] The second largest proportion was allocated to social housing, First Nations Housing and Northern housing at approximately 15.4 per cent of total infrastructure related funding and administered through the Canada Mortgage and Housing Corporation (CMHC) and Indian and Northern Affairs (INAC) in some cases.[6] The third largest component of funding was allocated to a mixture of provincial, municipal and First Nations, Territorial and some federal infrastructure—amounting to approximately nine per cent of total infrastructure related investments.[7] Many of the infrastructure investments that were chosen were often less complicated projects such as road expansion as opposed to more transformative projects such as transit for which the employment effects of stimulus spending are greater (CCPA, 2009, p.2). In many OECD countries, the infrastructure components of stimulus programs included transformative long-term projects (OECD, 2011).

The chart below details spending by major program area for Infrastructure Canada between the years 2008-2011 (in 2002 constant dollars).[8] Funding programs have significantly expanded in Infrastructure from but two major program areas in the 2008-09 fiscal year to 14 in the 2010-11 fiscal year. Some of this is one time funding, such as support for the G20 and G8 Summits. However, much of it represents a major program of investment into large infrastructure projects, particularly in areas that support trade such as the Asia Pacific Gateways and Corridors Initiative; the Ontario-Quebec Continental Gateway and Trade Corridor and; the Atlantic Gateway and Trade Corridor. These initiatives involve major partnerships between the federal and provincial and municipal governments to connect Canada to eastern, western and southern markets with significant funding attached to the development of border crossings, ports, airports, railway lines and major highways across the region.

5　Calculation includes funding for the programs Home Renovation Tax Credit; Enhancing the Energy Efficiency of Our Homes; increasing withdrawal limits under the Home Buyers' Plan and; First-time Home Buyers' Tax Credit as a proportion of all infrastructure-related funding measures. This figure excludes Knowledge Infrastructure.
6　Ibid.
7　Ibid.
8　Fields noted 'not applicable' (n/a) indicate funding has been discontinued.

Office of Infrastructure Canada	2008-2009	2009-10	2010-11
Infrastructure Stimulus Fund	n/a	n/a	2,271,425,616
Gas Tax Fund	n/a	1,716,386,457	1,605,461,467
Building Canada Fund—Major Infrastructure component	n/a	n/a	371,188,766
Provincial-Territorial Infrastructure	n/a	634,798,773	400,845,468
Canada Strategic Infrastructure Fund	n/a	1,470,607,922	307,676,621
Green Infrastructure Fund	n/a	n/a	31,313,027
Building Canada Fund—Communities component top-up	n/a	n/a	278,242,103
Building Canada Fund—Communities component	n/a	n/a	205,571,316
Municipal Rural Infrastructure Fund	n/a	n/a	134,073,573
Border Infrastructure Fund	n/a	n/a	62,129,383
Internal services	n/a	36,435,601	57,157,305
Economic analysis and research	n/a	8,004,135	963,660
Support for the G8 Summit 2010	n/a	n/a	4,189,538
National trails coalition	n/a	n/a	92,803
Infrastructure Investments	2,079,301,981	n/a	n/a
Policy, Knowledge and partnership development	10,382,264	n/a	n/a
Total	2,089,684,245	3,866,232,888	5,730,330,645

Chart 5. Office of Infrastructure Canada – Expenditure components by program type, millions of dollars, 2002 constant dollars.

The role of the federal government in municipal affairs has gone through waves of engagement and disengagement over the past decades. The Harper Government is publicly committed to the principles of 'open federalism' and seeks to adhere to the constitutional division of powers wherein municipalities are 'creatures' of the provinces. However, their strong role in infrastructure development and a particular orientation to trade is a major area of federal involvement—one that sets a strong direction for urban policy in Canada's biggest city regions. In this role, the federal government is a leader, committing vast sums of money to build partnerships that will reorient our urban regions around a trade agenda.

NATURAL RESOURCES

Unlike the Ministry of Transport, the Ministry of Natural Resources has been a relatively stable Portfolio.[9] The chart below shows the total budget by authority within the Natural Resources Ministry for the fiscal years 2006-2011 (in millions, 2002 constant dollars). As was seen in the case of Infrastructure Canada, the Department of Natural Resources leads in gains.

Ministry of Natural Resources, total budget by fiscal yr, milns of $ (2002 constant)

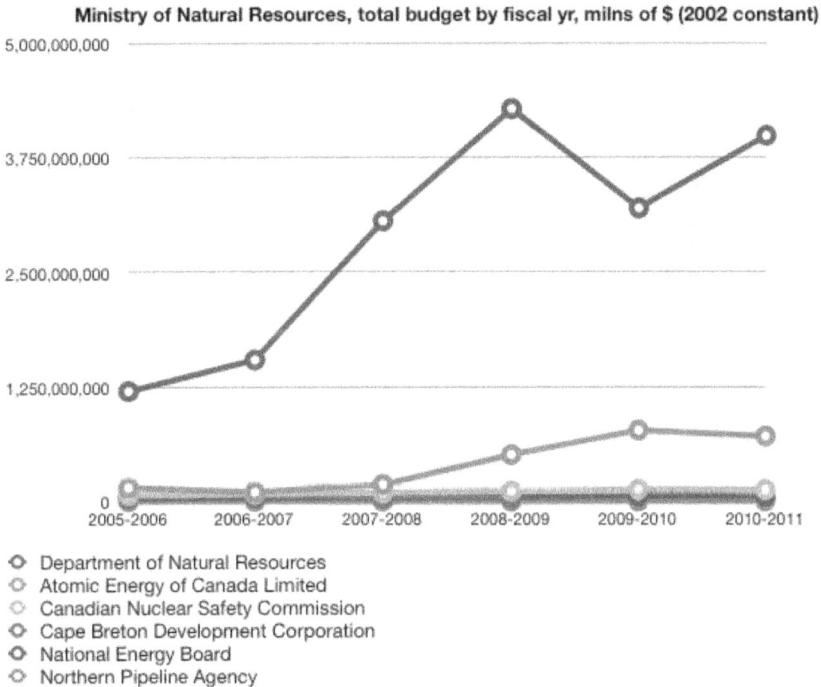

- ○ Department of Natural Resources
- ○ Atomic Energy of Canada Limited
- ○ Canadian Nuclear Safety Commission
- ○ Cape Breton Development Corporation
- ○ National Energy Board
- ○ Northern Pipeline Agency

Chart 6. Ministry of Natural Resources, total budget of authorities used by fiscal year, millions of dollars, 2002 constant dollars.

The Department of Natural Resources seeks to enhance the use and competitiveness of Canada's natural resources products. The Department conducts scientific research and technology development in the fields of energy, forests, mineral and metals and earth sciences. As a lead Department in the natural resources development they are involved in environmental assessments and their work must comply with the *Cana-*

9   It is composed of the Department of Natural Resources, Atomic Energy of Canada Limited, the Northern Pipeline Agency, the Canadian Nuclear Safety Commission, the National Energy Board and Cape Breton Development Corporation. The Cape Breton Development Corporation was disbanded in 2009.

dian Environmental Assessment Act and the *Cabinet Directive on the Environmental Assessment of Policy Plan and Program Proposals.* Chart 7 (below) shows expenditure components by program type for the Department of Natural Resources (millions of dollars, 2002 constant dollars). One can see that over the past few years, the Department has focused its attentions on adaptation management (including hazard risk management and climate adaptation). Some of these functions had previously been undertaken by Environment Canada and one can make the argument that environmental protection might be better placed there rather than a Department whose mandate is resource development.

Department of Natural Resources	2005-2006	2006-2007	2007-2008	2008-2009	2009-2010	2010-2011
Information dissemination and consensus building	174,029,995	n/a	n/a	n/a	n/a	n/a
Economic and social benefits	509,129,005	n/a	n/a	n/a	n/a	n/a
Environmental protection and mitigation	422,368,614	n/a	n/a	n/a	n/a	n/a
Safety and security of Canadians	29,216,589	n/a	n/a	n/a	n/a	n/a
Sound departmental management	68,529,345	n/a	n/a	n/a	n/a	n/a
Earth sciences	n/a	219,153,119	227,721,587	n/a	n/a	n/a
Earth sciences – Geomatics Canada	n/a	-484,981	2,873,446	923,434	416.203	-232,277
Energy	n/a	1,095.040,075	2,572,970,775	n/a	n/a	n/a
Sustainable forest	n/a	163,229,963	189,461,133	n/a	n/a	n/a
Minerals and metals	n/a	68,187,077	69,352,522	n/a	n/a	n/a
Economic opportunities for natural resources	n/a	n/a	n/a	3,413,526,095	1,868.236,335	2,155,784.196
Clean energy	n/a	n/a	n/a	491,876,859	735.597,438	1,218.663,252
Ecosystem risk management	n/a	n/a	n/a	150,796,095	143,429.486	181.756,142
Natural resources and landmass knowledge	n/a	n/a	n/a	118,816,451	104,001,675	87,556,435
Adapting to a changing climate and hazard risk management	n/a	n/a	n/a	94,002,226	57,637,155	55,749,031
Natural resource-based communities	n/a	n/a	n/a	17,397,271	10,020.631	11,625,600
Internal services	n/a	n/a	n/a		280.721,390	282,708,039
Total		1,203,273,547	1545125254	3,062,379,462	4287338433	3,200,060,313	3,993,610,420

Chart 7. Department of Natural Resources – Expenditure components by program type, millions of dollars, 2002 constant dollars.

The Prime Minister's efforts to promote Canadian exports abroad and natural resources in particular, has been a key feature of Canada's recent trade and foreign policy. Strong lobbying for the Keystone XL pipeline and the recent visits to China, Malaysia and Japan were aimed at increasing trade surpluses with these countries and underline the government's strategy to use economic growth as means of paying down the deficit in time for the next election. In a 2006 speech, Mr. Harper set out his vision of Canada as a "global energy superpower power" and was reportedly furious with president Obama's 2011 announcement to delay the Keystone XL pipeline for at least a year. Soon after, Harper had established energy exports as the government's new top strategic priority, with Asia seen as the key market to target, making Enbridge' Northern Gateway pipeline to the seaport at Kitimat BC an essential project (Wells and McMahon, 2012).

This context helps explain why environmental assessments have recently been streamlined and also the alacrity with which Prime Minister Harper appears to have backtracked in relation to China's record on human rights. As Corcoran observes "His [Mr. Harper's] previous issues with China appear to have been sidelined, replaced in part by some neo-Nixonian strategizing over potential economic advantage over the United States" (Corcoran, 2012). Heading to China, Mr. Harper set out his intentions and his hopes very clearly: "[a]s you know, our country is looking for new markets for our goods and services and China and the entire Asia-Pacific region is an area of tremendous opportunity," and added, "[w]e hope to expand on our strategic partnership with China and, in particular, we hope to deepen the economic and trade ties between our two countries" (Corcoran, 2012). This represents a significant shift in policy by the government and it remains to be seen how the US will react and how deeper trade ties with China and Asia will develop.

OPPORTUNISM AMIDST CRISIS: THE NARRATIVE OF AUSTERITY AND THE 2012 FEDERAL BUDGET

Having examined federal expenditures over the past several years, we turn here to the most recent federal budget to examine some of its implications for policy development in the near term. For several reasons, the 2012 budget can be seen as a watershed moment in a politically realigned Canada and speculation was intense leading up to its release. The Conservatives having secured a much sought after majority were finally in a position to define their political agenda without having to depend on the mercurial support of the opposition parties. Political opponents feared that the way was now clear for the Conservatives to push ahead with the implementation of the so-called *Harper Agenda*, particularly in view of the fact that both the NDP and Liberal parties had spent most of 2011-12 in limbo as they attempted to (re)establish long-term leadership and political direction. That said an uncertain and fragile fiscal and economic climate, a weak majority and a series of political scandals including the so-called "in and out" scandal, misuse of the G8/G20 border infrastructure fund and the "Robocall" election fraud made this a challenging environment within which to introduce an austerity budget. In particular it required the government to tread carefully as it balanced cuts in public spending with the fragile economic recovery and the political fallout that typically accompanies cuts in core services and benefits such as pensions and old age security spending.

When the Conservatives came to power in 2006 they inherited a budget surplus of $8-billion. In 2008, the government entered into a deficit due to falling tax revenue and higher spending. In its November 2011 economic update, the government projected Canada's deficit for 2011-2012 would be $31-billion, although recent indicators suggest it could be lower. In 2010-2011, Canada's actual deficit was $33.4-billion. Whether or not the 2012 budget is seen as draconian response to this size of deficit, the government's majority allied to its commitment to slay the deficit created an opportunity to prioritize its spending and program commitments in a way that was not conceivable in previous years.

As during the election campaign, Mr. Flaherty and the Prime Minister said repeatedly that jobs and economic growth are their first priority. Not surprisingly therefore, the first Harper majority government Budget on March 29th was titled and pitched as a *Jobs, Growth and Long-Term Prosperity Budget*, with links back to the Economic Action Plan from their Minority government years. Stressing that Canada has done relatively well in the global recession context and in job creation since 2009, Finance Minister Jim Flaherty emphasized instead the structural problems that Canada must now address both for long-term prosperity and "to ensure the sustainability of public finances and social programs for future generations" The structural fundamentalism of the Budget, that is, its greater focus on steps needed to ensure the full potential of the economy is intended to be the main message.[10] The Harper list of policies and initiatives (spending, tax and regulatory in nature) in their order of presentation include:

- Supporting Entrepreneurs, Innovators and World- Class Research
- Responsible Resource Development
- Expanding Trade and Opening New Markets for Canadian Business

---

10 On structural fundamentalism, see Doern et al, 2013, Chapter 3.

- Investing in Training, Infrastructure and Opportunity
- Expanding Opportunities for Aboriginal Peoples to Fully Participate in the Economy
- Building a Fast and Flexible Economic Immigration System
- Sustainable Social Programs and Secure Retirement
- Responsible Expenditure Management[11]

The budget cuts of $5.2 billion, mainly referred to in the final "responsible expenditure management" section are not highlighted although considerable attention is drawn in the Budget to the elimination of 19,200 civil service jobs. Among the agencies mentioned in the Budget to be eliminated outright are Assisted Human Reproduction Canada (beset with constitutional and court challenges) and the National Roundtable on the Environment and the Economy (an advisory body not favoured by the Conservatives, in part because of its climate change policy advocacy). Further budget cuts are planned to reach about $5 billion a year by 2014-2015 (see further discussion below of cuts and the strategic review process headed by Treasury Board President, Tony Clement).

Under the above structural themes other key particular initiatives were announced in Budget 2012). Among these are:

- Increase funding for research and development by small and medium-sized companies, including through a refocusing of the role of the National Research Council.
- In the resource development sphere, bring forward legislation to achieve the goal of "one project, one review" in a clearly defined period.
- Pursue new and deeper trading relationships, particularly with large, dynamic and fast-growing economies.
- Invest in First Nations education on reserve, including early literacy programming and other supports and services to First Nations schools and students.
- Move to an increasingly fast and flexible immigration system where priority focus is on meeting Canada's labour market needs.
- Gradually increase the age of eligibility for Old Age Security (OAS) and Guaranteed Income Supplement benefits from 65 to 67.

---

11 Government of Canada, 2012, p.5-11.

This change will start in April 2023 with full implementation by January 2029, and will not affect anyone who is 54 years of age or older as of March 31st, 2012.[12]

As these priorities and initiatives demonstrate, the government's response to the fiscal crisis has been influenced by the neoliberal framework and "commandments" outlined in the introduction. Just as the financial crisis in Canada was at least in part manufactured by domestic fiscal policy, the urgency with which the deficit is being tackled is just as much a question of politics as it is economics. In a political context it is important that the deficit is reduced quickly and, specifically, in time for the next federal election. Having already committed to return to a surplus position by then the question for the Conservatives appears to be *how* not *whether* to implement cuts. To this end much emphasis has been placed on strategic review. In Canada, "program reviews" that check all government spending have been a feature of public sector managing since the late 1970s. At that time these reviews were infrequent and usually responded to political promises that spending would be kept to a minimum. It was not until the late 1990s that such reviews became a routine feature of Canadian public management, culminating in "strategic reviews" introduced in 2006, and now "operational reviews" (not the same thing) introduced in 2011. These latter reviews are intended to find significant one-time cuts in services, rather than ongoing and permanent cuts as in the case of the former. "Strategic Reviews" were introduced to force departments and agencies to find critical savings and to use these savings to align with key government priorities. Such reviews are conducted every four years with the objective of finding five percent savings from low performing, low priority programs and services.

The goal of the latest strategic and operating review is to find ongoing savings of at least $4-billion a year by 2014-2015 from departments' total $80-billion operating budget. This represents only one part of total federal spending and includes the cost of staff and benefits etc. The rest of the spending, including $150-billion in program spending and transfers, are not part of the spending review. Consequently out of a total spending of almost $250-billion, including about $30-billion in interest on the federal debt, the government aims to cut spending by 1.5%. More than 60 departments have submitted plans to Cabinet for either five to 10 per cent cuts to their budgets, by finding operating efficiencies and examining the usefulness of programs.

---

12 Government of Canada, 2012, p.5-11.

The stated desire to avoid cuts in services is attractive to governments because it reduces the political fall-out with the electorate and provides the opposition and critics with less ammunition. The government's strategy is to present cuts as targeting inefficiency, red tape and redundant "back room" bureaucrats rather than services and benefits. In order to further reduce the political pain some commentators have suggested that Mr. Flaherty is also conducting a "strategy by stealth" approach to realizing cuts and deficit reduction (Reynolds, 2011). This view is predicated on two main patterns of action that have helped Minister Flaherty achieve "real dollar, per-capita austerity" over the each of the last 5 years without the kinds of protests and political fallout seen in other countries in response to austerity measures. First, Reynolds points to program spending increases that are less than the amount needed to keep pace with population-plus inflation adjustments. A budget prepared in this way will show nominal increases in national expenditure every year (averaging 2 per cent a year) even though they are, *de-facto*, cuts. Second, he points to Minister Flaherty's attempts to look for and weed out government programs that are no longer seen to serve a productive purpose.

By making small, incremental spending cuts, "here and there, hither and yon", he contends that Minister. Flaherty has provided the world with a good example of "responsible restraint – without inciting mobs" (Reynolds, 2011). Because these kinds of cuts are difficult to notice, he describes the process as "austerity on the quiet" (Reynolds, 2011). Clearly this approach is politically attractive as it avoids minus signs on the fiscal ledger, and it is harder for the opposition to galvanize resistance around specific or draconian cuts. Reynolds concludes it is an effective strategy that has managed to realize $10- billion of savings in recent years.

In spite of the political attractiveness of stealth as a means of achieving reductions many fiscal Conservatives would like to see more severe cuts, particularly in areas that have become political and ideological targets or simply to signal government priorities. Not surprisingly in this context, further job cuts are predicted for Environment Canada, in addition to the 776 already announced in 2011-12. Consistent with a neoliberal agenda, environmental assessments have been seen to slow down projects and the exploitation of natural resources across Canada, and in its northern regions in particular, and the government is keen to suspend these for projects pending, labeling them as excessive red tape and impediments to economic growth and jobs. Specific programs and green energy initiatives were also being pinpointed for cuts and/or eradication. The target of these proposed cuts are clearly green and renewable energy programs which, since the expansion of the Alberta tar sands, have increasingly come to symbolize the deepening ideological divide between Canada's left and right on energy and environmental policy as well as the splits between the provinces.

While Ontario and other provinces have begun to seriously invest in renewable energy programs, Alberta and Saskatchewan look to the federal government for policies that facilitate greater exploitation of oil and gas as well as other natural resources. Given the Harper Conservative's commitment to jobs, growth, increased trade and their western political base, it is no surprise that spending on the environment and in renewable energies continues to be vulnerable. Consequently the government has sought to minimize climate change as an issue, withdrawn from Kyoto and effectively given up the pretence of taking serious action to reduce emissions.

However, it is not just the substance of the 2012 budget that has caused concern; critics also point to the lack of transparency and informed debate that has been a constant feature of the process. Bill C-38, also called the *Jobs, Growth and Long-Term Prosperity Act*, tabled the 2012 budget as part of a so-called *omnibus bill*. Over 420 pages long, it has been described as a "statutory juggernaut" that introduces, amends, or repeals nearly 70 federal laws. It has been presented to the House of Commons in a manner that may be without close precedent in Canadian parliamentary history and has made proper parliamentary scrutiny impossible in the time available (Galvin, 2012). The Parliamentary Budget officer has also been concerned by the lack of reporting to parliament on the impact of the cuts announced in the 2012 budget as well as the previous two and is fighting to have details released by the government. Liberal MP John McCallum said this "slow oozing" of information over months erodes transparency and accountability and silences any debate at committees on what programs and services Canadians may be losing (May, 2012). He also expected this delay and "lack of transparency" since Treasury Board recently ordered departments not to include details about the reductions in their annual planning and priorities reports to Parliament (May 2012).

CONCLUSION

The policy practices of the Harper Government over the past few years have transformed much of what the state does and how it does it. The narrative of austerity has been formative in the ability of the Government to push through these transformative changes. In particular, the economic crisis and Canada's growing reliance on oil and gas for its economic wellbeing has allowed the government to shift policy direction in ways that might have seemed impossible when they came to power.

As this paper has shown, the crisis of austerity is at least in part a manufactured one—based on the decision to reduce taxation in a number of areas. This narrative of 'crisis' has been instrumental in reducing government involvement in a range of activities and in plans to decrease the size of the public service significantly. Numerous women's groups have lost their funding; the Roundtable for the Environment and the Economy has been disbanded; as has the Canadian Council on Learning.[13] These are but a small sample of groups and policy issues affected. At the same time, regulatory and oversight mechanisms are being eroded in such areas as trade and environmental assessments (Woods, 2012). While the government is divesting its involvement in many areas, it is increasing them in others—as we have shown through the Departments of Infrastructure and Natural Resources. Consequently, we argue that 'open federalism' is a serious misnomer and that 'strategic federalism' better describes the selective nature of the federal role under the Harper government.

Our analysis of Public Accounts has sought to take a look at overall spending patterns and focus on two examples, but the data holds many stories of interest. Rather than abandoning the neoliberal project, we believe that recent budgets, policies and priorities suggest that a more intense and comprehensive neoliberal agenda is emerging in Canada. Dissecting these changes and what they mean for the longer term will be a major task in the coming years. The well-documented restriction of information and control of communications complicates this task (Office of the Information Commissioner of Canada, 2010; The Professional Institute of the Public Service of Canada, 2011; Maher, 2011). But, such work will be pivotal in understanding how neoliberal policies, in the case of this Government, are being practiced. We hope to have contributed in some small way to this dialogue.

---

13 As of April 25, 2011, thirty-five women's organizations in Canada have had federal funding significantly cut or ended all together (Ad Hoc Coalition for Women's Equality and Human Rights 2011).

REFERENCES

Ad Hoc Coalition for Women's Equality and Human Rights (2011). http://www.womensequality.ca/

Bagnall, J. (2011, June 10). Afraid of 2012? Remember the Budget of 1995. *The Ottawa Citizen*. http://www.fcpp.org/publication.php/3797

Baker, A. (1999). Nebuleuse and the 'internationalization of the state' in the UK? The case of HM Treasury and the Bank of England. *Review of International Political Economy*, 6(1), 79-100

Bruno, J. (2012, February 27). The majority governing Conservatives are having a difficult time deciding what to cut, what to keep, and where to reallocate the scarce funds. *The Hill Times*. http://www.hilltimes.com/news/news/2012/02/27/expect-a- %E2%80%98watershed%E2%80%99-federal-budget-say-experts/29723

CCPA (2009). *2009 Budget Analysis*. Ottawa: Canadian Centre for Policy Alternative.

Cerny, P. G. (2004). *Mapping Varieties of Neoliberalism*. Paper prepared for presentation at the annual convention of the International Studies Association, Montreal, Québec, 17-20 March 2004 and the annual conference of the Political Studies Association of the United Kingdom, 6-8 April 2004. http://www.psa.ac.uk/cps/2004/cerny.pdf

Coen, D. & Roberts, A. (2012). A New Age of Uncertainty. *Governance: An International Journal of Policy, Administration, and Institutions*, 25(1) 5-9.

Corcoran, T. (2012, February 10). Panda politics: It's trickier than you think. *National Post*. http://opinion.financialpost.com/2012/02/10/panda-politics-its-trickier-than- you-think/

de Souza, M. (2012, April 6). Quebec Tories say Stephen Harper creating 'winning conditions' for referendum. *Postmedia News*. http://lifestyle.topnewstoday.org/culture/article/1969375/

Department of Finance (2010). Annual Financial Report of the Government of Canada Fiscal Year 2009–2010. http://www.fin.gc.ca/afr-rfa/2010/report-rapport-eng.asp

Department of Finance Canada. (2007). *Strong Leadership, a Better Canada: Economic Statement*. Ottawa: Government of Canada, October 30, 2007.

Department of Finance Canada. (2009). *Budget 2009: Canada's Economic Action Plan Backgrounder*. Ottawa: Government of Canada. http://www.fin.gc.ca/n08/09-011- eng.asp

Doern, G.B., A.M. Maslove and M.J. Prince. (2013). *Canadian Public Budgeting in the Age of Crises*. Ottawa and Kingston: McGill-Queens Press.

Easterbrook, W.T. & Watkins, M.H. (1984) The Staple Approach. In W.T Easterbrook & M.H. Watkins (Eds.), *Approaches to Canadian Economic History* (pp. 1–98). Ottawa: Carleton University Press.

Evans, B. & Albo, G. (2011). Permanent Austerity: The Politics of the Canadian Exit Strategy from Fiscal Stimulus. *Alternate Routes: A Journal of Critical Social Research*, 22, 7-28.

Fanelli, C. & Hurl, C. (2011). Janus-Faced Austerity: Strengthening the 'Competitive' Canadian State. *Alternate Routes: A Journal of Critical Social Research*, 22, 29-50.

Fekete, F. (2012b, March 16) Future of public service in hands of nine parliamentarians. *Postmedia News*. Retrieved September 30, 2012, from http://www2.canada.com/future+public+service+hands+nine+parliame ntarians/63 14885/story.html?id=6314885

Fekete, J. (2012a, March 10). Bureaucrats must shift to efficiency and constraint: Clement. *Canada.com*. http://www2.canada.com/topics/ news/story.html?id=6282995

Galloway, G. (2012, March 5). Spare veterans from budget axe, opposition says. *Globe and Mail Update*. http://m.theglobeandmail.com/news/ politics/ottawa- notebook/spare-veterans-from-budget-axe-opposition-says/article2358967/?service=mobile

Galloway, G. (2011, November 29). After the Tory witch-hunt against the CBC, who'll be next? *Globe and Mail*. http://www.theglobeandmail.com/ arts/television/after-the- tory-witch-hunt-against-the-cbc-wholl-be-next/article4179574/

Glavin, T. (2012, May 7). Something's fishy with Bill C-38. *National Post*. http://www2.canada.com/ottawacitizen/news/archives/story. html?id=cb8b39a4- f566-4e5a-a5c9-f3431c0dd554

Government of Canada (2009, January 27). Canada's Economic Action Plan. *Budget 2009*, tabled in the House of Commons by J.M. Flaherty, P.C., M.P. Minister of Finance.

Government of Canada (2010, March 4). Canada's Economic Action Plan, Year 2: Leading the Way on Jobs and Growth. *Budget 2010*, tabled in the House of Commons by J.M. Flaherty, P.C., M.P. Minister of Finance.

Government of Canada (2011). Infrastructure Stimulus Fund. *Infrastructure Canada*. http://www.infrastructure.gc.ca/prog/other-autres-eng. html#isf-fsi

Government of Canada (2012, November 11). *Jobs, growth and long term prosperity, Economic Action Plan 2012: the Budget in Brief*. Department of Finance. http://www.budget.gc.ca/2012/rd-dc/brief-bref-2012-eng. pdf

Gray, K. (2011, August 10). A defenseless economy. *The Ottawa Citizen*. *http://blogs.ottawacitizen.com/2011/08/10/a-defenceless-economy/*

Harmes, A. (2007). The political economy of open federalism. *Canadian Journal of Political Science*, 40(2), 417-437.

Harvey, D. (2003). *The New Imperialism*. Oxford: Oxford University Press.

Harvie, D. & Milburn, K. (2011, August 4). The zombie of neoliberalism can be beaten – through mass direct action. *The Guardian*. http://www. guardian.co.uk/commentisfree/2011/aug/04/neoliberalism-zombie-action-phone-hacking

Innis, H. (1956). *Essays in Canadian Economic History*. Toronto: University of Toronto Press.

Kipp, K. (2012, March 15). Most disabled access projects going to Tory ridings: documents. *Postmedia News. http://www. calgaryherald.com/business/Most+disabled+access+projects+going+ Tory+ridings+documents/6309515/story.html*

Krugman, P. (2010, July 1). Op Ed Column: Myths of Austerity. *The New York Times. http://www.nytimes.com/2010/07/02/opinion/02krugman. html*

Maher, S. (2011, November 30). Harper's PR obsession fostering paranoia and paralysis in the public service. *Canada.com*. http://www2. canada.com/news/maher+harper+obsession+fostering+paranoia+pa ralysis+public+service/5792000/story.html?id=5792000

May, K. (2012, March 14). Budget won't reveal details of PS cuts. *The Ottawa Citizen.* from http://www.ottawacitizen.com/opinion/op- ed/ Budget+reveal+details+cuts+Clement+says/6303389/story.html

MacKinnon, D. & Shaw, J. (2010). New State Spaces, Agency and Scale: Devolution and the Regionalisation of Transport Governance in Scotland. *Antipode*, 42(5), 1226-1252.

Nadeau, R. (2008, March 25). The Economist Has No Clothes: Unscientific assumptions in economic theory are undermining efforts to solve environmental problems. *The Scientific American*. http://www.scientificamerican.com/article.cfm?id=the-economist-has-no-clothes

Nguyen, L. (2012, February 24). Jim Flaherty says there 'shouldn't be any tax increases' in next budget. *Postmedia News*. http://www.theguardian. pe.ca/Business/2012- 02-24/article-2906460/Jim-Flaherty-says-there-shouldnt-be-any-tax-increases-in- next-budget/1

OECD [Organisation for Economic Development and Cooperation] (2011). Making the most of public investment in a tight fiscal environment: Multilevel governance lessons from the crisis. Paris: OECD.

Office of the Information Commissioner of Canada (2010). Special report to Parliament: Interference with Access to Information requests. Ottawa, Ontario.

Peck, J. & Tickell, A. (2002). Neoliberalizing space. *Antipode*, 34(3), 380–404.

PM of Canada (2006, March 21). Prime minister promotes open federalism. *Office of the Prime Minister of Canada*. Retrieved September 30, 2012, from http://pm.gc.ca/eng/media.asp?id=1123.

Public Works and Government Services Canada [PWGSC] (2010). *Public Accounts of Canada, volume II, Details of Expenses and Revenues.* Government of Canada, prepared by the Receiver General of Canada.

Public Works and Government Services Canada [PWGSC] (2005). *Public Accounts of Canada, volume II, Details of Expenses and Revenues.* Government of Canada, prepared by the Receiver General of Canada.

Public Works and Government Services Canada [PWGSC] (2006). *Public Accounts of Canada, volume II, Details of Expenses and Revenues.* Government of Canada, prepared by the Receiver General of Canada.

Public Works and Government Services Canada [PWGSC] (2007). *Public Accounts of Canada, volume II, Details of Expenses and Revenues.* Government of Canada, prepared by the Receiver General of Canada.

Public Works and Government Services Canada [PWGSC] (2008). *Public Accounts of Canada, volume II, Details of Expenses and Revenues.* Government of Canada, prepared by the Receiver General of Canada.

Public Works and Government Services Canada [PWGSC] (2009). *Public Accounts of Canada, volume II, Details of Expenses and Revenues.* Government of Canada, prepared by the Receiver General of Canada.

Public Works and Government Services Canada [PWGSC] (2011). *Public Accounts of Canada, volume II, Details of Expenses and Revenues.* Government of Canada, prepared by the Receiver General of Canada.

Pugliese, D. (2012, March 9). Opposition MPs say they'll now think twice about accepting Canadian Forces' invitations. *The Ottawa Citizen.* http://www.ottawacitizen.com/news/Opposition%20they%20 think%20twice%20ab out%20accepting%20Canadian%20Forces%20 invitations/6280032/story.html

Ruckert, A. (2006). Towards an Inclusive-Neoliberal Regime of Development: From the Washington to the Post-Washington Consensus. *Labour, Capital and Society,* 39(1), 34-67.

Ruckert, A. (2009). Periodizing Neoliberal Development Policy: From Destructive 'Roll Back' and Constructive 'Roll Out' to Inclusive Neoliberalism. Paper presented at the Annual Convention of the Canadian Political Science Association

Reynolds, N. (2011, September 6). Jim Flaherty: The master of stealth austerity. *The Globe and Mail.* http://www.theglobeandmail.com/report-on-business/rob- commentary/jim-flaherty-the-master-of-stealth-austerity/article627118/

Stiglitz, J. E. (2012). *The Price of Inequity: How Today's Divided Society Endangers our Future,* Norton: NY.

The Professional Institute of the Public Service of Canada (2011, July 28). Privy Council Muzzles Canadian Scientist. http://www.pipsc.ca/portal/ page/portal/website/news/newsreleases/news/072811

Varro, K. (2010). Re-Politicising the Analysis of 'New State Spaces' in Hungary and Beyond: Towards an Effective Engagement with 'Actually Existing Neoliberalism.' *Antipode*, 42(5), 1253-1278.

Veldhuis, N. & Lammam, C. (2012), March 5. The Chopping Block: Cut $10-billion now. *National Post*. http://opinion.financialpost.com/2012/03/05/the-chopping-block- cut-10-billion-now/

Wells, P. & McMahon, T. (2012, April 2). Oil Power. *Maclean's Magazine*, p.16.

Corcoran, T. (2012, March 6). The Chopping Block: Opinion. *National Post*. http://www.nationalpost.com/opinion/Where+Flaherty+begin/6255598/story.html

Williams, B. & McNeill, J. M. (2005). The Current Crisis in Neoclassical Economics and the Case for an Economic Analysis based on Sustainable Development. *U21 Global Working Paper, No. 001/2005*.

Williamson, J. (1990). *Latin American Adjustment: How Much Has Happened?* Washington, D.C.: Institute for International Economics.

Woods, M. (2012, April 17). Federal budget: Critics blast Ottawa's plan to overhaul environmental review process. *The Star*. http://www.thestar.com/news/canada/politics/article/1162871 — tories-introduce-sweeping-changes-to-environmental-assessments

Canada's Conservative Class War: Using Austerity to Squeeze Labour at the Expense of Economic Growth

—Toby Sanger[1]

INTRODUCTION

This time *was* different. In contrast with previous post-war recessions, the 2008/9 economic crisis was unquestionably caused by an internal crisis of capitalism. Canada's two previous recessions in the past half-century were directly caused by the federal government hiking interest rates to slow economic growth and reduce the pace of wage increases, ostensibly to reduce inflation. While the recent economic crisis was not caused by similar higher interest rate policies, *reactions* to it with an austerity agenda and other measures to suppress wages were designed to accomplish the same thing: a weakening of the power of workers in relation to capital and a further shrinking of labour's share of national income. This is despite the fact that the negative impacts of these economic policies on the distribution of national income and economic growth are now quite broadly accepted among economists. Even the International Monetary Fund (IMF) and the Organization for Economic Cooperation and Development (OECD) have publicly stated that a more equitable distribution of income would lead to stronger economic growth (IMF, 2011; OECD, 2011; 2012). However, Canadian and other governments have largely rejected these policies. The question is why?

This paper argues that the Conservative federal government's macroeconomic cyclical policies, characterized by austerity and additional neoliberal measures, are designed not to respond to short-term economic problems but to further entrench a shift in the national income away from labour to capital at the expense of stronger economic growth. This is evident in an analysis of the 2012 Conservative budget, which not only cut public spending, but also put in place measures that will

---

1   Toby Sanger is Senior Economist for the Canadian Union of Public Employees.

lead to a corrosion of wages, thereby reducing economic demand and making the state of household finances more treacherous. The absence of a political counter-weight to capital has meant that the half-hearted attempts at structural reform to reduce the likelihood of further financial crises have been overtaken by business-as-usual economic policies that will increase inequality, weaken economic growth and ultimately result in another cycle of economic crises. History suggests there will be little prospect of even moderate progressive change without increased social and political mobilization and the emergence of more radical threats to challenge the power of capital.

THIS RECESSION WAS DIFFERENT

In the three years prior to the start of the 1981/2 and 1990/1 recessions, the Bank of Canada almost doubled its short-term interest rate, which also pushed up medium- and longer-term rates (See Figure 1). This hiking of short-term interest rates to over 10 percent reduced investment, increased personal and business bankruptcies and pushed the unemployment rate to over 10 percent for four years after these recessions (Statistics Canada, 2012). The economic decline, lower government revenues, higher social spending and these higher interest rates also caused large increases in government deficits and deficit ratios (Finance Canada, 2012).

Coming out of these recessions, Canadian governments embarked on deficit-cutting crusades, largely through cuts to program spending along with public sector wage freezes and constraints to "share the pain" with public sector workers. Despite contractionary fiscal policies, Canada's economy was ultimately able to grow at reasonable rates coming out of these previous recessions because of expansionary monetary policies. As Figure 1 illustrates, the Bank of Canada cut its key interest rate by more than half following both the 1981/2 and 1990/1 recessions, providing a very large monetary stimulus for the economy. Lower interest rates relative to the United States also helped reduce the value of the Canadian dollar in the years following these recessions, providing a big boost to Canada's net exports.[2]

Canada faced a completely different situation in the 2008/9 recession. Instead of hiking interest rates, the Bank of Canada steeply cut its key lending rate going into the downturn. As the economic crisis

2   In the years following the early 1980s recession, the value of Canada's dollar declined from over US $0.86 in 1980 to US $0.71 in early 1986. Following the early 1990s recession, the value of Canada's dollar declined from a high of over US $0.88 in October 1991 down to below US $0.70 by 1998 (Statistics Canada, 2012).

progressed, the Bank of Canada further reduced its lending rate to record lows and has remained at close to historical lows since, with further monetary stimulus provided through "quantitative easing" and other extraordinary financial market measures.[3] Consequently, the Canadian economy has had little capacity to grow through further monetary stimulus as it did in the recoveries following previous post-war recessions. Instead, interest rates are widely expected to be increased, which will not only slow economic growth with lower investment, but are also likely to precipitate a long overdue 'correction' for Canada's housing market.

While Canada's federal Conservative government engaged in stimulus measures in its 2009 and 2010 budgets to bring the economy out of the financial and economic crisis, most of these measures were time-limited to two years only. Since then, the Harper government has strongly promoted contractionary fiscal policies both domestically and internationally, with successive spending cuts at the federal level and advocacy of fiscal austerity through the G20. These measures are causing unnecessary economic harm, particularly without the potential for offsetting monetary stimulus to mitigate the damage. As a result of austerity budgets, countries around the world including Canada are suffering from slow economic growth, with the U.K. and a number of other European countries forced into secondary recessions in 2012. With their economies weakening, these spending cuts have perversely increased the debt burdens of many countries instead of reducing them (Thomas and Jolly, 2012). As a result, even the IMF called for countries to focus on policies to strengthen growth over "fiscal consolidation" in its October 2012 World Economic Outlook (IMF, 2012).

While the 2008/9 financial and economic crisis was the *result* of internal crises of capitalism, these secondary recessions and resulting slow growth have been by *design*. As even traditionally neoliberal organizations such as the IMF have advised against these policies because they will slow economic growth, it is becoming ever more apparent that they are being implemented for political economy reasons: to strengthen the power of capital and weaken the power of labour as part of the longer term project of capital.

---

3   "Quantitative easing" involves central banks creating money to directly purchase assets such as bonds on financial markets. This is usually focused on longer-term assets in order to reduce longer-term interest rates.

LABOUR'S DECLINING SHARE

Successive contractionary fiscal policies together with other forms of direct and indirect wage suppression led to a steep decline in the rate of wage increases in both the private and public sectors following the post-war recessions. Figure 2 shows the rate of private and public wage increases in large collective agreements, illustrating sharp declines following both the 1981/2 and 1990/1 recessions. While inflation was also reduced, wage increases were lower, leading to real wage declines. These real wage declines took up to a decade of economic growth to recover from, especially for public sector workers. These periods of wage suppression ushered in a long-term shift in the share of national income from labour to capital.

Neoclassical economic growth models generally assume that labour and capital's shares of national income stay roughly constant over time: this was one of Kaldor's "stylized facts" about long-term economic growth (Kaldor, 1957). Fluctuations over the economic cycle are expected to occur – with more volatile corporate profits reducing capital's share and labour's share increasing during recessions – but over the long term these shares were expected to be fairly constant. Instead the past three decades have brought a longer-term decline in labour's share together with a long-term increase in capital's share of national income in both Canada and many other industrialized countries (OECD, 2012). The cyclical decline for profits in the recent recession was a short-lived blip in the long-term trend toward increasing shares of national income going to capital and diminishing shares going to labour (OECD, 2012). In the United States, labour's share recently reached its lowest recorded level since numbers were first kept in 1947, and more than 10 percent below its pre-2000 level (Federal Reserve Bank of St Louis, 2012).[4]

Within the household share of national income, inequality has also reached levels not seen since the 1930s, with a high share of the income gains going to the top one percent of the income distribution. The share of national income going to the top one percent reached 14 percent in 2007, almost double their share of the 1970s and 1980s (Veall, 2012). The shrinking share of labour in national income has become so significant

---

4   These figures underestimate the decline because much executive compensation, bonuses and stock options are actually included in labour income. The share of this top 1 percent recently escalated to the highest share of labour income since the 1930s (Hein, 2011, p.11-16). If the top 1 percent of income earners are excluded, the drop in labour's share of national income in Canada is close to double the rate when the wealthiest are included, from 1990 to the mid-2000s (OECD, 2012, p.115).

that even neoliberal organizations such as the OECD and the IMF have recently raised concern. The OECD included a chapter on "Labour Losing to Capital: What Explains the Declining Labour Share" in its 2012 Employment Outlook (OECD, 2012), following the IMF's chapter on "The Globalization of Labor" in their 2007 World Economic Outlook (IMF, 2007).

A recent OECD paper states clearly that declining labour shares and growing inequality are likely to slow down the economic recovery as well as endanger social cohesion. Together with the IMF's previous analysis on this issue, the OECD argues that the main factor reducing labour's share of national income has been technological change and capital deepening. In particular, the spread of information and communication technologies has led to the elimination of jobs involving routine tasks with machines leading to much greater polarization of employment and pay within the labour market.

This report (OECD, 2012) now acknowledges that neoliberal economic policies – those they have advocated for for decades – have had a significant impact in reducing labour's share of income. These include increasing trade and globalization, outsourcing, privatization, reduction in workers bargaining power and changes in collective bargaining. In terms of collective bargaining structures, it notes that governments and employers have used both centralized and decentralized bargaining structures – whatever works, often imposing settlements – to constrain wages, thereby reducing labour's share of pay and income.

Increasing financialization of the economy – switching from the principle of "retain and invest" to "downsize and distribute" – has also significantly weakened workers' bargaining power (Lazonick and Sullivan, 2000), as well as eroded economic growth. Other studies have found that levels of government spending and employment protection also have a strong impact on the distribution of national income between capital and labour (Harrison, 2002) Numerous studies have found that increasing globalization led to lower shares for labour in higher wage countries (Guscina, 2007). Labour's share in most other regions of the world also declined following increased globalization (Rodriguez and Jayadev, 2010; Tytell and Jaumotte, 2008). Increased openness to trade has been associated with higher income inequality in industrialized countries by many (Guscina, 2007), while employment protection policies are associated with lower rates of inequality. Inequality has also increased in most emerging countries, with the exception of some countries with antipoverty programs and strong social and employment protections, such as Brazil and Indonesia (OECD, 2011, p.51-64).

The shifts between these sectors are far greater when one considers accumulated capital rather than income. Following Keynesian national income accounting frameworks, analysis of our macro-economy focuses more on income than on capital measures. This is problematic (especially for a system called "capitalism") and is no doubt why so many economists remained blind to the growing imbalances of accumulated capital and the precariousness of a consumer debt-fuelled asset boom.

The balance sheets of corporate and household sectors reflect these shifts. Public attention is usually focused on the annual balance – deficits or surpluses – of the government sector. A more remarkable trend is the unprecedented shift in savings and surpluses from the household sector to the corporate sector in the 2000s. From at least 1960 until the late 1990s, the household sector recorded surpluses year after year which were invested in corporations to finance their capital investments. This relationship completely changed at the turn of this century. As Figure 4 shows, from 2000 onwards Canadian non-financial corporations have run massive surpluses (profits in excess of their capital investments), accumulating an additional $500 billion in cumulative surpluses. The total is even higher if the surpluses of banks and other financial corporations are included. These funds have been put into financial investments, used to reduce debt or buy back stock, or are sitting as excess cash or "dead money" as they were notably described by Bank of Canada Governor Mark Carney (Carmichael, 2012). By 2011, Canadian corporate debt-to-equity ratios reached record lows. Meanwhile, slow wage and income growth together with rising house prices resulted in unprecedented deficits for individuals and households and record rates of household indebtedness.[5]

THE ECONOMIC CRISIS AND THE CRISIS IN NEOLIBERAL ECONOMICS

While most Western governments continued to implement supply-side economic policies, these growing imbalances and inequalities created an ever more unstable economy. An overgrown and under-regulated financial sector, large pools of speculative financial investments and growth financed by household debt masked a stagnant underlying economy.

---

5   In the fourth quarter of 2011, the credit market debt of Canadian non-financial corporations had dropped to below 54 percent of the value of their equity, down from over 90 percent in 1994. On the other hand, the credit market debt of Canadian households reached a record high of over 163 percent in the second quarter of 2012, almost double the 85 percent rate it was in 1990 (Statistics Canada, 2012). The ratio of household debt to disposable income is now at record highs in Canada while these ratios have declined in other countries. For instance, in the United States household credit market debt has declined by about 7 percent in gross terms from 2007 to 2012 (Federal Reserve Bank of St Louis Economic Research Data, 2012).

When the financial house of cards finally started to collapse in 2007/8, it sparked a financial crisis, credit crunch, evaporation of business credit and an economic crisis, marking the first downturn in global GDP since the 1930s. Fortunately, governments around the world had learnt from the Great Depression and responded relatively swiftly and in a coordinated fashion, providing extraordinary sources of credit to business, bailing out the financial industry, reducing interest rates to all-time lows (in some cases negative) and introducing fiscal stimulus spending measures to counteract the economic downturn and prevent an even deeper economic decline. The almost complete reversal of neoliberal supply-side policies that had ruled for decades belied previous claims that that they were impossible or would be damaging for the economy. The fact that neoliberal organizations like the IMF and the OECD now acknowledge that growing income inequality is damaging for the economy is a significant reversal for these organizations after decades of advocating supply-side trickle-down economic policies (IMF, 2011; OECD, 2011, 2012).[6] It also reflects a growing crisis within neoliberal economics.

In Canada, Don Drummond, former chief economist of TD Bank and former federal Associate Minister of Finance, recently confessed that, despite governments implementing most of the public policy changes he had advocated – including tax cuts, free trade, competition, labour market flexibility deregulation, etc – productivity in Canada had actually deteriorated (Drummond, 2011). This confession followed just five years after he claimed all economists agreed on these policy measures – and after advocating that Ontario cut its public spending at twice the rate as during the 1990s! (Drummond, 2011; Sanger, 2011).

Also notable, the former chief and deputy chief economist of Canada's Department of Foreign Affairs and International Trade, Dan Ciuriak, recently co-authored a paper publicly questioning the alleged benefits of trade policy and other conventional wisdoms of economics, including supply-side economic measures, privatization, labour market flexibility, and other market-based incentive measures in their provocatively entitled paper, "What if Everything We Know About Economic Policy Is Wrong?" (Ciuriak and Curtis 2011).

Despite this very fundamental questioning and repudiation of neoliberal economic policies by former advocates (even if they did not offer

6   While these organizations have reflected similar concerns in some of their other policy prescriptions for Canada and other countries, they may not be reflected in more extensive reconsiderations of their approach. Often their concern is focused on how inequalities in the distribution of *personal* income might threaten "social cohesion" rather than on how changes in the distribution of *national* income are affecting economic and political relations.

alternatives), there has been no such questioning of these policies by Canada's federal Conservative government. Instead, they accelerated the implementation of these policies despite ample evidence that some of these measures will likely weaken economic growth.

Canada's Conservative government initially denied that the country was in recession in late 2008. Only when a coalition of opposition parties threatened to replace them as government did they acknowledge there was a real problem, proroguing Parliament and implementing stimulus spending measures. The discretionary fiscal policy that resulted was far more expansionary than in previous recessions in Canada, and in particular government capital investment increased at a far faster pace.[7] Still, stimulus measures were unbalanced: spending measures and those benefiting workers or households were time-limited and temporary while tax cuts for business were made permanent.

NEOLIBERAL AUSTERITY AND MANUFACTURED RECESSIONS

Following this close brush with worldwide depression and questioning of the validity of neoliberal economics, many hoped it would lead to some positive structural measures to stabilize the economic system and at least marginally reduce inequalities, as had eventually happened after both the 19th Century "Long Depression" and the 1930s Great Depression. By 2012, such hopes had pretty much evaporated. Instead, crude Keynesian policies drove up deficits, which were subsequently used to justify austerity budgets, cuts to employment protection, retirement security, social spending, other government programs and the weakening of environmental regulations. At the same time, businesses had not used their accumulated and growing surpluses to make productive investments, exacerbating the problem of stagnation.

The Conservative government's focus on spending cuts belies the fact that the federal government is in a much better fiscal situation than after previous recessions. While government deficits increased as a result of the economic crisis and stimulus measures, as a ratio of GDP they are still far below the rates they reached during the 1990s. With low borrowing rates, debt servicing costs for Canadian governments are about half of what they were during the mid-1990s (Figure 5).

---

7   Statistics Canada figures show that general government gross fixed capital formation (investment) increased to a share of 4.75 percent of Canada's economy (GDP) in the fourth quarter of 2010 from a low of below 3 percent a decade earlier, an increase of over 50 percent. In contrast, during the recessions of the early 1980s and 1990s, government capital investment increased to no more than 4 percent of the economy, hikes of only about 10 percent (Statistics Canada, 2012).

The on-going shift in national income and accumulated surpluses towards capital mean that Canada's non-financial corporations were, by 2012, sitting on over $526 billion in excess cash, up 42 percent since the recession ended in mid-2009. This amount is equivalent to 30 percent of GDP: just a small proportion could provide a significant boost to the economy and to household incomes. As Bank of Canada Governor Mark Carney stated, Canadian companies are in "historically rude health, have the means to act -- and the incentives," calling their surpluses "dead money" (Carney, 2011; Carmichael, 2012). Despite exhortations from Carney and Finance Ministers in the provinces and federally, corporations have done little to invest their surpluses back into the economy (Isfeld, 2012). In response, the obvious route would be for governments to tax this excess cash and use it to undertake productive investments, redistribute income and reduce household debt and inequality through the expansion of public services or direct transfers. While public spending quite appropriately increased during the recession, it remains a relatively small share of the economy. In fact, total public spending of all governments in Canada as a share of GDP dropped to at least a 30 year low just prior to the economic crisis (Figure 6). The increase during the past few years is as much a result of the shrinking of the underlying economy as it is of increased public spending: with a growing economy, this ratio will gradually decline.

With existing fiscal policies, the federal government would be in a structural surplus of over $25 billion, as the Parliamentary Budget Officer demonstrated in his September 2012 Fiscal Sustainability Report (Parliamentary Budget Officer, 2012b). In other words, as the economy grows to its full capacity, the federal deficit would soon be eliminated. In addition, federal and provincial deficits could be eliminated much faster with a few fair tax measures, there is no need for deep spending cuts and austerity measures to balance these budgets.

Instead, we should see public spending cuts as politically-driven, constituting "Janus" or two-faced austerity (Fanelli and Hurl, 2010). Fanelli and Hurl examined how Conservative budgets between 2006 and 2010 had constitutionalized neoliberalism and used austerity arguments to weaken labour and social protections while at the same time fuelling capital accumulation through tax cuts, privatization and increased neoliberalism. After winning a majority in the 2011 federal election, the Conservatives' political and economic agenda became even more transparent in what some described as their "transformative" 2012 budget (Ibbitson, 2012). Extending Fanelli and Hurl's analysis, I now examine the 2011 and 2012 budgets and their impact on the distribution of national income between capital and labour.[8]

CONSERVATIVE BUDGETS, THE ATTACK ON WORKERS' WAGES AND LABOUR'S SHARE

The 2011 and 2012 federal Conservative budgets have focused on constraining public and private sector wages, reducing employment protections and weakening workers' bargaining power; expanding free trade and corporate property rights; increasing resource extraction and weakening environmental protections; reducing taxation of capital; and implementing selective austerity and increased privatization. As we have seen above, each of these is associated with shrinking labour's share of national income, increasing capital accumulation and increasing inequalities.

CONSTRAINING PUBLIC AND PRIVATE SECTOR WAGES

Public sector wage constraints and freezes have been politically justified for fiscal reasons, garnering public support as a fair way for public sector workers to "share the pain" along with private sector workers suffering from the economic crisis. This is despite evidence that wages and salaries in the public sector are, on average, very similar to wages for similar jobs in the private sector but are much more equitable, with less of a wage gap for women and lower paid workers, and less excessive compensation at the top (Sanger 2011b). Much less overtly disclosed was one of the federal government's reasons for constraining public sector wages, which was to suppress wage increases in the private sector as well. In a court affidavit, in response to a court challenge of the federal government's wage constraint measures by the Association of Justice Counsel, Canada's Associate Deputy Minister of Finance, Paul Rochon (2011, p.20), stated: "The ERA's [Expenditure Review Act] policy objectives were complementary elements of the government's larger economic and fiscal policy. These objectives were threefold:

1. to help reduce upward pressure on private sector wages and salaries;
2. to provide leadership by showing restraint and respect for public money; and
3. to manage public sector wage costs in an appropriate and predictable manner that would help ensure the ongoing soundness of the government's fiscal position."

---

8 The focus here is very much on the federal government, although some provincial governments have also implemented similar measures.

This was a rare admission of the government's broader economic objectives: to squeeze private sector wages and ultimately reduce labour's share of national income; but Canada is of course not alone on this. The European Central Bank previously published a number of studies urging governments to squeeze public sector wages so that private sector wages would also be reduced "in order to enhance economic stability and competitiveness in the Economic and Monetary Union" (Holm-Hadulla et al, 2010, p.4; Afonso and Gomes, 2010; Fernàndez-de-Córdoba et al., 2009; Lamo et al., 2008). The subsequent policies of many governments in Europe to cut public sector wages were developed and implemented with this in mind.

After winning a majority government in the 2011 federal election, the Conservatives made their objective of squeezing workers' wages much more transparent in their 2012 budget. While some measures were rationalized for fiscal reasons, others were focused at more directly limiting wage growth in the private sector. First, the government announced new rules to allow employers to pay temporary foreign workers wages 15 percent below the prevailing rate, and fast-tracked approvals for skilled workers to no more than ten days (less time than it takes Canadian banks to clear cheques on foreign banks). Second, the Conservatives eliminated Employment Insurance (EI) benefits for claimants who fail to take jobs at up to less than 30 percent below their previous wage. As well, they abolished the Employment Insurance Tribunal and delegated EI appeals to a much smaller centralized Social Services Tribunal also responsible for dealing with Canadian Pension Plan and Old Age Security (OAS) appeals, with members directly appointed by the federal government, thereby eliminating balance and local input into the appeals process and directly enforcing the government's directives. Third, the government eliminated the federal Fair Wage and Hours of Labour Act, meaning that contractors on federal construction jobs can pay their workers as little as the minimum wage, accelerating the proverbial race to the bottom (CUPE, 2012).

These measures follow the Harper government's repeated curtailment of the right to strike by legislating workers under federal jurisdiction back to work with little hesitation, including rail workers at Canadian Pacific, airline workers at Air Canada and postal workers at Canada Post. In the case of postal workers, they also directly intervened to reduce wage increases below the rates previously offered by their employer. These actions sent a strong message that this federal government would not allow workers to exercise their right to collectively withdraw their labour through strikes, thereby undermining Canada's system of free collective bargaining (Fanelli and Lefebvre, 2011).

One of the most controversial measures in the 2012 Budget – the increase in the retirement age to 67 to qualify for OAS benefits – was rationalized and promoted by the Harper government as a necessary change required to ensure that public pensions would be fiscally sustainable. As the Finance Minister Jim Flaherty (2012, p.6) stated in his budget speech, "Today it is clear we must take action to ensure the sustainability of the Old Age Security program, which is the largest spending program of the federal government." However the increase in the age of retirement was made much more for political and labour market reasons – to increase the supply of labour by requiring workers to work longer before collecting retirement benefits – than for fiscal reasons. Canada's Parliamentary Budget Officer, Kevin Page, released a report in 2012 demonstrating that the federal government's OAS and Guaranteed Income Supplement (GIS) programs are already on a fiscally sustainable path. While the costs of these benefits are forecasted to rise to a peak of 3.2 percent of GDP by 2031 from the current level of 2.2 percent of GDP, they are then set to ultimately decline to 1.8 percent of GDP – below current rates (Parliamentary Budget Officer, 2012a, p.ii).

The federal Conservative government's move to increase the age of retirement was introduced together with other measures to directly increase incentives for later retirement followed lobbying by the Canadian Chamber of Commerce (CCC) for changes to get seniors to work more, but went further than the CCC was prepared to publicly advocate (Canadian Chamber of Commerce, 2011).

Layoffs of public sector workers and cuts in the 2012 federal budget will reduce employment by approximately 40,000. Job losses increase to well over 100,000 when taking account of cuts in the previous two budgets and spending cuts by provincial governments wages (Parliamentary Budget Officer, 2012a; 2012b). Together with cuts to public services, these job losses will also weaken workers' bargaining power and lead to a broader erosion of wages.

EXPANSION OF FREE TRADE AGREEMENTS
AND CORPORATE PROPERTY RIGHTS

The Conservative government's relentless pursuit of free trade deals with countries and trading blocs around the world are also a major factor in strengthening the power of corporate capital, weakening labour and limiting the democratic powers of governments. The federal government now has eighteen different sets of free trade agreements in negotiation or discussion and has concluded six others in the past three years (Canada Department of Foreign Affairs and International Trade, 2012). Gaining better access for trade of goods is actually a minor element of most of these deals: the real interest is in eliminating "non-tariff barriers" – such as local content provisions and marketing boards – and expanding corporate property rights, including patent protection.

In fact, Canada's trade balance with countries that it has signed major trade deals has become worse than with countries that it doesn't have trade deals with. As Jim Stanford has noted, "If the policy goal (sensibly) is to boost exports and strengthen the trade balance, then signing free trade deals is exactly the wrong thing to do" (Stanford 2012, n.p.).

INCREASING RESOURCE EXTRACTION AND WEAKENING OF ENVIRONMENTAL PROTECTIONS

The Conservatives' 2012 federal budget bill also significantly expanded the power of corporate capital over Canada's natural or environmental resources through numerous measures that roll-back environmental protections and accelerate resource extraction (Sierra Club of Canada, 2012). These included the elimination of and deep cuts to environmental protection programs and protective legislation to the extent that it was even criticized by a former Conservative minister of fisheries (Halifax Chronicle Herald, 2012). It has also gone on the attack against environmental organizations, denouncing them as "extremists" funded by foreign money, threatening their charitable status and, in a move redolent of the McCarthy and Bennett era, adding some of them to the list of potential terrorists along with anti-capitalist groups. This follows the Harper government's leadership in scuttling the Kyoto Accord and resistance to any significant measures to address climate change. Weakened environmental protections and increased resource extraction significantly increases capital accumulation by speeding the appropriation of natural resource rents.

REDUCING TAXATION OF CAPITAL

Capital accumulation has also been significantly increased through cuts to corporate and capital taxes at the federal level and strong pressure and billions in support from the federal government to provinces to reduce corporate tax rates and remove sales taxes from business inputs. Corporate tax rates have been cut even further despite evidence that these tax cuts have not stimulated investment but, on the contrary, have been associated with declining rates of business investment (Figure 7). Instead, these corporate tax cuts have been far more successful at increasing capital accumulation at the expense of labour, in addition to increasing deficits to provide a rationale for selective austerity measures.

SELECTIVE AUSTERITY AND PRIVATIZATION

Selective austerity measures have included elimination of funding for civil society organizations, including any involved in "advocacy". Many of these measures have been discussed elsewhere (see, for example, Fanelli and Hurl 2010). However, recent measures expanded the involvement and control of capital over public services and public policy in some notable ways beyond the traditional scope of commercialization, contracting-out, public-private partnership and asset-sale privatizations beyond that already being implemented. These include providing business employers with much greater say over the selection of permanent immigrants (in addition to the often exploitative power they have over temporary foreign workers), use of development assistance funds to help promote Canadian mining firms abroad, exploring the use of social impact bonds and introducing legislation to allow private ownership of First Nations land (Mendleson, 2012; Leblanc, 2012; Wingrove, 2012).

CONCLUDING REMARKS

With current economic policies in place, prospects for a healthy recovery will remain meager in Canada. Lower interest rates cannot provide the stimulus for economic recovery they did following previous recessions. Household debt is at record levels and a housing price bust is imminent. Business is failing to reinvest its growing surpluses into productive capital investments and export expansion is largely limited to resources. With Canadian governments slashing public spending, contractionary fiscal policy is creating the conditions for another lost decade.

The federal Conservative government has not only used the economic crisis as an opportunity to impose selective austerity measures which are slowing the economy, but are also using it to accelerate neoliberal economic policies that will further shrink labour's share of income and increase that of capital. This is being done at a time when the economic crisis has provoked a number of high profile neoliberal economists to question their fundamental economic policies and prescriptions.

With the bankruptcy of neoliberal economic policies, it is difficult to reach any other conclusion except that the Conservative government is continuing to aggressively implement neoliberal policies for political reasons: to expand the power of capital and to weaken the power of labour in a continued class war. As Warren Buffett, one of the wealthiest men in the world, once stated: "There's class warfare, all right, but it's my class, the rich class, that's making war, and we're winning." (Stein 2006).

One of the great achievements of neoliberal economic theory was the perpetuation of the illusion that economics is a science and that its analysis can be divorced from consideration of economic and political power, as well as human and social behavioral considerations. While some in the economics profession may continue to cling to these illusions, many are moving beyond it. For example, Joseph Stiglitz, the prominent New Keynesian economist and Nobel-prize winner, is only one of many who are now declaiming how appropriation of political and economic power by a small elite is endangering our future but also entreating them to support new policies (Stiglitz, 2012). But entreaties to the one percent to embrace different economic policies will likely have little effect unless the alternatives are starker and they feel more threatened.

It may be largely forgotten now but at the time of the last major global crisis of capitalism, John Maynard Keynes felt compelled to address the power of vested interests in his conclusion to *The General Theory* (Keynes, 1936, n.p.)

"the ideas of economists and political philosophers, both when they are right and when they are wrong, are more powerful than is commonly understood. Indeed the world is ruled by little else. Practical men, who believe themselves to be quite exempt from any intellectual influences, are usually the slaves of some defunct economist. Madmen in authority, who hear voices in the air, are distilling their frenzy from some academic scribbler of a few years back. I am sure that the power of vested interests is vastly exaggerated compared with the gradual encroachment of ideas. Not, indeed, immediately, but after a certain interval; for in the field of economic and political philosophy there are not many who are influenced by new theories after they are twenty-five or thirty years of age, so that the ideas which civil servants and politicians and even agitators apply to current events are not likely to be the newest. But, soon or late, it is ideas, not vested interests, which are dangerous for good or evil."

These concluding comments of Keynes were clearly made in a different world. The threats to capital and the elite were far more present with the strength of the Soviet Union and growing appeal of socialism in the West. His ideas and approach provided a much more palatable alternative for the vested interests than the other threats they were facing in the world of ideas and politics at that time.

While conventional, Keynesian, new Keynesian and even post-Keynesian economic solutions may appear convincing to some on their own, even their marginal changes have little chance of being adopted unless the growing power of the "vested interests" also considers them in their interests – or at least, a lesser threat than the alternatives.

For some in this class, the Occupy Movement is starting to have that effect. American billionaire Jeff Greene recently warned (Pressier, 2012, n.p.):

> "There are all these people in this country who are just not participating in the American Dream at all. Right now, for some bizarre reason, a lot of these people are supporting Republicans who want to cut taxes on the wealthy. At some point, if we keep doing this, their numbers are going to keep swelling, it won't be an Obama or a Romney. It will be a Hollande. A Chávez."

While neoliberal economic policies are being increasingly questioned and abandoned by economists, politicians – including Canada's Conservative federal government – continue to implement them for purely political and ideological reasons: to further concentrate economic and political power among the owners of capital and to weaken the power of labour. With these conditions, it should be increasingly apparent that there will be little prospect of even moderate change without increased social and political mobilization and the emergence of more radical threats to challenge the power of capital.

FIGURES

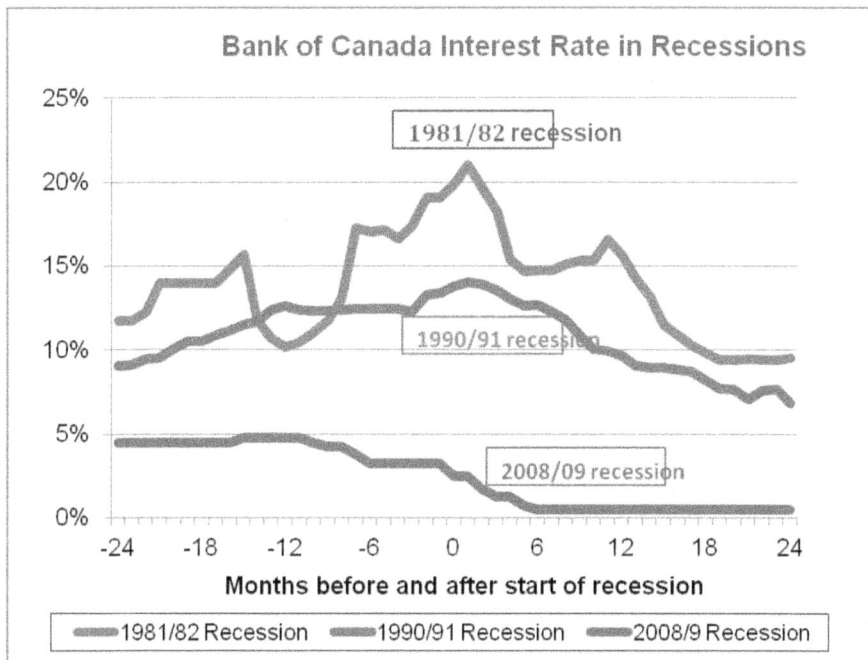

Bank of Canada Interest Rate in Recessions

1981/82 recession

1990/91 recession

2008/09 recession

Months before and after start of recession

1981/82 Recession   1990/91 Recession   2008/9 Recession

Figure 1
Source: Bank of Canada interest rates: Bank of Canada Rate.
http://www.bankofcanada.ca/rates/interest-rates/

Shattering the Myth of Canadian Exceptionalism

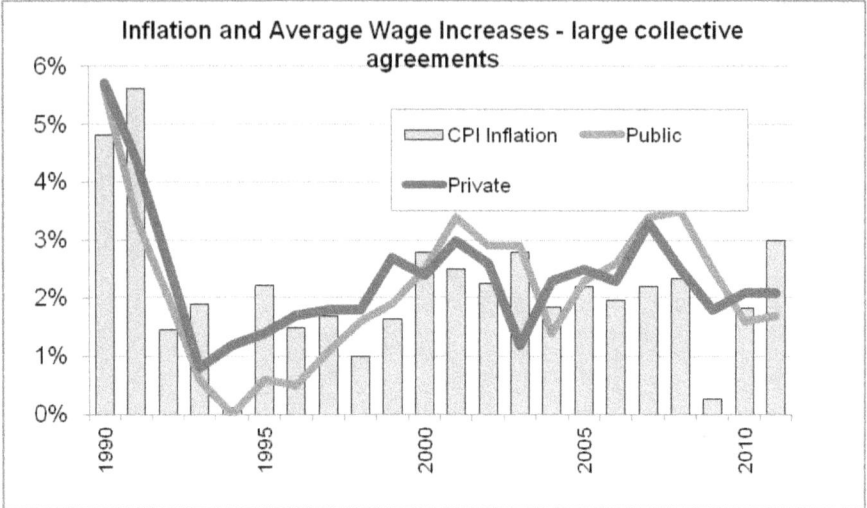

Figure 2
Sources: Statistics Canada *Consumer Price Index* (Cansim Table 326-0021);
Human Resources and Skills Development Canada *Annual Wage Settlements*. http://www.hrsdc.gc.ca/eng/
labour/labour_relations/info_analysis/datas/wages/in dex.shtml

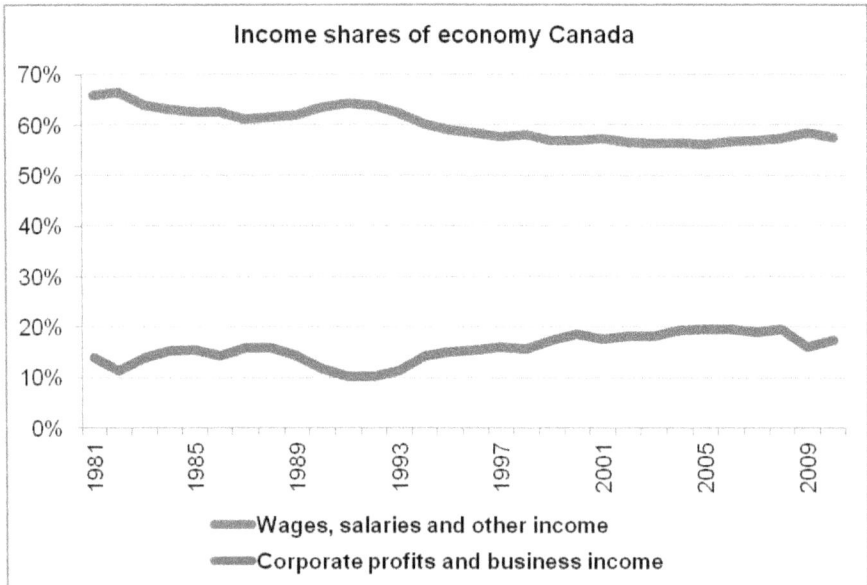

Figure 3
Source: Statistics Canada *GDP Income-based* (Cansim table 380-0001).

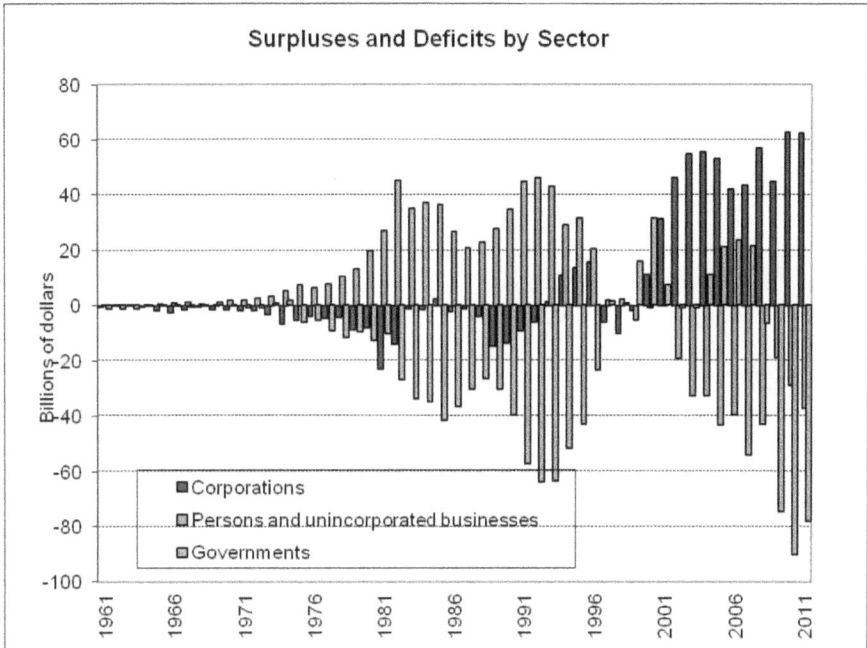

Figure 4
Sources: Statistics Canada, *Financial Flows* (Cansim Tables 378-0018, 378-0019 and 378-0040).

Shattering the Myth of Canadian Exceptionalism

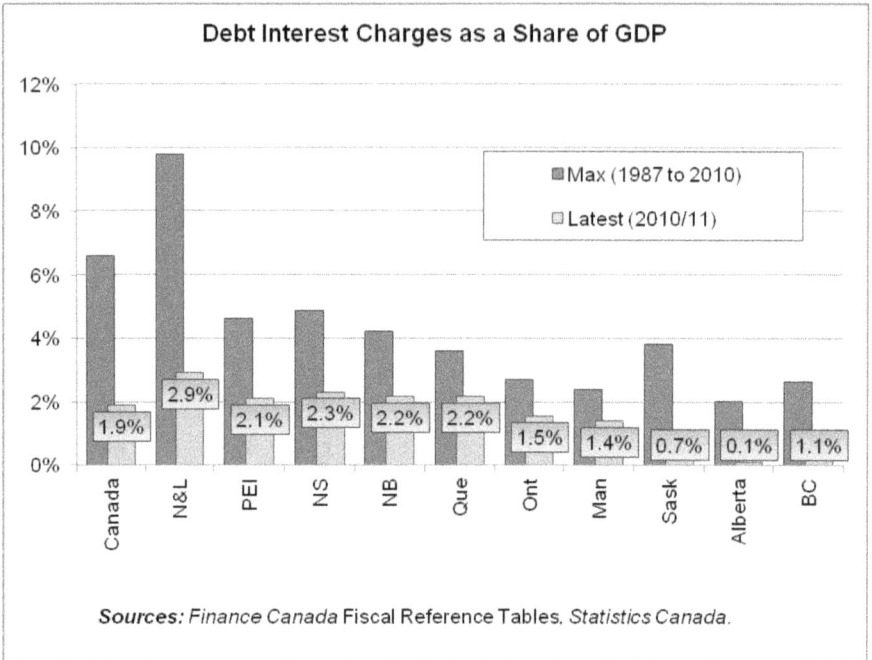

Debt Interest Charges as a Share of GDP

Max (1987 to 2010)
Latest (2010/11)

1.9%   2.9%   2.1%   2.3%   2.2%   2.2%   1.5%   1.4%   0.7%   0.1%   1.1%

Canada | N&L | PEI | NS | NB | Que | Ont | Man | Sask | Alberta | BC

Sources: Finance Canada Fiscal Reference Tables. *Statistics Canada.*

Figure 5
Source: Statistics Canada, Fiscal Reference Tables, http://www.fin.gc.ca/pub/frt-trf/index-eng.asp

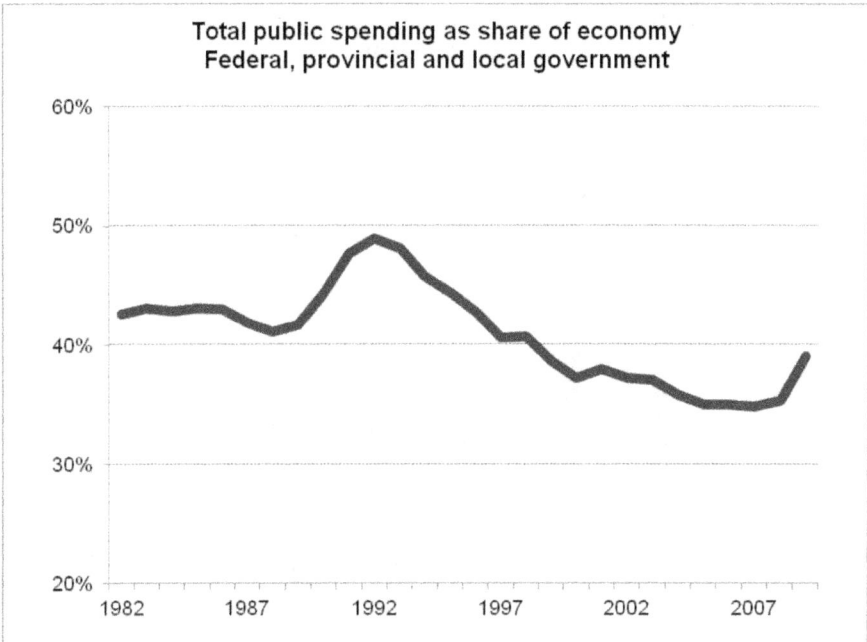

Figure 6
Source: Statistics Canada *Provincial and Territorial Economic Accounts Data* Tables 1 and 6. (Publication #13-018X). http://www.statcan.gc.ca/pub/13-018-x/2011001/tab-eng.htm

Shattering the Myth of Canadian Exceptionalism

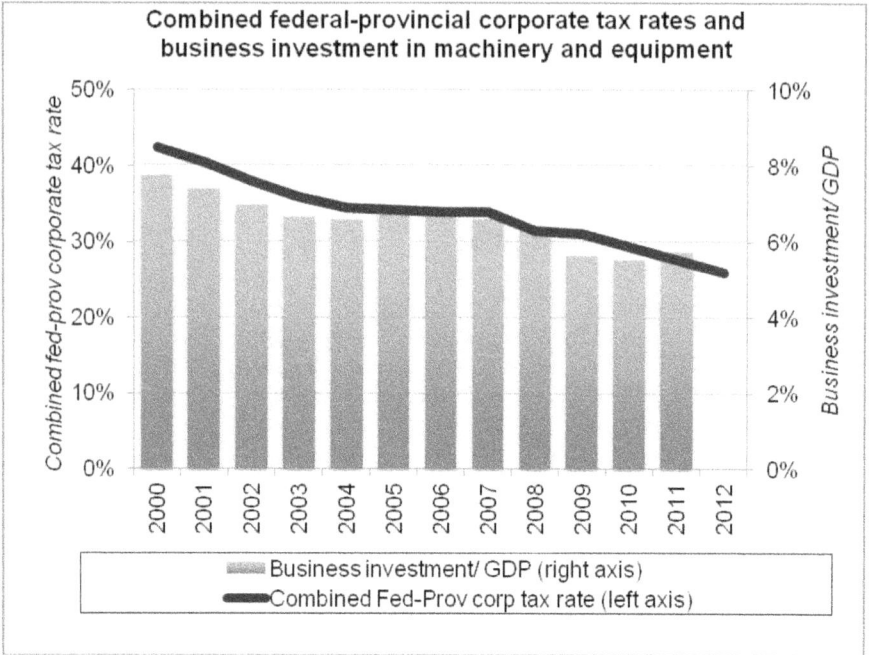

Figure 7
Sources: Statistics Canada, *GDP Expenditure-based* (Cansim Table 380-0002); OECD Tax Database (Part II, Table II.1). http://www.oecd.org/tax/taxpolicyanalysis/oecdtaxdatabase.htm

REFERENCES

Afonso, A. and Gomes, P.M. (2010). Interactions between Private and Public Sector Wages. *IZA Discussion Papers 5322, Institute for the Study of Labor* (IZA).http://ftp.iza.org/dp5322.pdf

Canadian Chamber of Commerce. (2011, December). *Incenting Seniors to Continue Working.* http://www.chamber.ca/images/uploads/Reports/2011/1112IncentingSeniors_to_ ContinueWorking.pdf

Carmichael, K. (2012, August 22). Free up 'dead money,' Carney exhorts corporate Canada. *The Globe and Mail.* http://www.theglobeandmail. com/report-on-business/economy/free-up-dead- money-carney-exhorts-corporate-canada/article4493091/

Carney, M. (2011, December 12). *Growth in the Age of Deleveraging.* Speech to the Empire Club of Canada/Canadian Club of Toronto. http://www. bankofcanada.ca/2011/12/speeches/growth-in-the-age-of- deleveraging/

Ciuriak, D. and Curtis, J.M. (2011, April 1). *What If Everything We Know About Economic Policy is Wrong?* http://dx.doi.org/10.2139/ssrn.1839647

Canada Department of Foreign Affairs and International Trade. (2012). *Negotiations and Agreements.* http://www.international.gc.ca/trade-agreements-accords-commerciaux/agr- acc/index.aspx?view=d

Canadian Union of Public Employees. (2012, March 29). Conservative's small-minded budget kills jobs and fails Canadians: CUPE's analysis of the 2012 federal budget. http://cupe.ca/budget/federal-budget-analysis

DeCloet, D. (2009, October 24). Civil servants: It's time to share the pain. Globe and Mail. http://advisor1.dynamic.ca/servlet/ArticleNews/story/gam/20091024/RDECLOET 24ART1922

Drummond, D. (2006). The Economists' Manifesto for Curing Ailing Canadian Productivity. *International Productivity Monitor, Centre for the Study of Living Standards,* 13, 21-26. http://www.csls.ca/ipm/13/IPM-13-drummond-e.pdf

Drummond, D. (2011). Confessions of a Serial Productivity Researcher. *International Productivity Monitor, Centre for the Study of Living Standards,* 22, 3-10. http://www.csls.ca/ipm/22/IPM-22-Drummond.pdf

Fanelli, C. and C. Hurl. (2010). Janus-Faced Austerity: Strengthening the 'Competitive' Canadian State. In Fanelli, C., C. Hurl, P. Lefebvre and G. Ozcan (Eds.), *Saving Global Capitalism: Interrogating Austerity & Working Class Responses to Crises, Alternate Routes 2011* (pp. 29-50). Ottawa: Red Quill Books.

Fanelli, C. and P. Lefebvre. (2011). The Ottawa and Gatineau Museum Workers' Strike. Precarious Employment and the Public Sector Squeeze. In Fanelli, C. and P. Lefebvre (Eds.), *Uniting Struggles: Critical Social Research in Critical Times, Alternate Routes 2012* (pp. 121-146). Ottawa: Red Quill Books.

Flaherty, J. (2012, March 29). The Budget Speech. *Government of Canada*. http://www.budget.gc.ca/2012/rd-dc/speech-eng.pdf

Guscina, A. (2007).Effects of Globalization on Labor's Share in National Income. *International Monetary Fund Working Papers 06/294*. http://www.imf.org/external/pubs/ft/wp/2006/wp06294.pdf

Hein, E. (2011). Distribution, 'Financialisation' and the Financial and Economic Crisis – Implications for Post-crisis Economic Policies. *MPRA Paper 31180, University Library of Munich, Germany*. http://www.ipeberlin.org/fileadmin/downloads/working_paper/ipe_working_paper_ 09.pdf

Federal Reserve Bank of St Louis Economic Research Data. (2012). *Nonfarm Business Sector: Labor Share (PRS85006173)*. http://research.stlouisfed.org/fred2/series/PRS85006173?rid=47&soid=22

Fernàndez-de-Córdoba, G. (2009). Public and private sector wages interactions in a general equilibrium model. *Working Paper Series 1099, European Central Bank*. http://www.ecb.int/pub/pdf/scpwps/ecbwp1099.pdf

Finance Canada. (2012). Fiscal References Tables. http://www.fin.gc.ca/frt-trf/2012/frt-trf-12-eng.asp

Halifax Chronicle Herald. (2012, June 10). Ex-ministers assail changes to fisheries protection. *Halifax Chronicle Herald*. http://thechronicleherald.ca/thenovascotian/105518-ex-ministers-assail-changes- to-fisheries-protection

Harrison, A.E. (2002). Has Globalization Eroded Labor's Share? Some Cross-Country Evidence. *University of California at Berkley and NBER, mimeo*. http://mpra.ub.uni-muenchen.de/39649/1/MPRA_paper_39649.pdf

Holm-," H. (2010). Public wages in the euro area - towards securing stability and competitiveness. *Occasional Paper Series 112, European Central Bank*. http://www.ecb.europa.eu/pub/pdf/scpops/ecbocp112.pdf

Ibbitson, J. (2012, March 29). Flaherty's plan forces you to expect less from Ottawa. *Globe and Mail*. http://www.theglobeandmail.com/news/politics/flahertys-plan-forces-you-to- expect-less-from-ottawa/article627560/

IMF. (2007). *World Economic Outlook*. http://www.imf.org/external/pubs/ft/weo/2007/01/data/index.aspx

------ (2011, September). *Why Inequality Throws Us Off Balance, Finance and Development*. 48(3). http://www.imf.org/external/pubs/ft/fandd/2011/09/index.htm

------ (2012, October). World Economic Outlook,. http://www.imf.org/external/pubs/ft/weo/2012/02/index.htm

Isfeld, G. (2012, September 25). Flaherty urges businesses to open wallets, forge partnerships with emerging economies. *Financial Post*. http://www.ottawacitizen.com/mobile/business/fp- business/Flaherty+urges+businesses+open+wallets+forge+partnerships+with/72 97401/story.html

Kaldor, N. (1957). A model of economic growth. *The Economic Journal*, 67(268), 591-624.

Keynes, J.M. (1936).*The General Theory of Employment, Interest and Money*. Cambridge: Cambridge University Press. http://www.marxists.org/ reference/subject/economics/keynes/general- theory/ch24.htm

Lamo, A. (2008). Public and private sector wages - co-movement and causality. *Working Paper Series 963, European Central Bank*. http://www.ecb.europa.eu/pub/pdf/scpwps/ecbwp963.pdf

Leblanc, D. (2012, September 6). CIDA funds seen to be subsidizing mining firms. *Globe and Mail*. http://m.theglobeandmail.com/ news/politics/cida-funds-seen-to-be-subsidizing- mining-firms/ article1360059/?service=mobile

Mendleson, R. (2012, April 20). Canada Immigration: Jason Kenney's Reforms Will See Employers Selecting Newcomers. *Huffington Post*. http://www.huffingtonpost.ca/2012/04/20/canada-immigration-employers-pick- newcomers_n_1439992.html

OECD. (2011, December). *Divided We Stand: Why Inequality Keeps Rising*. http://www.oecd.org/els/socialpoliciesanddata/49170475.pdf

OECD. (2012, July). *Employment Outlook 2012*. http://www.oecd-ilibrary.org/ employment/oecd-employment-outlook- 2012_empl_outlook-2012-en

Parliamentary Budget Officer. (2011, February 8). Federal Fiscal Sustainability and Elderly Benefits. *Office of the Parliamentary Budget Officer*. http://www. parl.gc.ca/PBO-DPB/documents/Sustainability_OAS.pdf

Parliamentary Budget Officer. (2012a, April 24). *PBO Economic and Fiscal Outlook*. http://www.parl.gc.ca/pbo-dpb/documents/EFO_April_2012.pdf

Parliamentary Budget Officer. (2012b, September 27). *Fiscal Sustainability Report*. http://www.pbo-dpb.gc.ca/files/files/FSR_2012.pdf

Pressier, J. (2012, July 29). The Other Barbarians at the Gate. *New York Magazine*. http://nymag.com/news/business/themoney/jeff-greene-2012-8/

Radice, H. (2011). Cutting Government Deficits: Economic Science or Class War? In Fanelli, C., C. Hurl, P. Lefebvre and G. Ozcan (Eds.), *Saving Global Capitalism: Interrogating Austerity & Working Class Responses to Crises, Alternate Routes 2011* (pp. 87-102). Ottawa: Red Quill Books.

Rochon, P. (2011, April 11). Rochon Affidavit at para. Cited in Respondents Factum. Ontario Superior Court of Justice, CV-10-404604, p. 20. http:// ajc-ajj.net/files/library/02_-_AGC_Factum_Part_1_of_3.pdf

Rodriguez, F. and A. Jayadev. (2010).The Declining Labor Share of Income. *Human Development Research Papers (2009 to present) HDRP-2010-36, Human Development Report Office, United Nations Development Programme*. http://hdr.undp.org/en/reports/global/hdr2010/papers/ HDRP_2010_36.pdf

Sanger, T. (2011a). *Fair Shares: How Banks, Brokers and the Financial Industry Can Pay Fairer Taxes*. Ottawa: Canadian Centre for Policy Alternatives.

------ (2011b). Battle of the Wages: Who gets paid more, public or private sector workers? Ottawa: Canadian Union of Public Employees.

------ (2012). Austerity Doesn't Work: Ontario can balance its budget while improving public services and tax fairness. Ottawa: Canadian Union of Public Employees.

Sierra Club of Canada. (2012). The Harper Budget: Assault on the Environment for Big Oil profits: Roundup of Canadian Environmental NGO Responses. http://www.sierraclub.ca/en/main-page/harper-budget-assault-environment-big- oil-profits-roundup-canadian-environmental-ngo-respo

Stanford, J. (2012, May 21). The troubling truth about free trade. *Globe and Mail*. http://www.theglobeandmail.com/commentary/the-troubling-truth-about-free- trade/article4186695/

Statistics Canada. (2012). *Cansim Database*. (Labour Force Cansim Table 282-0002; Exchange rates Cansim Tables 176-0049; Debt ratios Cansim tables 378-0123 and 378-0124; Investment shares of the economy Cansim table 380-0064) http://www5.statcan.gc.ca/cansim/

Stein, B. (2006, November 26). In Class Warfare, Guess Which Class is Winning. *New York Times*. http://www.nytimes.com/2006/11/26/business/yourmoney/26every.html

Stiglitz, J. (2012). *The Price of Inequality*. New York: W. W. Norton & Co.

Thomas, L. Jr. and D.Jolly. (2012, October 22). Despite Push for Austerity, European Debt Has Soared. *New York Times*. http://www.nytimes.com/2012/10/23/business/global/despite-push-for-austerity- eu-debt-has-soared.html?_r=0

Tytell, I. & F. Jaumotte. (2008). How has the Globalization of Labor Affected the Labor Income Share in Advanced Countries? *IMF Working Papers 07/298, International Monetary Fund*. http://www.imf.org/external/pubs/ft/wp/2007/wp07298.pdf

Veall, M. (2012). Top Income Shares in Canada: Recent Trends and Policy Implications. *Canadian Journal of Economics*, 45(4), 1247-1272.

Wingrove, J. (2012, August 6). Ottawa's plan to allow private property on reserves reignites debate. *Globe and Mail*. http://www.theglobeandmail.com/news/politics/ottawas-plan-to-allow-private- property-on-reserves-re-ignites-debate/article4466019/

Stabilizing Privatization: Crisis, Enabling Fields, and Public-Private Partnerships in Canada

— Heather Whiteside[1]

Public-private partnerships (P3s) – or "cooperative ventures between the state and private business" (Linder, 1999, p.35) – are now commonly used in Canada to deliver public infrastructure such as hospitals, highways, water treatment facilities, and schools. However, despite their growing popularity, P3 arrangements are seldom able to provide better value for money than traditional public procurement given the higher costs associated with private financing and for-profit service delivery. Problems of this sort were only further compounded during the recent global financial crisis as private financing became more expensive and difficult to secure, leading to several project delays and cancellations across the country (Mackenzie, 2009). With the onset of a new round of fiscal austerity as of late, one might reasonably expect that this policy would be scrapped in favour of lower cost public procurement. Instead, as of 2010, the P3 model is flourishing once again. This is particularly problematic given that these arrangements link important public services to highly volatile global financial markets and poorer value for money leads to additional unnecessary costs over the long run.

The relatively quick recovery of the P3 model in the face of recent and longstanding concerns requires explanation. One obvious driver is neoliberal ideology and its dogged commitment to privatization. Yet however accurate this explanation may be, on its own it is inadequate since it tells us very little about the specific policy forms that these normative commitments take. To this end, attention is paid here to the changes in public infrastructure decision-making that have occurred

---

1   Heather Whiteside is a Ph.D. candidate in the Department of Political Science at Simon Fraser University. She is the co-author of *Private Affluence, Public Austerity: Economic Crisis & Democratic Malaise in Canada* (with Stephen McBride), and has published articles in journals such as *Studies in Political Economy*, *Health Sociology Review*, and *Socialist Studies*.

over the past decade which shore up the ideological underpinnings of privatization via P3. This is not to suggest that the normatively-based preference for P3s has disappeared, but it does point to its normalization within a public sector reoriented toward greater market dependence. This has helped to promote P3s over the long run and to stabilize their use more recently despite the growing list of drawbacks.

This article makes two interrelated arguments. First, in Canadian jurisdictions most enthusiastic for P3s – Ontario and British Columbia – P3 proliferation is encouraged through important changes within government made to capital planning procedures and bureaucratic decision-making, and new forms of institutional support for privatization. This constellation of new arrangements will be referred to here as a 'P3 enabling field'.[2] These provincial enabling fields normalize P3 use through the routinization, institutionalization, and depoliticization of this policy. *Routinizing* P3 implementation involves the creation of infrastructure planning protocols and routines that deeply embed the language and calculus of the private for-profit sector into the heart of public policy making. *Institutionalizing* support for P3s has been advanced through the creation of new capital planning procedures and public authorities, both of which create an air of permanency for this policy. Finally, *depoliticization* through provincial P3 enabling fields helps to obscure the normative basis of P3 use by making it appear as though privatization is merely a pragmatic decision. Depoliticization also occurs through the actual shift from public to private authority, making it both a strategy and a reality.

However, given that P3 markets are vulnerable to the volatility of global finance, existing problems with the model (such as poor value for money) are exacerbated during times of crisis which can readily lead to collapsed/abandoned deals and crises of faith on the part of policy makers. This recently occurred when newly initiated projects – those in the high risk bidding or construction stages – were hard hit in 2008/9 when access to capital markets narrowed significantly. Thus the second argument made here flows from the first: the subsequent stabilization and recovery of P3 use in Canada after 2009 relates in large part to the routinizing, insti-

---

2 The use of this term has been inspired by, though differs from, Jooste and Scott's (2012) discussion of P3 enabling fields. For them an enabling field is composed of a "network of new 'enabling organizations' (public, private, nonprofit)" (2012, p.151). These organizations include specialized P3 units, Auditors General, private consultants, and advocacy organizations. While these actors are no doubt crucial to the maturation of P3 markets, by focusing only on organizations (essentially the 'institutional support' category of the enabling field as conceptualized here) their concept of an enabling field ignores legislation, capital planning frameworks, and supportive secondary reforms which are particularly important for P3s in Canada.

tutionalizing, and depoliticizing effects of provincial P3 enabling fields. This has led to the curious condition that P3s are now increasingly the new 'traditional' mode of public infrastructure procurement despite their longstanding inability to live up to the promises made by proponents.[3]

These arguments will be substantiated through a series of steps. First, the article discusses the (misleading) basis on which P3s are often justified in Canada, and how problems with the private financing component in particular were compounded by the recent financial crisis. Second, it describes the principal features of the P3 enabling fields that have been set up in Ontario and BC, and examines how they routinize, institutionalize, and depoliticize privatization policy.

PUBLIC-PRIVATE PARTNERSHIPS

The Canadian public sector is becoming increasingly reliant upon capitalist markets to deliver 'public' infrastructure and support services at all levels of government, and P3s are a leading way in which this occurs. P3 policy is typically passed off as a new and innovative approach to 'alternative service delivery' (e.g., see Hodge and Greve, 2005, p.7-8), as though partnering with for-profit partners is simply one innocuous option among many. However, P3s contribute to a transformation in the social relations of power, and therefore they should be more precisely understood to be a form of what David Harvey (2003) calls 'accumulation by dispossession'.

Reminiscent of 'original accumulation' as described by Marx, dispossession involves the expansion of capitalist market relations in a number of ways, namely through the creation of new opportunities for profit making and by redistributing assets, thereby enhancing the breadth and depth of capitalist accumulation (Harvey, 2003). This form of market expansion is achieved by incorporating into the realm of private accumulation that which has come to exist 'outside' of these circuits of capital (ibid). Through this predatory mechanism, privatization opens up new investment and profit-making opportunities in three distinct ways.

As discussed by Ashman and Callinicos (2006), privatization can involve commodification, recommodification, and/or state restructuring. Their qualification of Harvey's argument is an important contribution as

---

3　This applies to hospital re/development in particular. Though the numbers fluctuate over time, hospital P3s make up the majority of all P3 projects in BC and Ontario, particularly with projects that cost in excess of $50 million (for up-to-date project lists see Partnerships BC, n.d.; Infrastructure Ontario, n.d.). This has been relatively consistent over the past decade due to the strategic targeting of health care infrastructure in provincial infrastructure renewal plans.

privatization is not a homogenous process. Commodification turns assets that were not previously commodities into private property which can be bought and sold in capitalist markets; recommodification converts what was once produced privately but subsequently taken over by the state back into a commodity; and restructuring creates a reliance upon private for-profit provision (ibid, p.121-123). P3s can involve commodification and/or recommodification, depending on the project, as well as state restructuring. The latter feature is of principal interest here and its key elements (routinization, institutionalization, and depoliticization) will be examined in subsequent sections.[4]

Like other forms of privatization (e.g., selling state assets), P3s create new markets for capital through re/commodification. Restructuring via P3s intensifies market dependence and awards greater authority and decision-making over public policy to private for-profit investors. Sometimes labeled 'privatization by stealth' (e.g., CUPE, 2003), P3s also allow for dispossession within potentially unprofitable or especially sensitive areas which would not otherwise be suitable candidates for more overt privatization initiatives. However, an important distinguishing characteristic of the P3 model is that while it features dispossession, state obligations to provide that particular good or service are not severed (Grimsey and Lewis, 2004, p.55). In other words, should the purported benefits of a P3 project fail to materialize, the public sector (i.e., taxpayer) ultimately remains on the hook.

Policy makers make several misleading claims to justify P3 use. Transferring projects risks away from taxpayers and onto the shoulders of private partners is often touted as the central advantage of the P3 model (Hodge and Greve, 2005). The most common risks attributed to infrastructure projects are those relating to the site (tenure, access, suitability), design and construction (delays, weather, cost overruns), operation and maintenance (cost overruns), and financing (interest rate fluctuation, inflation). While these are indeed important concerns, the risks addressed in P3 contracts are restricted to those which can be insured against through market actors, thus excluding other forms of risk relevant to the public sector.[5] For instance, this involves ignoring social concerns related to privatization (e.g., more precarious working conditions and lower quality services) and the creation of long run risk when the public sector is locked in to more

---

4 Other aspects of P3s as accumulation by dispossession, particularly as this relates to the Canadian public health care system, are addressed in Whiteside, *forthcoming* 2013.

5 Furthermore, the Auditor General of Ontario argues that a well-designed public procurement contract can adequately protect the public from many of these risks (especially cost overruns, delays, and design flaws). See Ontario Auditor General, 2008.

expensive, inflexible, multi-decade P3 agreements. Further, in practice risk transfer is often illusory given that private consortia build these costs into the price of their bids, and thus acceptance of risk translates into the anticipated profit margin of the private partner. This essentially cancels out public sector gains whilst the private partner is fully compensated by the state (Cohn, 2004, p.8). Risk transfer is a very lucrative arrangement for the private partner, with investors earning real rates of return of roughly 15-25 percent per year (Gaffney et al., 1999, p.116; Hodge, 2004, p.162).

Financial risk transfer played a large role in the justification of early P3s in Canada (see Loxley, 2010). These arguments rely on the belief that infrastructure ought to be funded by private firms, and financed by loans, particularly when government funds are scarce. In Canada this rationale is in part ideological (i.e., the perception of public debt as a sign of mismanagement) and in part practical due to fiscal austerity. However P3s cannot actually reduce the financial obligations of the state, they are only able to mask costs since traditional infrastructure tends to be paid for upfront while P3s tend to be structured as lease arrangements, spreading payments out over time. Whether or not P3s can actually deliver value for money and cost savings over the long run therefore becomes of primary concern.

Proponents base value for money (VfM) arguments on risk transfer as well as the neoclassical assumption that competition (in this case for the P3 contract) combined with the profit-maximizing behaviour of the private sector will result in lower overall project costs (Loxley, 2010, p.2-3).[6] There are a number of problems with these claims, the most important being the suggestion that private sector cost superiority will actually lead to lower public sector costs rather than being absorbed by the private partner in the form of higher profit (Vining and Boardman, 2008, p.15). These arguments also do not take into account social concerns produced by reducing labour costs and through a relaxation of standards (e.g., environmental, design, hiring and training). Finally, claims that value for money is achieved through 'on time' and 'on budget' delivery must, of course, be confirmed through the empirical record. In Canada like elsewhere many P3s have been delivered late and there have been serious cost overruns (e.g., see Edwards and Shaoul, 2002; McKee et al., 2006; Mehra, 2005).

Compounding these more straightforward financial concerns is the methodological deception that occurs with VfM calculations. A central component of any VfM assessment is a comparison between the cost

---

6   See Spronk, 2010 for a discussion of the normative assumptions used to justify privatization on the basis of 'economic efficiency'.

of a P3 in relation to a public sector comparator (PSC) – a hypothetical model created to represent the traditional delivery method. A key part of this process involves the application of a discount rate to the project costs in order to estimate the "cost of capital over time" which allows for considerations such as interest and inflation (Partnerships BC, 2005, p.19). Yet the choice of which discount rate to use is not a neutral decision, it is both political and controversial. The higher the discount rate, the more attractive the P3 option becomes since it favours expenditure in later years relative to that which is spent now (Gaffney et al., 1999, p.117). As Loxley (2012; 2010) indicates, even though there is no universally agreed upon discount rate, rates used to calculate VfM in Ontario and BC are well above the UK's best practice rate of 3.5%, often by 1-3 percent respectively. This practice makes it appear as though a P3 offers better value even in cases where cost savings fail to materialize.

PUBLIC-PRIVATE PARTNERSHIPS AND THE 2008/9 GLOBAL FINANCIAL CRISIS

Many of the long-standing problems that accompany P3 projects were made even worse by the recent global financial crisis. The most obvious impact was the ratcheting up of costs associated with the private finance portion of newly initiated partnerships. Prior to 2007 government borrowers in Canada were able to secure interest rates that were, on average, 2 percent lower than those charged to private borrowers, but between 2007 and 2009 this increased to an average of 3 or 4 percent – making P3s nearly 70 percent more expensive than publicly funded infrastructure (when measured in present value terms) (Mackenzie, 2009, p.2). Transaction costs also increased as the timeframe for negotiations was lengthened due to financial market instability (Drapak, 2009). This impacted P3 value for money as any unbiased assessment would have to favour the traditional procurement model on these grounds alone.

Along with increased costs came the implications of the credit crunch and changes in financial market dynamics. When the option to secure monoline wrapped bonds disappeared during the subprime meltdown, the main source of private financing used by P3s was suddenly eliminated.[7] Together these developments posed serious challenges for newly initiated projects (those that were in the bidding and construction stages) and led to a series of delays, renegotiations, and collapsed deals in 2008/9.

---

7   A monoline wrapped bond refers to when companies take out insurance against the risk that they will default on their debt ('monoline'), and by using a high quality insurance group ('wrapped') debtors are able to secure very high credit ratings, leading to lower interest rates (see Tett, 2007 for further detail).

In Canada the effects of the financial crisis began to show in mid-2008 and most projects that reached financial close at this time were smaller in scope and required only short term financing (Canadian Council for Public-Private Partnerships [CCPPP], 2009, p.1). Several high profile and high cost deals also faced serious challenges during this time. With the Port Mann Bridge P3, one of the private partners (Macquarie Infrastructure Group) was unable to come up with the requisite $700 million and as a result the Province of British Columbia was forced to renegotiate the agreement in order to keep the project going (Hunter, 2009). This renegotiation occurred just weeks before construction was scheduled to begin. With the Fort St. John Hospital P3 project, also in BC, financial market instability meant that a new private partner was needed to bailout the original private equity partner that had been contracted to finance the $268 million hospital (Mackenzie, 2009, p.11). Further, although the BC provincial government remained committed to actively pursuing P3 projects throughout the crisis, stimulus fund spending targeted speedier traditional infrastructure projects and decision makers suspended the requirement that P3s be first considered for all large infrastructure projects (Mackenzie, 2009, p.10).[8]

Other pro-P3 provinces faced similar problems. In Ontario, for example, the Niagara Health Systems P3 project, originally scheduled to begin construction in spring 2009, was delayed for several months when the private financing portion fell through (Mackenzie, 2009, p.12). A new private financing partner then stepped in. Rather than abandon P3 policy altogether, the province temporarily moved away from partnerships which relied on private financing.

Equally troublesome were the problems posed for operational projects. Based on the assumption that projects could be refinanced periodically at projected rates, many existing P3s have secured financing for a shorter term than the life of the project. As Mackenzie (2009) suggests, the rationale underpinning privately financed P3s therefore had a built-in expectation that the credit-fueled bubble would continue indefinitely. There was little prudence demonstrated despite P3-proponents often justifying partnerships on the basis of fiscal austerity, and promoters ignored the possibility of a looming financial crisis. Fiscal recklessness such as this led Scotland's Finance Minister John Swinney to label the use of private financing associated with P3s "one of the worst excesses of the age of financial irresponsibility" (Fraser, 2009).

---

8   The requirement that P3s must be first considered for all large infrastructure projects has since been re-imposed.

Crises of faith began to emerge in Canada's public sector as well. While labour unions and public service advocacy groups have long been vocal and determined opponents of P3s, the global financial crisis and its immediate aftermath also led several policy makers to publicly question their use. For instance, Quebec Health Minister Yves Bolduc stated in 2009 that "P3s were not a religion" for his party (Canadian Union of Public Employees, 2009). The Treasury Board President, Minister of Transport, and Minister of Municipal Affairs also cast doubt on the future of P3s in that province, and several proposed P3s were scrapped in favour of public procurement (ibid).

Altogether, the new and longstanding problems and widening opposition could have easily nurtured a movement away from the P3 model. That it has since rebounded was never inevitable, but rather the legacy of the P3 enabling fields created nearly a decade earlier. This constellation of initiatives stabilized the P3 model during the darkest days of the financial crisis and helped it subsequently recover given the reorientation of public policy and public sector decision-making that had been initiated several years earlier.

P3 ENABLING FIELDS

In light of their troubled track record, governments seeking not to abandon P3 policy but to normalize its use have restructured and reoriented certain key elements of their public sectors. In addition to the expansion of, and enhanced public sector dependence on, capitalist markets that accompanies dispossession, P3s have also come to entail the application of private sector logic and rationale to public infrastructure and service delivery. These new rules, and the institutions that have been created to enforce and promote them, are conceptualized here as forming a 'P3 enabling field'. Over the long run, enabling fields promote dispossession through state restructuring, and on a more immediate level they help stabilize P3 policy during times of crisis – as witnessed in the wake of the 2008 global financial crisis.

The P3 enabling fields set up by Canada's key P3 enthusiasts – the BC and Ontario provincial governments – are composed of several crucial elements, including new capital planning frameworks, and new forms of institutional support for privatization.[9] The capital planning changes relevant to these provinces are: BC's Capital Asset Management Frame-

---

9   There are other legislative and supportive secondary reforms which have also been implemented although these contain elements unique to particular sectors (e.g., transportation and health) and therefore will not be addressed here.

work (CAMF) and Ontario's Infrastructure Planning, Financing and Procurement Framework (IPFP) and Alternative Financing and Procurement (AFP) model. New institutional support for P3s is now provided by specialized P3 units, named Partnerships BC and Infrastructure Ontario.

P3 Enabling Fields		
	BC	Ontario
Capital planning frameworks	CAMF (2002)	IPFP (2004); AFP (2004)
Institutional support	Partnerships BC (2002)	Infrastructure Ontario (2005)

CAPITAL PLANNING FRAMEWORKS

In May 2002, the Capital Asset Management Framework (CAMF) was introduced in BC to serve as new "rules of the road" for public infrastructure development, governed by five best-practice principles: sound fiscal management, strong accountability, value for money, protecting the public interest, and competition and transparency (BC Ministry of Finance, 2002, p.1-2). The CAMF applies province-wide and all ministries, public sector agencies, and public organizations must now comply with these rules when seeking approval and funding for infrastructure projects.

When it was first introduced, the Ministry of Finance made an effort to present the CAMF as being pragmatic, claiming that it "does not predetermine that every project will be a public-private partnership" (BC Ministry of Finance, 2002, p.1). The Value for Money CAMF document furthermore states that: "the framework does not assume that any one sector [public or private] is inherently more efficient in building and operating public assets. Instead, it emphasizes that capital decisions will be based on a practical, project-specific assessment of a full range of options" (BC Ministry of Finance, n.d., p.5). Yet pragmatism is more rhetorical than real since the CAMF also dictates that all capital project proposals in excess of $50 million must *first* be considered as P3s.[10] Cohn (2008, p.89) suggests that the CAMF shifts the bias away from traditional public procurement by "chang[ing] the terms of debate regarding P3s. Instead of explaining why a P3 was justified, it [is now] necessary to explain why a P3 (or some other form of alternative service delivery) [is] *not* being employed".

Less obvious but equally important are the implications of its focus on market-oriented notions of risk and the heavy emphasis placed on

---

10 From 2002-2008 this stipulation applied to all proposals above an even lower threshold of $20 million (since 2008 those in the $20-$50 million range are subject to a P3 screen which is used to determine whether a more comprehensive P3 evaluation should proceed) (BC Ministry of Finance, 2008).

identifying and valuating risk throughout the CAMF procedures. Before a project can move beyond the initial proposal stage it is subjected to a risk-based assessment which assumes that additional responsibilities bring greater risks, and thus risk can be mitigated and minimized through partnership agreements. This creates an innate bias against public financing and ownership given that *any* new infrastructure project taken on by a public sector agency is assumed to generate risk. Risks are then monetized and added onto publicly delivered projects, penalizing public procurement even though these risks may be entirely hypothetical. Reliance upon the private sector to reduce risk also ignores the potential for cost savings that can be achieved through risk pooling (i.e., publicly financing a large number of projects), which can amount to a huge loss for the citizen and taxpayer. Mackenzie's (2007, p.iv) study of Alberta P3 schools found that "for every two schools financed using the P3 model, an additional school could be built if they were all financed using conventional public sector financing."

The CAMF also enshrines a market-based notion of what defines the public interest. Under the CAMF this feature of policy making is to be determined through criteria such as assessing service outcomes (mediated by monetary relations) and monitoring the performance of service providers (using market-based contracts). This is an extremely narrow conception of the public interest and does not take into consideration other concerns such as the contradiction that exists between profit-making and commercial confidentiality on the one hand, and democratic oversight and local control on the other (see Wood 1995 for more on this tension).

Initiated in July 2004, Ontario's Infrastructure Planning, Financing and Procurement Framework (IPFP) is similar to BC's CAMF given that it outlines the strategies that will be used when developing (planning, building, financing and managing) new public infrastructure projects across the province. Like the CAMF, the IPFP framework enshrines five key principles in the planning, financing, and approval of project proposals submitted by Ministries, municipalities, and other public sector entities: the public interest is paramount, value for money must be demonstrated, appropriate public ownership/control must be preserved, accountability must be maintained, all processes must be fair, transparent, and efficient (Ontario Ministry of Public Infrastructure Renewal [MPIR], 2004, p.9). These are presented as a pragmatic, technocratic approach to infrastructure investment but there is an explicit emphasis on "innovative engagement of the private sector to leverage expertise and capital" (MPIR, 2004, p.17); and P3s must be considered for all projects over \$20 million. Of the nine infrastructure and procurement models discussed in the IFPF, eight are P3s (MPIR, 2004, p.21-22), and the public procurement option is only recommended for very minor investments (MPIR, 2004, p.24). A risk-focus is present here too, as is an emphasis on value for money which incentivizes private financing and procurement.

In 2003 Dalton McGuinty, while campaigning for Premier of Ontario, vowed to scrap the province's first P3 hospitals which had been recently initiated by his predecessor Mike Harris. However, not only did these particular deals go forward (although some renegotiation did take place), but attempts to depoliticize P3s were soon initiated when the newly elected McGuinty government rebranded them as 'Alternative Financing and Procurement' (AFP) projects. Though improvements have been made when compared to how P3s were previously developed (e.g., see Ontario Auditor General, 2008), there is no specific legislation in place to ensure that IPFP principles are upheld and in practice AFP projects are still P3s. Both involve partnering with for-profit private consortia for the design, construction, financing, and operation of public infrastructure and support services. P3 industry insiders and advocates also confirm that they see no substantial difference between the P3 and AFP models (e.g., see Ontario Standing Committee on Government Agencies, 2008, p. 1530), as did the Minister of Health when initially presenting AFP to the private sector (CCPPP, 2005).

An important feature of AFP as it applies specifically to Ontario's health sector which is worth highlighting here is the 2006 decision by the Ministry of Health and Long Term Care to exclude what they call 'soft support services' from future hospital deals (Block, 2008, p.2). This means that P3 hospitals in Ontario now involve only hard facility services such as maintenance, security, and operation of the physical plant but not care-related services like housekeeping, dietary, and laundry services. There is no such exemption in BC though some recent P3 hospital deals have excluded cleaning services.

Why exactly soft services were excluded in Ontario is a multifaceted issue. The Canadian Union of Public Employees (CUPE) and the Ontario Health Coalition (OHC) claim that this was largely the result of a series of community-initiated plebiscites organized by the OHC which indicated overwhelming community support for the proposition that new hospital projects be kept fully public. A plebiscite in Hamilton, for example, returned a vote of 98% in favour of this proposition (OHC, 2006). From a more cynical perspective, soft support services may have been exempted from P3 hospital project agreements not due to community activism but instead because of the serious and ongoing problems that have resulted from their incorporation within early project agreements in that province (see Ontario Standing Committee on Public Accounts, 2009, p.1340). It is therefore likely that this exemption serves two purposes: assuaging some public concerns whilst helping to make P3s run smoother in the future. By serving as both a concession offered to opponents and a pragmatic modification to the P3 model, overall this development has helped ensure the longevity of the P3 model in Ontario's public health care sector. There is also no guarantee that this exemption of soft services will be maintained in the future.

NEW FORMS OF INSTITUTIONAL SUPPORT

New forms of institutional support for P3s are the backbone of the enabling field. The creation of specialized government agencies, or 'P3 units', best exemplifies this component. P3 units promote and evaluate these projects and act as repositories of knowledge which facilitates policy learning by building government expertise surrounding the complex bidding, negotiation, and operational phase of P3 projects (Rachwalski and Ross, 2010). The presence of these P3 units has been essential to the entrenchment of privatization within the public sector. The role of the P3 unit extends beyond the more prosaic activities outlined on their websites and in policy documents as they must translate global policy models and dispossession imperatives, ensuring that this unfolds in ways which meet local needs whilst simultaneously ensuring profitability for global investors.

Without the institutional support that P3 units provide, problems experienced with individual projects would not readily transform into a sophistication of the local P3 model but instead could easily lead to its abandonment. Dispossession via P3s is relatively unique from other types of privatization since even though individual projects are locked in through multi-decade contracts, the model itself must be continually renewed through new projects and thus it contains a future-oriented component. This means that committed policy makers must take into consideration the long run implications of decisions made today. P3 units are currently the central way to ensure that this happens in BC and Ontario. As Jooste and Scott (2012, p.150) put it: "The move toward private participation in infrastructure does not simply substitute private sector capacity for public sector capacity, *it requires new forms of public sector capacity to be developed to overcome [P3] challenges*" (emphasis added).

The need for new forms of public sector capacity to facilitate dispossession was resolved in BC and Ontario through the creation of Crown corporations (in 2002 and 2006, respectively). This organizational form is significant given that in some countries greater political control is retained through the development of expertise and P3 unit-like roles within line departments (e.g., Mission d'Appui aux PPP in France and Parapublica in Portugal; see Farrugia et al., 2008). The use of Crown corporations, an arm's length quasi-public organizational form, has a long history in Canada and has been used for many different purposes ranging from economic development to cultural preservation (Whiteside, 2012). Yet something entirely new appears to have occurred in the past decade with P3 units: the use of Crown corporations to facilitate dispossession. This occurs not through their sale but through their very existence – they are developed by the state to manage and encourage privatization in other areas of the public sector. Thus the Crown corporation is now being used to extend market-led restructuring in Canada's public sector.

These Crown corporations also help root market rules and norms within the public sector, and this is role appears to be expanding as their purview grows. With Partnerships BC this expansion is both internal and external to the province. Within the province, greater use of P3s means that Partnerships BC has been gradually taking over the roles previously played by the BC Building Corporation (BCBC) (McKellar, 2006). Created in 1977 to manage public sector real estate, land, and infrastructure, BCBC is thus being increasingly replaced with a commercialized Crown corporation oriented toward privatization. Further, as indicated in its 2011 annual report (Partnerships BC, 2011), its future strategy includes diversifying its client base. This involves selling its expertise to other jurisdictions without P3 units and pushing the P3 model into new sectors within the province.

The roles assigned to Infrastructure Ontario have also been greatly expanded over the years and it is now responsible for many different aspects of infrastructure and land development in the province: from large P3 infrastructure development and operation in 2005 to small infrastructure loans (offered to municipal borrowers only) in 2006 when it absorbed the Ontario Strategic Infrastructure Financing Authority (OSIFA), and more recently in 2011 it took on the responsibilities of the Ontario Reality Corporation (ORC) (the manager of government owned and occupied land and buildings) (see Infrastructure Ontario, 2011). This has not only given Infrastructure Ontario a greater degree of permanence within the province but it also means that its P3-specific tasks are increasingly normalized within the day-to-day operations of government.

In order to assist jurisdictions without a P3 unit, in 2007 the federal government has also increased its commitment to P3s through the creation of PPP Canada Inc. as a way of promoting and assisting P3 development across the country (especially at the municipal level). Once the P3 market deteriorated sharply with the financial crisis in 2008, PPP Canada Inc. also began to engage in 'extensive discussions' throughout 2008/9 with the provinces/territories, private sector stakeholders and other federal organizations to gauge the nature and extent of public sector support needed to ensure that new projects were started and that recently initiated projects reached financial close. Through these efforts PPP Canada determined its priority would be to help ease the "significant roadblock" to P3 projects posed by the financial crisis (PPP Canada, 2009). In furtherance of its mandate to "develop the Canadian market for public-private partnerships," it has received funding commitments from the federal government of $2.8 billion per annum for 2011-2013 (PPP Canada, 2009). PPP Canada also teamed up with Export Development Canada to provide surety, bonding support, and co-lending to enable troubled P3 projects to proceed (ibid). In contrast, fiscal austerity is making a comeback in most other areas of government.

Enabling field support cannot ultimately resolve all the problems associated with P3s but it does make them easier to implement, smoothes out and regularizes the process, and promotes privatization. And to the degree that some policy learning takes place then P3s may in fact perform slightly better – or at least appear to. The real significance of the enabling field is thus the way in which it creates a 'common sense' that permeates public sector processes and decision-making. This insulates the P3 model from crises through routinization, institutionalization, and depoliticization.

ROUTINIZATION

Routinizing dispossession within the public sector involves the development and normalization of protocols which facilitate the selection of P3s. There are two important components here: the language of the enabling field (and an entrenchment of risk, derived through calculations of relatively short term costs and value for money, as the primary focus of decision-making) and the normalization of a market-based and market-reliant view of how the 'public interest' is to be conceptualized and upheld. This is accomplished not through grand overt offenses but instead through mundane, technocratic procedures.

Given the market-oriented nature of this form of decision-making, the language of the enabling field is part rhetoric and part reality. The rhetoric of public provision as being inherently riskier and of poorer value for money demonizes traditional projects and incentivizes privatization. For this reason P3 development remains a highly normative process as adherence to, and support for, logics of dispossession require a strong ideological commitment to privatization. However, even though the establishment of routines surrounding P3 selection may initially be normatively-based, once enabling fields are up and running normalization can proceed through its everyday routines. Thus normalized and normative processes are not mutually exclusive. Rhetoric is further transformed into reality when, as Larner (2000, p.33) describes, discourse comes to constitute the institutions and practices of decision makers. After nearly a decade of developing most/many large infrastructure projects as P3s, and of placing an importance on particular conceptions of risk, the public interest, and value for money, the normative basis of the P3 option is shored up in ways that transcend narrow ideological dogma.

Self-referentiality also characterizes P3 policy as assumptions and biases are recirculated and used to justify future P3 selection. This is paradoxical given that P3s remain, on the face of it, superior only when judged against a public sector comparator (PSC). Yet since a PSC is merely a hypothetical scenario and values alien to privatization policy (such as public provision in order to allow for collective decision-making and democratic accountability) are inherently penalized, the role of the PSC is not actually that of engaging with alternatives to P3s – instead it is often a device used to mask these normative aspects through technocratic procedures. Reinforcing this is the presumption that large infrastructure projects ought to be first considered as a P3. Even when improvements are made to overcome past problems, P3 policy innovations (e.g., exempting some services, standardizing contracts and bidding procedures) involve moving the privatization agenda forward, not searching for public alternatives.

INSTITUTIONALIZATION

An important element in the shift to P3s as the new 'traditional' is the institutionalization of this model as the de facto standard way in which large infrastructure projects are delivered in BC and Ontario (especially hospital projects). The term 'institutionalization' is used here to denote a number of different things. First, the root word – institution – should be taken to literally represent the creation of new public sector agencies (P3 units) which act as centres of expertise for P3 development protocols. Another way to think of institutionalization is the way in which new 'rules of the game' are formalized through the enabling field and come to shape future decisions, connoting a new system of action and a reorientation of standards and decision-making.[11] P3 units and new capital planning procedures tailored to privatization therefore lead to a change in the rules of the game, the norms of the public sector, and the social processes and actions repeated by decision-makers.

An increasing permanence is also suggested by the use of the term institutionalization: these agencies and protocols are no longer expendable and temporary, but are indicative of a regulatory shift. As captured by Selznick (1957, p.16-17), "institutionalization is a process... to 'institutionalize' is to infuse with value beyond the technical requirements of the task at hand". When P3 development begins to shed its reliance upon external validation through reference to previous traditional methods, it begins to take on a life of its own (as the new 'traditional'). Institutionalization should therefore be conceptualized in process-based terms. In Selznick's (1957) description, institutionalization is something which happens to an organization over time but with the enabling field it is obvious that increasing permanence can also be sped up by state policy. In fact both evolution and entrenchment are visible with P3 units and the norms and procedures they embody and reproduce.

This is not to say that processes relating to the evolution of the enabling field are unidirectional and heading ineluctably toward a situation where P3s are *the* hegemonic model for all public sector infrastructure projects. This category of institutionalization equally captures how different moments of P3 policy are crystallized (i.e., the ways in which challenges are dealt with, created, and absorbed). These challenges come from many directions: neutralizing and accommodating P3 opponents; making good on election promises (or at least appearing to – i.e., AFP in Ontario); dealing with the inherent problems and conflicts associated with privatization and economic crises; and adjusting to the tensions associated with marketized state restructuring. As Larner (2000, p.20) suggests, "the emergence of new forms of political power does not simply involve the imposition of a new understanding on top of the old ... [it] involves the complex linking of various domains of practice, is ongoingly contested, and the result is not a foregone conclusion". In other words, P3 development and the 'lock-in' of the privatization model is not a foregone conclusion by any stretch; the argument being made here is that the whole purpose behind enabling fields and institutionalization is to provide for some semblance of permanency even though dispossession via P3s requires constant renewal and therefore ongoing political/ideo-

---

11 See Burnham, 1999 on rules-based forms of state management and depoliticization.

logical commitment. As mentioned above, efforts by CUPE and the OHC to politicize P3 use in Ontario's public health care sector clearly stand out as an example of how effective, targeted resistance can lead to tangible changes in P3 policy.

DEPOLITICIZATION

Depoliticizing privatization policy, or how dispossession now proceeds largely through technocratic decision-making rather than grand normative gestures, is another key implication of the P3 enabling fields in BC and Ontario. Peter Burnham (2001, p.127) connects depoliticization to a particular governing strategy which "plac[es] at one remove the political character of decision-making". This benefits state managers by redirecting blame and dampening expectations whilst still allowing them to retain control. More than merely rhetoric, depoliticization also relies on new bureaucratic practices and a shift from discretion-based to rules-based regimes in particular (Burham, 2001, p.130-1). The routines of the new capital planning and procurement frameworks and P3 units correspond to this conceptualization. It is also suited to describing the P3 enabling field as it deals with the internal transformations that occur with state restructuring, and indicates that depoliticized decision-making remains simultaneously political in nature

In addition to Burnham's (2001) version of depoliticization (which deals mainly with internal state restructuring) we must specifically add the privatization dimension. Colin Hay (2007, p.80-87) provides this in his description of three forms of depoliticization: when issues are demoted from the governmental to the public sphere, from the public sphere to the private sphere, and from the private sphere to the realm of necessity. Depoliticization is therefore a process with many faces.

Changes that have occurred with P3s and the creation of enabling fields generally fall within the first two categories of depoliticization. Most obviously it involves shifting decision-making from the public sphere into the profit-oriented private sphere. This moment captures the new authority and influence awarded to the private consortia representatives who now influence individual projects, and the private consultants, accountants, auditors which form the private technocracy that informs policy and evaluates projects. In addition, when issues are demoted from the governmental sphere to the public sphere it means that public infrastructure and service decisions are no longer primarily managed through the formal democratic arena (where decision-makers are accountable and public deliberation takes place), but instead are shifted into the far less transparent realm of bureaucratic management (conducted by public or quasi-public agencies). This is the realm of the public technocracy and where officials become fairly insulated from public accountability (i.e., P3 units).

Like with routinization, depoliticization can become a reality in the sense that decisions are actually shifted into the private sphere, however it is also remains a powerful rhetorical tactic used by policy makers attempting to duck responsibility for, or reduce the visibility of, privatization. As Ascoli and Ranci (2002, p.14) suggest, marketization will always remain politicized since it "changes the direction in which [government] policies are developing" making it "an eminently political process, which redistributes rights and power, modifies policy networks and the institutional context in which [public] policy is made, and influences the ways in which welfare needs are defined." Furthermore, since public infrastructure delivered via a P3 remains a political responsibility (with the governmental sphere ultimately on the hook for funding, procuring, and broadly overseeing the operation of new public infrastructure and support services), this form of privatization cannot be truly depoliticized given that issues are never entirely demoted to the private sphere.

CONCLUSION

Routinizing, institutionalizing, and depoliticizing P3 development is an ongoing process, not a stationary state. It is increasingly 'locked-in' through various changes and innovations in the P3 enabling field. Provincial enabling fields have become more sophisticated over time, leading to P3 project proliferation and the entrenchment of privatization particularly in the area of large infrastructure projects. Since this process requires policy learning and P3 program evolution, elements of these P3 enabling fields in Ontario and BC have been altered in response to market changes and community activism. However, so long as this involves changes made to *how* P3s proceed and not *whether* P3s proceed, adaptations have ultimately strengthened the model overall.

Nothing presented here should be taken to suggest that jurisdictions without enabling fields are not, or have not been, developing P3s. Whether at the provincial or municipal level, most provinces in Canada have developed at least one P3 in the past, although outside of BC and Ontario these efforts have been far more sporadic. At the federal level there are also several operational P3s and the Harper Conservatives have implemented a P3 screen (federal funding through the Building

Canada initiative is tied to the use of P3s) and a P3 unit (PPP Canada). However, due to the constitutional division of powers, the sectors with projects most suitable for partnership agreements are mainly located within provincial jurisdiction (e.g., hospitals, schools, highways, water treatment facilities) which inherently limits the number of federal P3s.

Furthermore, the argument made here is not that enabling fields unequivocally force Ministries and other public authorities to choose the P3 procurement model. Mainly what enabling fields do, as the name would suggest, is *enable* P3s by simplifying processes, and encouraging, supporting and promoting their use. Some items compel public authorities to consider P3s (i.e., CAMF and IPFP) but even these are mere frameworks which could be easily altered, transcended, or ignored if the political will to do so existed. Instead it is the sheer bulk of the enabling field which acts as a form of soft lock-in by shifting the bias away from traditional public procurement. Soft lock-in also helps depoliticize these activities just as P3s themselves depoliticize dispossession through technocratic decision-making.

Enabling fields also help P3s weather crises, whether the crisis is related to financial market volatility or a loss of faith in the model. We have recently seen this in action as routinizing and institutionalizing P3 adoption played an important role in helping to avert widespread P3 abandonment after the 2008/9 crisis. This has allowed the P3 model to retain its privileged policy position in Ontario and BC, despite all of its drawbacks.

Changes in P3 markets and policy have nonetheless occurred over the past five years. It is likely that the global volume of annual P3 deals will not return to the heyday of 2002-7 given that this was an era of cheap credit and euphoric financialization (CCPPP, 2009, p.1). Concerns around debt refinancing have also led to the inclusion of clauses within Ontario's P3 hospital project agreements which stipulate that financial gains reaped through debt refinancing must now be shared with the relevant public hospital board (Loxley, 2010, p.110). A reversal of some elements of privatization enabling legislation has also occurred. Most notably, in 2007 the Supreme Court of Canada sided with BC's Hospital Employees Union, and other health sector unions, in their fight against BC Bill 29-2002 (the *Health and Social Services Delivery Improvement Act*) which unilaterally rescinded provisions in signed collective agreements and paved the way for unprecedented privatization of health care support staff in the province. This forced changes to similar unconstitutional provisions in P3-related legislation (BC Bill 94-2003 *The Health Sector*

Partnerships Agreement Act) as well. More recently, in 2011/12 the Province of Manitoba took an important step toward expanding protections for the public with its Bill 34 (*The Public-Private Partnerships Transparency and Accountability Act*) which requires greater public consultation and involvement of officials such as the provincial Auditor General and fairness monitors.

These victories and initiatives help dampen the more deleterious effects of dispossession but they do not entirely counter it, nor do they root out the specific elements of privatization-driven state restructuring that have occurred over the past decade. A greater focus on P3 enabling fields would be useful for opponents as it helps to uncover the ways in which privatization by stealth proceeds through the support of even more obscure changes being made to public sector decision-making in some jurisdictions. Resistance must therefore be not only directed at the outcomes of P3 use (i.e., dispossession) but also at the processes encouraging and supporting P3 selection (i.e., enabling fields). This includes politicizing the institutionalization, routinization and normalization of the market-based rationale that informs P3 policy and reorients public sector decision-making.

REFERENCES

Ascoli, U., & Ranci, C. (2002). The Context of New Social Policies in Europe. In U. Ascoli, & C. Ranci (Eds.), *Dilemmas of the Welfare Mix*. NY: Kluwer.

Ashman, S., & Callinicos, A. (2006). Capital Accumulation and the State System. *Historical Materialism, 14*(4), 107-131.

BC Ministry of Finance. (n.d). Overview. *Capital Asset Management Framework*. http://www.fin.gov.bc.ca/tbs/camf_overview.pdf

BC Ministry of Finance. (2002, May 30). New Framework, Agency to Guide Public Building. *News Release*. http://www2.news.gov.bc.ca/nrm_news_releases/2002FIN0001-000023.htm

BC Ministry of Finance. (2008, November 7). Province Raises Capital Standard Threshold for PPPs. *Information Bulletin*. http://www2.news.gov.bc.ca/news_releases_2005-2009/2008FIN0019-001677.htm

Block, S. (2008). *From P3s to AFP*. Ontario: Canadian Centre for Policy Alternatives. http://www.policyalternatives.ca/sites/default/files/uploads/publications/Ontario_Office_Pubs/2008/From_P3s_to_AFPs.pdf

Burnham, P. (1999). The Politics of Economic Management in the 1990s. *New Political Economy*. 4(1), 37-54.

Burnham, P. (2001). New Labour and the Politics of Depoliticization. *British Journal of Politics & International Relations*, 3(2), 127-149.

Canadian Council for Public-Private Partnerships (CCPPP). (2005). Ontario Infrastructure Minister Announces New Infrastructure Agency & Financing Method. *For the Record*. http://www.pppcouncil.ca/pdf/caplanfu2.pdf

Canadian Council for Public-Private Partnerships (CCPPP). (2009). *The impact of global credit retraction on the Canadian PPP market*. Toronto: Canadian Council for Public-Private Partnerships. http://www.pppcouncil.ca/pdf/credit_retraction_report_summer2009.pdf

Canadian Union of Public Employees (CUPE). (2003). *Exposing PPPs*. http://cupe.ca/public-private-partnerships/exposingppps

Canadian Union of Public Employees (CUPE). (2009). *Quebec Government Backs Away From P3s*. http://cupe.ca/privatization-watch-june-09/Quebec-backs-away-from-P3s

Cohn, D. (2004). The Public-Private Partnership "Fetish": Moving beyond the rhetoric. *Revue Gouvernance, 1*(2), 2-24.

Cohn, D. (2008). British Columbia's Capital Asset Management Framework: moving from a transactional to transformative leadership on public-private partnerships, or a "railroad job"? *Canadian Public Administration, 51*(1), 71-97.

DiMaggio, P.J., & Powell, W.W. (1991). Introduction. In W. W. Powell, & P. J. DiMaggio, (Eds.) *The New Institutionalism in Organizational Analysis*. Chicago: University of Chicago Press.

Drapak, F. (2009). *How the financial crisis has changed the market for PPPs.* http://www.slideshare.net/FilipDrapak/financial-crises-and-public-private-partnership-by-filip-drapak

Edwards, P., & Shaoul, J. (2002). Partnerships: for better, for worse? *Accounting, Auditing & Accountability Journal, 16*(3), 397-421.

Farrugia, C., Reynolds, T., & Orr, R. J. (2008). *Public-Private Partnership Agencies: A Global Perspective.* Collaboratory for Research on Global Projects, Stanford University. Working paper #39. http://crgp.stanford.edu/publications/working_papers/Farrugia_etal_PPPAgencies_WP0039.pdf

Fraser, I. (2009, April 19). John Swinney slams PFI legacy. *The Sunday Times.* http://business.timesonline.co.uk/tol/business/economics/article6122170.ece

Gaffney, D., Pollock, A. M., Price, D., & Shaoul, J. (1999.) The private finance initiative. *British Medical Journal, 319*(7202), 48-51.

Grimsey, D., & Lewis, M. K. (2004.) *Public Private Partnership.* UK: Edward Elgar.

Harvey, D. (2003). *The New Imperialism.* Oxford: Oxford University Press.

Hay, C. (2007). *Why We Hate Politics.* Cambridge: Polity Press.

Hodge, G. (2004). Risks in public-private partnerships: Shifting, sharing or shirking? *Asia Pacific Journal of Public Administration, 26*(2), 155-179.

Hodge, G., & Greve, C. (Eds). (2005). *The Challenge of Public-Private Partnerships: Learning from International Experience.* UK: Edward Elgar.

Hunter, J. (2009, January 29). Province takes on larger share of toll-bridge project. *Globe and Mail,* p. S1.

Infrastructure Ontario. (n.d.) *Projects.* http://www.infrastructureontario.ca/Templates/Projects.aspx?id=36

Infrastructure Ontario. (2011). *2010-2011 Annual Report.* http://www.infrastructureontario.ca/WorkArea/DownloadAsset.aspx?id=2147488402

Jooste, S. F., & Scott, W. R. (2012). The Public-Private Partnership Enabling Field: evidence from three cases. *Administration & Society, 44*(2), 149-182.

Larner, W. (2000). Neoliberalism: Policy, Ideology, Governmentality. *Studies in Political Economy, 63,* 5-25.

Linder, S.H. (1999). Coming to Terms with the Public-Private Partnership. *American Behavioral Scientist, 43*(1), 35-51.

Loxley, J. (2010). *Public Service, Private Profits.* Black Point: Fernwood.

Loxley, J. (2012). Public-Private Partnerships After the Global Financial Crisis: Ideology Trumping Economic Reality. *Studies in Political Economy. 89,* 7-37.

Mackenzie, H. (2007). *Doing the Math: why P3's for Alberta schools don't add up.* Alberta: Canadian Union of Public Employees. http://cupe.ca/updir/cupe_alberta_doing_the_math.pdf

Mackenzie, H. (2009). *Bad Before, Worse Now.* Ontario: Hugh Mackenzie and Associates. http://www.cupe.bc.ca/sites/default/files/Bad%20Before%20Worse%20Now%20_final_%20_2_.pdf

McKee, M., Edwards, N., & Atun, R. (2006). Public-private partnerships for hospitals. *Bulletin of the World Health Organization, 84*(11), 890-896.

McKellar, J. (2006). Alternative Delivery Models: the special purpose corporation in Canada. In O. Kaganova, & J. McKellar (Eds.), *Managing Government Property Assets: international experiences.* Washington, D.C.: The Urban Institute Press.

Mehra, N. (2005). *Flawed, Failed, Abandoned.* Ontario: Ontario Health Coalition. http://cupe.ca/updir/Flawed.Failed.Abandoned.P3s.pdf

North, D. C. (1990). *Institutions, Institutional Change and Economic Performance.* Cambridge: Cambridge University Press.

Ontario Auditor General. (2008). Brampton Civic Hospital Public-Private Partnership Project. *2008 Annual Report of the Auditor General of Ontario.* http://www.auditor.on.ca/en/reports_en/en08/303en08.pdf

Ontario Health Coalition. (2006, March 27). *Hamilton joins more 50,000 Ontarians in saying no to privatized P3 hospitals.* http://www.web.net/~ohc/Hamiltons/March272006HamiltonRelease.pdf

Ontario Ministry of Public Infrastructure Renewal (MPIR). (2004). *Building a Better Tomorrow: Infrastructure Planning, Financing and Procurement Framework for Ontario's Pubic Sector.* Ontario: Queen's Printer.

Ontario Standing Committee on Government Agencies. (2008, September 17). *Agency Review: Ontario Infrastructure Project Corp. (Infrastructure Ontario).* Hansard Committee Transcripts. http://www.ontla.on.ca/web/committee-proceedings/committee_transcripts_details.do?locale=en&Date=2008-09-17&ParlCommID=8859&BillID=&Business=Agency+review%3A+Ontario+Infrastructure+Projects+Corp.+%28Infrastructure+Ontario%29&DocumentID=23205

Ontario Standing Committee on Public Accounts. (2009, March 25). *2008 Annual Report, Auditor General: Ministry of Energy and Infrastructure, Ministry of Health and Long-Term Care.* Hansard Committee Transcripts. http://www.ontla.on.ca/web/committee-proceedings/committee_transcripts_details.do?locale=en&Date=2009-03-25&ParlCommID=8861&BillID=&Business=2008+Annual+Report%2C+Auditor+General%3A++Ministry+of+Energy+and+Infrastructure%2C+-+Ministry+of+Health+and+Long-Term+Care&DocumentID=23744

Partnerships BC. (n.d.) *Projects.* http://www.partnershipsbc.ca/files/projects.html

Partnerships BC. (2005). *Project Report: Achieving Value for Money. Abbotsford Regional Hospital and Cancer Centre Project.* Victoria: Partnerships BC. http://www.partnershipsbc.ca/files_2/documents/020705_PBCAbbotsford.pdf

Partnerships BC. (2011). *2010/2011 Annual Report.* Victoria: Partnerships BC. http://www.partnershipsbc.ca/files/documents/pbc-annualreport-15jun2011.pdf

PPP Canada. (2009). *Annual Report 2008-2009.* Ottawa: PPP Canada. www.p3canada.ca/_files/file/PPP-Annual-Report_EN.pdf

Rachwalski, M. D., & Ross, T. (2010). Running a Government's P3 Program: special purpose agency or line departments? *Journal of Comparative Policy Analysis, 12*(3), 275-298.

Scott, W. R. (1995). *Institutions and Organizations.* London: SAGE.

Selznick, P. (1957). *Leadership in Administration.* NY: Harper & Row.

Spronk, S. (2010). Water and Sanitation Utilities in the Global South: Re-centering the Debate on "Efficiency". *Review of Radical Political Economics, 42*(2), 156-174.

Tett, G. (2007, November 16). How Monoline Market Works. *Financial Times.* http://www.ft.com/cms/s/0/4465d6c8-93e5-11dc-acd0-0000779fd2ac.html#axzz1V8mVqfao

Vining, A. R., & Boardman, A. E. (2008). Public-private partnerships in Canada: Theory and Evidence. *Canadian Public Administration. 51*(1), 9-44.

Whiteside, H. (2012). Crises of Capital and the Logic of Dispossession and Repossession. *Studies in Political Economy, 89,* 59-78.

Whiteside, H. (forthcoming 2013). Tarnished yet tenacious: examining the track record and future of public-private partnership hospitals in Canada. In Y. Atasoy (Ed.), *Global Economic Crisis and the Politics of Diversity.* London & New York: Palgrave MacMillan.

Wood, E. M. (1995). *Democracy Against Capitalism: renewing historical materialism.* Cambridge: Cambridge University Press.

When Resistance Isn't Futile: Understanding Canadian Labour's Fight for Decent Pensions

— Joel Davison Harden[1]

In recent years, the Canadian Labour Congress (CLC) – the political voice for over 3.2 million union members in English Canada – waged a "Retirement Security for Everyone" campaign. At the core of the campaign were three demands: doubling future Canada Pension Plan (CPP) benefits; eliminating retiree poverty; and creating a federal insurance system for workplace pensions. From 2009-2010, the campaign was the top priority for Canadian unions with most allocating significant attention and resources to the effort. Many consider this the best work Canadian unions have done since the "free trade" battles of the late 1980s (Wilson, 2011).

During the height of the CLC's pension campaign, employers and governments were compelled to acknowledge union perspectives. Important legislative reforms were introduced while thousands of ordinary union members shared common demands articulated through their own experience. This article describes how the campaign took shape, and its lessons for progressive strategy. Of any, the importance of bottom-up, inclusive activism was reinforced by this example, far more of which must happen if unions want effective anti-austerity campaigns in tough political conditions. Despite the many challenges facing unions, effective resistance isn't futile with an educated, empowered, and confident union membership.

There are four distinct phases to the CLC's pension campaign explored here. The first involved the years preceding the 2008 financial crisis when unions were hamstrung by an expert-led focus on pension

---

1 Joel Davison Harden is an Ottawa-based writer and activist. He was the previous Registrar of the Labour College of Canada, and Director of the Labour Education Department at the Canadian Labour Congress. I sincerely thank the following reviewers who offered helpful advice and comments: Alan Zuege, Govind Rao, Rebecca Schein, and Ingo Schmidt. Any mistakes that remain are mine alone.

issues, and stymied by a stalemate in Canada's pension debate. This period then gave way to a second "discovery phase" from 2006-2008 as the CLC grappled with the complexity of pension issues on the one hand, and the need for inclusive pension activism (of relevance to union and non-union workers) on the other. By the autumn of 2009, with an effective campaign in place, the CLC entered into a third "capacity development phase" where hundreds (perhaps thousands) of activists received training on pension issues. Once a critical mobilization point was achieved, substantial momentum developed for pension reforms, with a wide array of observers crediting the CLC for driving the discussion. By the end of 2010, however, the CLC pension campaign entered a tough fourth phase of limited opportunity for activism on pension issues. A key factor was the federal government's decision to withdraw interest in CPP expansion, but the CLC also suffered from a drop in bottom-up pension activism. What follows is an attempt to grasp the lessons learned over the entirety of these four campaign phases.

CANADA'S PENSION STALEMATE ENDS (2005-2006)

The years preceding the CLC's pension campaign are best understood against the "tech wreck" of 2000-2002, when dot com firms became investor nightmares. Robert Brown, an actuary and academic from the University of Waterloo, reflected on Canada's pension debate at the height of this crisis. His conclusion was instructive: the key issue in Canada was an unwillingness from unions to exchange defined benefit (DB) workplace pensions for individual account arrangements (2001). The biggest reason was the simplicity and security of DB plans, which allowed workers to predict their future pension based on years of service, best average or career salary, and a certain percentage of earnings. With this in mind, the rest of this article refers to DB plans as "decent pensions", unlike RRSPs, 401k's, or so-called "defined contribution" plans where retirement benefits are based on the performance of pension investments and prevailing interest rates at the moment of a worker's retirement. DB pensions are decent because of the pension promise that underpins them; benefits, at least in theory, are predictable, and union negotiators were reluctant to let them go (though some felt compelled to make that choice). As a result, the number of workers covered by DB plans in Canada, unlike other countries, increased from the mid 1970s to 2004 (even as the percentage of workers enjoying DB plans dropped by 7 percent from 1992 to 2005) (Statscan, 2005; Townson, 2009). A major source of DB plan growth came from women in the Canadian public sector.

By 2004, Bob Baldwin – then a CLC pension specialist – wrote about a stalemate produced by these conditions (2004). One end of this stalemate was the failure of pension industry lobbyists to succeed in major campaigns of privatization. In the 1990s they had campaigned unsuccessfully to transform the CPP/QPP into a system of individual accounts. Industry lobbyists took a further hit when the tech wreck devastated pensions, particularly market-linked individual accounts. It was hardly a time to suggest that Canadians should fend for themselves.

But if conditions were not ideal for Canada's pension industry, they were more troublesome for unions. By 2005, a third of working-age Canadians (18-64) had no personal retirement savings, and only 30 percent contributed to Registered Retired Savings Plans (or RRSPs, the Canadian version of the American 401k) (Statistics Canada: 2006). Of the 17 million workers in paid employment in 2005, almost 11 million (or 62 percent) were not part of any workplace pension plan (Statistics Canada, 2005). Organized labour had negotiated pensions for union members, but decent coverage had not spread widely outside the public sector. By 2005, barely 20 percent of private sector workers had decent pensions, and this had much to do with the growth of precarious, non-union work, and the stalled position of union organizing in general. This regrettable situation posed major problems for unions' intent on advancing the progressive side of Canada's pension debate.

The pension industry was first in attempting to break this stalemate. In the summer of 2005, the Association of Canadian Pension Management released a paper entitled Back from the Brink: Securing the Future of Defined Benefit Pension Plans (ACPM, 2005). Its key demand was control of the surplus that accrued on a yearly basis when pension investments performed well, and a call for less stringent pension funding rules. Without question, these arguments were made at an opportune time.

By 2005, the U.S. housing market was in full stride, and finance capital was building a new speculative bubble. In 2005 and 2006, as employers sought control of pension surplus, this bubble was peaking. Any financial organization (or employer with the access to pension fund investments) was freeing up available cash to get in on the game, either through listed trades on stock markets or via the shadow banking system of over-the-counter derivatives trading (Blackburn, 2007). The fight over pension funding and surplus was therefore a fight over a lucrative source of profit, among the most generous in all of global capitalism.

What frustrated Canadian employers were regulations and court rulings that made ownership of pension surplus unclear, and therefore subject to extensive legal battles. In a unionized environment, collective bargaining agreements often specified ownership of pension surplus be negotiated or shared. It faced a similar challenge in efforts to weaken pension funding rules. By 2005, unions were in no mood to offer that consent, and politicians were nervous about being perceived as advocates of an insecure pension system. Nonetheless, the intensity of the moment forced governments to intervene, and facilitate discussion on this issue. In November 2005, the Canadian federal government hosted a "Work to Retirement Roundtable" at Wilson House (where the Meech Lake Accord Constitutional negotiations were once held in 1987). What transpired there spoke to the status of Canada's pension debate.

Following a brief introduction by federal government facilitators, both union and industry leaders staked out positions. Employer executives wanted more "fairness" and "flexibility" to facilitate the growth of decent pensions. Union leaders insisted that meant strengthening (not weakening) the existing pension system, notably the well-being of DB plans. Government facilitators looked on with increasing unease – there was no clear consensus on the key issues. Both sides were dug in, with no apparent appetite for compromise. Industry was attempting to break the 2004 stalemate, but unions were not budging.

At the same time, the stalemate was already unraveling under the force of other pressures. In the private sector, many employers were following through on threats to convert DB plans into less secure arrangements. The cost of public sector worker pensions was (and remains) a frequent source of banter among the usual pundits. To effectively counter these attacks, the CLC needed a vision for change that could compete with the industry-employer view, and unite a broad coalition for progressive reform. But first, the CLC needed its own analysis of the pension industry, and a better sense of the industry's role in the architecture of global capitalism. As the next section explains, a series of important research discoveries would allow this to happen.

2006-2007: THE CLC IN DISCOVERY MODE ON PENSIONS

Starting in early 2006, research surfaced which undermined industry arguments, and helped clarify the CLC's positions in Canada's pension debate. Since the ACPM's Back From the Brink paper, industry lobbyists claimed (to some degree of success) that funding rules restricted the growth of decent pensions. Curiously enough, an article for an industry magazine, the *Pensions and Benefits Monitor* (by Greg Hurst, an influential pensions consultant from Vancouver), demolished this position (2006).

What stood in the way of decent pension coverage, Hurst argued, were employers who viewed pension plans as "cash management tools". In the 1980s and 1990s, high interest rates generated huge windfalls for pension funds, often to the point where most were fully funded from investment returns alone. In these situations, pension rules in Canada allow employers to pursue "contribution holidays", an unfortunate practice that continues to this day.

Research from elsewhere confirmed Hurst's analysis. Quebec's pension regulator has estimated that over $2.9 billion was taken in contribution holidays by employers from 1991 to 2000 (Gold, 2006). Bernard Dussault, the former Chief Actuary of the Canada Pension Plan from 1992-1998, insists this led to the hobbled funding condition of pension plans in general, and their lack of preparation for the leaner years of 2001-2003 and 2008 (2009). Thanks to contribution holidays, employers did not maintain a "rainy day" fund to cushion the blow of market slumps. Instead, they could redirect pension surplus for other purposes – the details for which will never be known.

Hurst painted a picture that did not fit with the industry's explanation, and it gave rise to lively debate in progressive circles. Union researchers soon questioned whether "cupboard is bare" arguments by employers on pensions had any merit, and they quickly found grist for their mill. In April 2006, non-financial employers enjoyed a "net lending position" (or balance sheet surplus) of $80.6 billion, and the International Monetary Fund documented a similar trend worldwide (Tomas, 2006; Cardarelli et al, 2006).

Two years later, a report from Desjardins Securities, a financial services firm, explained Canadian employers had operating profits 18.3 times the size of their pension liabilities (Gibson et al, 2008). An average-sized employer, the report argued, could pay down pension liabilities with just one to two months of profit, or a year's worth of operating cash flow. The April 2006 issue of Benefits Canada (a widely-read industry magazine) noted the pension industry had grown to a size of $1.3 trillion, larger than the total of all goods and services sold in Canada the previous year (Cakebread, 2006). The following month, a British study posed more ambitious questions. According to the authors, the industry push for pension privatization (in Canada and elsewhere) was part of a more ambitious effort:

"Pension privatization is not really about pensions at all, but about extending capital markets, the free movement of capital, and changing the role of the state. The philosophy of [pensions] has changed over the twentieth century because politics has changed ... The critical issue is not a choice between the state and the private sector, nor the precise balance between a basic pension and a supplemental one, nor non-funding versus funding, nor general taxation versus contributions based on income. Instead, it is the question of whether financial institutions, financial markets and the "free movement of capital" should play leading roles in social welfare. Debates about pensions cannot ignore the effects pension schemes have on relationships between finance and industry, investment, and the broader social and economic implications of the stock-market approach to welfare or social security." (Minns and Sexton, 2006, p.35-36).

Robin Blackburn, a British historian, took this analysis even further (2007). For him, the attack on decent pensions was not just about creating freer reign for global finance, it was primarily an attempt to restore employer profitability which had gradually slipped since the mid-1970s. If employers and finance executives could access retirement savings, these substantial funds could be diverted to the lucrative paper chase of stock traders and ticker boards. Empowered by a new political context, employers could siphon off money meant for pensions to invest in various financial products, earning a tidy sum in the process. Over time, many did precisely this, but the perks were temporary if employers remained on the hook for a workers' pension. Hence the industry-employer preference to close decent pensions, and opt for schemes where workers bear the risk of market slumps.

Seen in this light, the attack on decent pensions was part of what Blackburn called the "financialization" of capitalism in general. In the course of a few short decades, pension funds were no longer sources of "patient capital", facilitating the lending of money to create investment and jobs. Instead, in a relatively short period of time, they became enmeshed in a paper chase where rampant speculation and fee extraction trumped reasonable judgement. As this happened, precious little went to genuine economic expansion, or what Jim Stanford has called the "real economy" (1999; 2008). In fact Stanford explains that, at the height of recent financialization, every dollar of investment in real production was eclipsed by a hundred dollars in pure speculation (Stanford, 2008). Such speculative activity was permitted by loose financial regulation in US stock markets, the heart of the system. Stock traders and ticker boards, propelled by the heavyweights of global finance, were ballooning a bubble of massive proportions, and often using workers' retirement savings to supply the hot air. The attack on pensions, while profitable, also had the additional benefit of disciplining unions, and taking back much of the postwar compromise in which workplace pensions emerged.

Soon enough, as the CLC grasped this bigger picture, they began challenging the framework for pension discussions in general. In a submission to Finance Canada on pension reform, CLC President Ken Georgetti made this explicit:

> "In a letter to Minister Flaherty dated March 27, 2005, I expressed the CLC's deep regret that the federal review of defined benefit pensions was taking place in a context where corporate lobbyists were guiding the discussion. This has been confirmed in recent months with the government's proposed [pension funding] regulations, which read like a wish list for the pension industry. The federal debate on defined benefit pensions – and retirement security for all Canadians – must be refocused, and reflect the cooperative values most Canadians share. In the twenty-first century, after eight decades of federal pension policy, it should no longer be acceptable for any working Canadian to retire into insecurity. A secure, enjoyable retirement should be the reward for decades of contributions to one's community and Canada's economy." (Georgetti, 2006, p.7).

At a federal government "pension policy dialogue" in 2007, the CLC also came out swinging. Why should unions, they asked, take hits in pension rights after years of employer contribution holidays? Why should consumers be charged ridiculous fees (so-called "Management Expense Ratios") for the mutual funds sold by Canada's financial sector (see: Korma et al, 2006)? And, above all, given most workers are without decent pensions or significant retirement savings, what is the government's vision to ensure retirement security for everyone?

The CLC soon realized that power brokers were ignoring such questions. Instead, debate remained focused on one thing: closing decent pensions, increasing employer access to pension surpluses, and weakening pension funding rules. At government pension consultations in 2006-2007, these objectives were repeatedly sought. Finance Minister Jim Flaherty wrote to the Congress of Union Retirees of Canada responding to their concerns about Canada Pension Plan benefits. At that time, Minister Flaherty insisted the CPP status quo was acceptable, and that current contribution rates "will remain unchanged" (2007). The letter confirmed what the CLC already knew: in 2007, there was little appetite to expand the modest CPP benefits available to all in paid employment.

Given these realities, the CLC faced tough conditions. It had gone through a valuable discovery phase, gained a broader awareness of pension issues, and expressed it well to reporters and politicians. These interventions made an impact, but they had not shifted the industry and employer framework that defined Canada's pension debate. Through polling research, the CLC had confirmed union members wanted action on pension reform, but the kind of reform was unclear. Most union activists, while an important voice in communities across Canada, were not informed players in the pension debate. Given this situation, union leaders and researchers were labour's political action team, and that limited group ensured less political influence.

For that to change the CLC needed a "capacity development phase" that could empower union activists to engage in pension activism; this activist core could then recruit others, and apply pressure to waverers and opponents. But for that to happen, a clear and compelling vision was required. If this was done well, politicians would face constituent anger (and electoral consequences) for not championing a more adequate, fair and secure pension system. As many have explained, Canadian history had seen this happen before, particularly when pensioners were involved (Finlayson, 1989; Deaton, 1989; Morton, 1987).

A golden opportunity soon presented itself: the CLC had pledged to hold a pension conference in late 2007, and union activists were motivated to participate. But what kind of conference would this be? Would it feature technical workshops of use to pension specialists, or a clear and compelling vision for pension reform? Between these two choices, unions leaders picked the latter, and at times to the dismay of their pension specialists. The 3rd CLC Pension Conference theme was *Move Forward Together or Fend for Yourself? The Future of Canadian Pensions*, and offered a clear indication that labour had grasped the bigger picture.

The conference was structured around political demands and aimed to refocus the CLC's pension work. A discussion paper was circulated that prioritized CPP expansion, improved public pensions, and a federal system of pension insurance (CLC, 2007). Three hundred and thirty-five delegates participated, making it the most successful event the CLC had held in some time. All delegates were registered on a "CLC Pension Activism" email list, which proved useful given mobilizations that happened later. One could sense union confidence on pensions was building. Debbie Marantz, a pension representative for the Communications, Energy, and Paperworkers Union, captured this in a report to her Executive Board:

"The 3rd Annual CLC Pension Conference from November 1 to 3 in Ottawa was meant to energize those attending and to assist them in focusing on labour's campaign to protect pensions and retirement security. And, may I say, for myself and everyone else who had the opportunity to attend, it did that and a lot more." (2007, p. 5).

2008-2010: CRISIS AND OPPORTUNITY FOR LABOUR ON PENSIONS

By 2008, the CLC shifted into action on pensions, and not a moment too soon. In April, the viral impact of Wall Street's defective investments was clear, setting off a chain of events well documented by others (Ferguson, 2012; McNally, 2010). The resulting slump, at its worst, caused stock markets to plummet by 52 percent and pension funds worldwide lost $5 trillion USD in assets (over three times the size of Canada's economy in 2008) (OECD, 2009).

At first, Canada's federal government denied these problems seeped North of the 49th parallel. In his economic and fiscal update of November 21, 2008, Finance Minister Jim Flaherty announced a budget surplus, and Prime Minister Stephen Harper speculated about "buying opportunities" in plummeting stock markets (as cited in Palmer, 2008). In a further bizarre move, a clawback on party financing was also announced (canceling, among other things, the $1.75 per vote federal political parties had received since 2003) which forced the hand of the government's opposition. A constitutional crisis followed, with a coalition of opposition parties threatening to oust the federal government from power.

To avoid that outcome, the federal government introduced a range of economic measures (which now meant forecasting a deficit of $64 billion) (Harper, 2008). Among these measures were new rounds of consultations on pension reforms, which the CLC rightly saw as an opportunity to advance its agenda for progressive change. After organizing an initial round of public forums on the economic crisis in January 2009, the CLC began a nationwide process of pension education sessions empowering union activists to attend federal pension consultations en masse. This proved to be challenging given details for consultations were often released a week before they were held, but the member response was unlike anything the CLC had seen in decades.

The first consultation took place in Ottawa on March 13, 2009, and union activists accounted for most of the 150 people in attendance. This hardly surprised officials who were aware of labour's focus on pension issues. What shocked them, however, were ideas that came from the front of the room. Bernard Dussault, the Chief Actuary of the Canada Pension Plan and Old Age Security from 1992-1998, had been invited as an expert to share his thoughts on specific reforms to federally-regulated pension plans. But Dussault, a major player in the CPP debates of the 1990s, did not restrict his comments to such narrow parameters. He instead proposed a dramatic expansion of CPP benefits that would eventually see all Canadians earn 70 per cent of their salary in retirement (Dussault, 2008). It was a case to shift the Canadian pension system to a "medicare" model, and away from its largely "fend for yourself" design. The direct losers would be banks and financial services companies who would almost certainly forego RRSP clients. Dussault's vision shook the pension establishment, and labour now realized it had a powerful ally in the case for pension reform.

As the consultations moved to six other Canadian cities, halls were filled with angry union members and retirees. Soon after, a conference room in Halifax meant for eighty participants was swamped by 150 people. Loretta Kent, a worker based at AV Pulp and Paper in Nackawic, New Brunswick, shared one of many compelling pension stories heard that day. Loretta's employer had declared bankruptcy in 2004 after underfunding the pension plan for five years. As a result, her pension went from 92 per cent funded to 48 per cent funded. When the employer emerged from bankruptcy protection, Loretta and her co-workers realized how much they lost given Canada's unfair bankruptcy rules, which rank workers' pensions at the bottom of an employer's list of creditors. For Loretta, it meant $400 in pension after sixteen years of service. Not $400 a month, or $400 a year, but a one-time post-bankruptcy payout of $400 (Kent, 2009). After she spoke, the entire room (industry experts included) stood and applauded her courage in sharing this story.

In Toronto, a room for 150 was packed by over 300 participants. One after another, they berated the government for failing to adequately protect their pensions, and provide decent options for the next generation. As Len Wallace, a retiree leader for the Canadian Autoworkers Union (CAW) spoke, heads nodded around the room: "Why should politicians and CEOs," he fumed, "get amazing pension plans, but not fight to ensure everyone else gets the same? What's the message to young people there? Do our kids have to be politicians and CEOs to retire with dignity?" (Wallace, 2009).

In Vancouver, a room meant for 225 was filled well beyond capacity, and once again retirees in particular made their presence felt. Art Kube, past-President of the Council of Senior Citizens Organizations of B.C., reminded government officials not to use consultations to delay reform. "Consultation is fine, and talking is fine," Kube said, "but we've had many years of that. We want action. And let me remind you of the obvious: seniors vote and we vote for people who care about pensions. You get this issue wrong, and you could be out of a job" (Kube, 2009).

The 2009 federal pension consultations confirmed what union leaders had said all along: pension anxiety was wide and deep, and action was required to fix the system. The CLC had prepared briefings and materials for union participants in the consultations, and these proved useful for the predictable deflections that came from the front of the room. A joint submission by seven federal employers (employing over 50 percent of all federal sector workers) once again demanded greater access to pension surplus and weaker pension funding rules (Air Canada et al, 2009). As they made these demands, the pension stories shared by workers and retirees became a powerful source of resistance. It was difficult to seek concessions in rooms filled with people facing an insecure pension future.

On April 23, 2009, yet another event added to labour's pension momentum. Following a call from the CAW, over 15,000 people demonstrated at the Ontario Legislature in Toronto to "protect our pensions." Rally participants included angry Nortel Networks workers and pensioners (facing significant concessions from a bankrupt employer), irate CAW members, and several concerned citizens who came for their own reasons. A Toronto "Stewards Assembly" held two weeks later (called by the Toronto and York Region Labour Council) drew over 1800 participants, from rank and file union stewards and elected union officials, and pensions were a hot topic. The *Globe and Mail* – a widely-read newspaper in English Canada among intellectuals and policymakers – took close notes at both events, capturing several compelling stories for an influential series than ran six months later (entitled "Retirement Lost"). Union activists realized that politicians could no longer, after bailouts for finance companies in 2008, ignore pleas to fix Canada's pension system. Momentum for change was starting to build — pension anger and anxiety had traction in the mainstream press and public mind.

In the midst of these opportune conditions, the CLC released its latest vision for pension reform (CLC, 2009b). Its July 2009 discussion paper — entitled Adequacy, Security, Fairness: Labour's Proposals for the Future of Canadian Pensions – proposed three core demands:
1. Doubling future CPP benefits through a phased-in increase of 60% to worker and employer contributions;
2. A 15 percent increase to the Guaranteed Income Supplement to federal Old Age Security Pensions (amounting to a $100 per month boost for low-income pensioners at a yearly cost of $1.2 billion);

3. Implementing an insurance system to protect workplace pensions should an employer declare bankruptcy, to a value of $2500 per month (pp. 6-8).

These demands formed the backbone of the CLC's Retirement Security for Everyone campaign launched on September 7, 2009, and elements of this vision were soon evident well beyond progressive circles. On September 11, 2009, the Provinces of Saskatchewan, Alberta and British Columbia threatened to "go it alone" on pension reform in the absence of coordinated action from Ottawa, and referenced CPP reform among other options (D'Alliesio, 2009). On September 15, the Financial Post ran a lead story entitled "pensions loom as election issue" that featured angry Nortel retirees, and quoted CLC Chief Economist Andrew Jackson on labour's plan to expand the CPP (Mazurkewich, 2009).

The following day, David Dennison, President and CEO of the CPP Investment Board (CPPIB), commented on the public debate over the fund's future (Dennison, 2009). The CPPIB had usually restricted its public relations to investment issues, but Dennison confirmed the depth of Canada's pension problems, and acknowledged a range of potential CPP reforms (including the CLC's proposal). On October 16, the *Globe and Mail's* "Retirement Lost" was released, beginning with these words:

> "Canadians can no longer assume they will retire with security. Many are seeking increasingly scarce work while others flail as their once-flush retirement accounts hemorrhage. A Globe and Mail series beginning today shows that the crisis in Canadian pensions is not looming; it is here, and has been for some time. A concerted national effort, involving changes in policy, behaviour and mindset from governments, businesses, unions, pension overseers and individual Canadians, is needed to repel the crisis." (McNish et al., 2009).

A week later, over three thousand Nortel workers and retirees joined union activists on Parliament Hill, demanding justice for a company once thought to the jewel of Canada's "Silicon Valley North". Earlier that month, Nortel CEO Mike Zafirovski appeared before the House of Commons Finance Committee, and was forced to account for demanding a 30 percent reduction in pensioner cheques while authorizing a $45 million bonus plan for top executives (CBC, 2009). This was a "hairshirt" moment for corporate Canada, and the CLC did much to publicize the exuberant heights to which executive pay and pensions had soared.

Politicians promised reforms due to an unrelenting wave of negative publicity, mobilizations, and appeals for change. After being ignored or dismissed by the pension establishment, the logjam that kept progressive options off the table had been broken.

Almost immediately, Canada's federal political parties began jostling for position on pension issues. The New Democratic Party and Bloc Quebecois supported the CLC's demands, while the Liberal Party proposed an expansion of the CPP through a private sector model. The ruling Conservatives, however, were cool to any ambitious plans. Reacting to the Liberal proposal, federal Finance Minister Jim Flaherty accused his opponents of a "knee-jerk reaction to a serious issue", while his staff warned against policy ideas that might "saddle taxpayers with big obligations" (cited in Chase, 2007). This was the first sign of a counter-attack to the CLC's new momentum on pensions, with more to come soon.

As Provincial, Federal and Territorial Finance Ministers prepared to meet in December (in Whitehorse, Yukon Territory), similar appeals continued from government reports and spokespersons. Jack Mintz, a public policy professor based at the University of Calgary, wrote a report for the Whitehorse meeting which emphasized the strength of the existing pension system (2009). Bob Baldwin, the former pension CLC expert, produced a study for the Ontario Government which downplayed ambitious reform, preferring instead to suggest "key subordinate questions", and hint at "mixing and matching" various policy ideas (2009, p. 76, 78).

"Fend for yourself" advocates seized on the ambiguity produced by these claims. The Canadian Bankers Association released a paper calling for raised RRSP limits (2009), while the C.D. Howe Institute published a study attacking federal public service pensions (using, critics charged, questionable assumptions to balloon the perceived costs) (Laurin and Robson, 2009). David Dodge, former Governor of the Bank of Canada, likened an expansion of the CPP to a "nanny state solution", and urged Finance Ministers to embrace policy options that allow "choice" in retirement planning (as cited in Scoffield, 2009).

These arguments gave politicians an excuse to deflect appeals for substantial reform, but they confirmed the CLC's pension campaign had traction. The Province of British Columbia said as much through its own independent study (also shared with Finance Ministers) that discussed CPP reform in positive terms (2009). Nevertheless, the Whitehorse talks ended with no commitment to reform, and most space given to dismissals from Mintz and others. The positive outcome was a pledge to hold further public hearings, leave "no policy option off the table", and articulate a clear direction on pension reform at the next Finance Ministers meeting in June 2010.

If Whitehorse was a tough moment for the CLC campaign, it was also clear that momentum for progressive options had not stalled. In fact, the CLC's lesson from Whitehorse was that more grass-roots mobilization was needed to push politicians in the right direction. So, from January to April 2010, the CLC worked with others in organized labour to host large pension forums, many of which invited attendees to share their own pension anxieties and concerns. The anger expressed at these forums generated more political action as labour activists pressed local politicians, held rallies and occupied constituency offices of pension industry supporters. This second wave of bottom-up pension activism quickly morphed into a movement for pension justice.

The movement's climax happened in March 2010, when the CLC and Ontario Federation of Labour hosted a "Pension Summit" in Toronto that offered space to divergent perspectives to debate the way forward. Almost six hundred delegates attended, including Federal Finance Minister Jim Flaherty, Canadian Federation of Independent Business CEO Catherine Swift, Pension Consultant Keith Ambachtscheer, and influential employer-side actuary Malcolm Hamilton. These voices, unlike usual, did not dominate the proceedings. Union delegates posed tough questions, and soon realized how brittle the "fend for yourself" establishment was. It was a moment where organized labour discovered a sense of its power, and one could feel received wisdom starting to shift. Incredibly, this shift was also on display a month later at an elite pension conference hosted by Jack Mintz at the University of Calgary.

Ken Georgetti was invited to speak on a panel with industry heavyweights (who, we can presume, were expected to lay waste to the CLC pension campaign). But when Robert Brown (a former top executive for Price Waterhouse Coopers) spoke after Georgetti, he told a stunned audience that expanding the Canada Pension Plan was likely the "best of all available options" (Georgetti, personal interview, 2010). Georgetti nearly tumbled from his chair, and that reaction was modest compared to Mintz's gaping jaw. Without question, the CLC notched a minor victory in the heart of Canada's conservative policy establishment. In June, this was followed by a resolution passed at the Federation of Canadian Municipalities Convention, where delegates (including the Mayors of Canada's large cities) backed he CLC's call to expand the CPP. The call for pension reform was making an impact at the highest official levels of Canadian politics.

This was confirmed in June 2010 when federal Finance Minister Jim Flaherty announced a new consensus among his colleagues for pension reform. The policy direction, he argued, would involve a "modest expansion of the Canada Pension Plan", while encouraging the financial sector to offer new retirement savings products (as cited in Curry, 2010). Alberta stressed its objections to the CPP reform, but it emerged as a lone voice doing so (with, perhaps, some support from right-leaning Saskatchewan as well). Union activists celebrated the result, and took pride in creating an historic moment in Canada's long-running pension debate. The rest of the summer, however, was unkind to organized labour. By the time union activists returned for Labour Day weekend, CPP reform was sputtering in the top levels of the federal government. In November, the federal government unveiled legislation enabling Pooled Registered Pension Plans (PRPPs), the latest "fend for yourself" policy option (Department of Finance, 2010). PRPPs would be voluntary in nature, and did not even require employer contributions. Critics from across the political spectrum argued PRPPs would do little to expand the scope of workplace pension coverage.

The CLC fumed about PRPPs receiving higher priority than CPP reform, and this fact was confirmed a month later when Prime Minister Stephen Harper confirmed the latter was officially off the table. "Canadians", Harper insisted, "are looking for options ... not a hike in their CPP premiums" (as cited in Scoffield, 2010). The union reaction was furious: Flaherty's constituency office was occupied by enraged protesters, and the CLC would later announce two access-to-information requests aimed at exposing who undermined CPP reform. Prior to a meeting of Finance Ministers in late December, a joint letter from the Governments of British Columbia, Ontario, Prince Edward Island, New Brunswick, Manitoba, and Nova Scotia urged the federal government to re-commit to CPP expansion, but this overture was rebuffed by Flaherty at a meeting the following week. The window of opportunity evident months earlier was abruptly closed.

LOOKING FORWARD: HOW DID IT HAPPEN? HOW CAN IT HAPPEN AGAIN?

Despite this unfortunate result, the CLC's pension campaign is a good news story in otherwise tough times for unions. As observers sift through the tea leaves of this experience, it will be important to understand where the CLC's clout on pensions came from, and how it can be restored. At a time when many question the political capacity of organized labour, this was an example of collective action winning positive results. Not mentioned in the above narrative, for example, were legislative changes Canadian governments felt compelled to make given widespread pension activism. These included guaranteed wage payouts in the event of corporate bankruptcies, strengthened rights for pension plan members, and guidelines to prevent federal sector employers "walking away" from unfunded liabilities in their pension plans. These were not the specific objectives the CLC sought, but significant in their own right, and more than could have been won without any activity at all. They also offer important lessons about what kind of activism is effective in today's challenging times.

The first is the necessity for unions, where possible, to pursue broad and inclusive campaigns. In 2007, the CLC made the crucial decision to depart from an expert-led focus on pensions, and embrace demands that bridged the concerns of union and non-union workers. In this vein, the decision to champion CPP reform and public pensions was important; industry critics could not easily criticize unions for being "self-interested", and non-union workers could be credibly told the CLC was fighting for everyone. The opposite would have happened if the focus had been protecting the pensions of unionized workers. Such defensive campaigns do not appeal to a wider public grown weary from decades of "fend for yourself" economic policy (in pensions and elsewhere). If organized labour is unable or unwilling to mount broad campaigns, employers will do so, and redirect public anger against "privileged unions". This is why US labour's recent pursuit of the Employee Free Choice Act was doomed to fail, and the CLC learned a similar lesson after a vigorous pursuit of federal "anti-scab" legislation in 2007 (Harden, 2007).

These goals, while important, will not appeal to a broad enough base, and will cater to the perception that unions are driven by self-interest. To regain momentum, unions must demonstrate their capacity to win victories for all workers. This was the first strength of the CLC's pension campaign — it offered a compelling vision of "retirement security for everyone", and forced opponents to defend a flawed status quo.

The second strength of the CLC pension campaign was its efforts to harness the fears, energies, and dreams of everyday union members. When it first realized an opportunity to mobilize on pension issues, the CLC could have simply presented its spokespersons to "multi-stakeholder" meetings and media opportunities. Instead, following the advice of Marshall Ganz (2001; 2009) and others, the CLC did that and much more. It recognized the power of workers' stories, and invited them into a focused campaign. For that to happen, the CLC financed an extensive, two-year process of pension education, at first to intervene in federal government hearings, but later to ensure inspired advocacy took place in every region possible.

As CLC campaigners criss-crossed the nation, they empowered union members to argue the merits of improved public pensions through the realities of a retiree on their street. The argument for pension insurance, likewise, was articulated locally as a backstop to prevent more Nortels, Abitibi-Bowaters, or AV Pulp and Papers (as referenced in Loretta's story above) from tearing communities apart. The costs of CPP expansion were explained as a sacrifice of a few take-out coffees or magazine subscriptions per month. From these local, accessible perspectives, union activists could speak from a position of strength, recruit supporters, and apply significant pressure to intransigent decision-makers. To this the CLC added an array of attractive materials which activists would colour with local stories (which were often more difficult for politicians to dispute). This was a welcome departure from CLC's earlier pension education efforts – intermittent regional courses, and research papers published for a specialist audience.

Solid research would remain a key element of the campaign, but a newly-mobilized layer of pension activists gave the CLC renewed agency on pension issues. This vindicated those who insist that "staffing up" or "hyper-professionalizing" takes unions away from their source of strength: the activism of union members (Clawson, 2008). If the grassroots of organized labour take ownership of campaigns, mass participation can happen, and much is possible. If union activists are compelled to act as a stage army, far less enthusiasm can be expected. For genuine success, labour's rank and file must be the authors of change.

Relatedly, the need to sustain local activism is third and final lesson from the CLC's campaign and it is likely the most challenging to understand. During the CLC's capacity development phase, it was never clear how bottom-up mobilizations would continue beyond appeals to politicians or mobilizations for various events. And yet, many of the campaign's most impressive moments came because activists themselves scored blows against the forces of pension austerity. The mass meetings, rallies, and sit-ins happened because union members gained a sense of their power, and focused it against a common adversary.

By June 2010, an apparent victory (through CPP reform) caused many to think change was coming. The truth, of course, was otherwise — and blame is hard to allocate about why this perception was widespread. The CLC leadership urged vigilance following Flaherty's June 2010 announcement, and called on local pressure to "get the job done". Pension activists sent in numerous requests for additional campaign materials and further trainings, many of which came to fruition. However one interprets the federal government's final decision, they clearly believed that betraying an earlier pledge would not entail significant political consequences.

As it happened, this turned out to be true – in Canada's May 2011 Federal Election, the ruling Conservatives won their first majority government. CLC supporters (particularly the NDP) also did well, but not well enough to ensure greater adequacy, fairness, and security for Canada's pension system. That weighty task remains, and it is one organized labour must take seriously. If capitalism's crisis-prone history portends anything, it is more economic slumps and major assaults on the living conditions of workers. When (and not if) that happens, unions must present a vision of change that inspires action, rather like the 99 percent visionaries whose protest encampments challenged the world's financial elite, or the Quebec student movement who (as these words were written) held fast in the face of enormous pressures. Canada's unions, despite their many challenges, can be a similar political force. This is possible, even probable, but only likely with the active involvement of labour's rank and file; their activism is the best means of ensuring resistance isn't futile, both for today and numerous battles ahead.

REFERENCES

Air Canada et al. (2009, March 5). Joint submission to the Department of Finance Canada on its January 2009 pension plan consultation paper. http://www.fin.gc.ca/consultresp/pdf/040-Joint-Submission-Department-of- Finance-March5th-FINAL.pdf.

Allemang, J. (2012, May 2). The sorry state of our unions. *Globe and Mail*. p. F1.

Association of Canadian Pension Management (ACPM). (2005). Back from the brink: securing the future of defined benefit plans. http://www.acpm.com/resources/7/pdf/ACFD2B.pdf

Bakvis, P. (2005). Social security models and the neoliberal challenge. http://library.fes.de/pdf-files/gurn/00019.pdf.

Baldwin, B. (2004). Pension reform in Canada in the 1990s. What was accomplished, what lies ahead? Ottawa: Canadian Labour Congress.

Baldwin, B. (2009, October). Research study on the Canadian retirement income system [prepared for the Ministry of Finance, Government of Ontario]. http://www.fin.gov.on.ca/en/consultations/pension/dec09report.html.

Blackburn, R. (2003). *Banking on death or investing in life: the history and future of pensions.* London: Verso.

Blackburn, R. (2007). *Age shock: how finance is failing us.* London: Verso.

Blackburn, R. (2006, May/June). Finance and the fourth dimension. *New Left Review.* 39, 39-70.

Government of British Columbia (2009, December). Options for increasing pension coverage among private sector workers in Canada [report prepared for the Steering Committee of Provincial/Territorial Finance Ministers on pension coverage and retirement income adequacy]. http://www.fin.gov.bc.ca/pension_plan_options_paper.pdf.

Brown, R. (2001). The Shift to Defined Contribution Pension Plans: Why Did It Not Happen in Canada? *North American Actuarial Journal,* 5(3), 65-77.

Cakebread, C. (2006, April). Top 40 money managers report: trillion dollar baby. *Benefits Canada.* http://www.hfconferences.ca/top40/pdfs/top40reportApril.pdf.

Canadian Bankers Association. (2009, November 23). Modernizing Canada's retirement savings system. http://www.cba.ca/contents/files/submissions/sub_20091209_pension_en.pdf.

Canadian Labour Congress. (2007). Move forward together, or fend for yourself? The future of Canadian Pensions. http://www.canadianlabour.ca/news- room/publications/move-forward-together-or-fend-yourself-future-canadian- pensions-3rd-clc-pensi.

Canadian Labour Congress. (2009a). Response by the CLC to the Department of Finance Pension consultation paper. http://www.canadianlabour.ca/sites/default/files/pdfs/2009-03-26-Federal- Pension-Review-EN.pdf.

Canadian Labour Congress. (2009b). Security, adequacy, and fairness: labour's proposals for the future of Canadian pensions. http://www.canadianlabour.ca/news-room/publications/security-adequacy-fairness-labour-s-proposals-future-canadian-pension.

Canadian Broadcasting Corporation (CBC). (2009, November 26). Nortel approves more exec raises. *CBC News Business.* http://www.cbc.ca/news/business/story/2009/11/26/nortel-raises-document.html.

Cardarelli et al. (2006). Awash with cash: why are corporate savings so high? *World Economic Outlook.* New York: International Monetary Fund.

Chase, S. (2009, October 27). Parties square off on federal pension reform: Liberals vow they would take a more activist role and expand CPP, Tories warn of spiraling costs. *Globe and Mail*. http://www. theglobeandmail.com/news/politics/federal-parties-square-off-on-pension-reform/article4215126/.

Chevreau, J. (2009, November 5). Canadians get the MERs they deserve. *Financial Post*.http://www2.canada.com/victoriatimescolonist/news/business/story.html?id= 1de8b905-d81e-4f4c-a772-f9d296e736ff.

Clawson, D. (2008). *The next upsurge: labor and the new social movements*. Ithaca, NY: Cornell University Press.

Curry, B. (2010, June 13). Flaherty pushes for expanded CPP. *Globe and Mail*. http://www.theglobeandmail.com/report-on-business/flaherty-pushes-for- expanded-cpp/article1602737/.

D'Aliesio, Renata. (2009, September 11). Western provinces pitch regional pension program. *Calgary Herald*. http://www.canada.com/vancouversun/news/business/story.html?id=747fca14- 170d-4de3-9e43-982626f37e3d&k=9970.

Deaton, Richard. (1989). *The political economy of pensions: power, politics and social change in Canada, Britain, and the United States*. Vancouver: UBC Press.

Department of Finance, Government of Canada. (December 2010). Framework for pooled registered pension plans. http://www.fin.gc.ca/activty/pubs/pension/prpp- irpac-eng.asp.

Dennison, D. (2009, September 16). The Canadian model: moving from affordability to sufficiency [remarks made to the 16h Annual Conference of Social Security Actuaries and Statisticians]. http://www.cppib.ca/files/CPPIB_Speech_- _ISSA_Conference__Sept_16_2009_.pdf.

Dussault, B. (2009). Global solution to the Canadian pension crisis: expansion of the CPP. Presentation to the Department of Finance, Government of Canada, on "Federal regulation of private pension plans, Ottawa, ON, Canada.

Ferguson, C. (2012). Predator nation: corporate criminals, political corruption, and the highjacking of America. New York: Random House.

Finlayson, D. (1989). *Whose money is it anyway? The showdown on pensions*. Toronto: Viking.

Flaherty, J. (2007, March 18). Debate on CPP reform [Letter to the Congress of Union Retirees of Canada].

Ganz, M. (2001, August). The power of story in social movements [presentation to the Annual Meeting of the American Sociological Association]. Anaheim: California. http://www.hks.harvard.edu/organizing/tools/Files/MG%20POWER%20OF%20S TORY.pdf.

— — — (2009, March). Why stories matter. *Sojourners*. http://sojo.net/magazine/2009/03/why-stories-matter.

Georgetti, K. (2006, March 16). It's time to refocus Canada's pension debate [Open letter to the Hon. Jim Flaherty, Federal Minister of Finance, Government of Canada].

Gibson, P. et al. (2008). *Research comment: could a pension crisis be next?* An analysis of pension shortfalls in Canada and the US. Toronto: Desjardins Securities.

Gold, M. (2006). Current Pension Issues and Trends. http://www.share.ca/files/Current_Pension_Issues_and_Trends_M._Gold.pdf.

Harden, J. (2007, May/June) Unions learn from defeat of anti-scab bill. *Relay*, 17, 18-19.

Harper, S. (2008). Sound foundations and open doors: Canada's blueprint for short and long-term success [remarks to the Asia Pacific Economic Cooperation CEO Conference]. http://www.pm.gc.ca/eng/media.asp?id=2323.

Harvey, D. (2005). *A brief history of neoliberalism.* New York: Oxford.

Hurst, G. (February 2006). Lies, damned lies, and Canada's private pensions funding crisis. *Pension and Benefits Monitor.* http://www.bpmmagazine.com/02_archives/2006/february/lies_canada_private_pension_funding.html.

Kent, L. (2009, March 21). My story about A/V Pulp and Paper. Presentation to the Department of Finance, Government of Canada, on "Federal regulation of private pension plans. Halifax, NS, Canada.

Korma et al. (2006, May). Mutual fund fees around the world. http://randsco.com/_img/blog/0702/fees.pdf.

Kube, A. (2009, April 12) Oral remarks made to the Department of Finance, Government of Canada, on "Federal regulation of private pension plans". Vancouver, BC, Canada.

Laurin, A. and Robson, W. (December 2009). *Supersized Superannuation: the startling fair-value cost of federal government pensions.* Backgrounder No 122. Toronto: C.D. Howe Institute.

Marantz, D. (2007). Report from the 3rd CLC Pension Conference [Letter to CEP National Executive Board].

Mazurkewich, K. (2009, September 15). Pensions loom as election issue. *Financial Post*, p. A4.

McCullough. M. (2009, November 22). Why there is no retirement crisis. *Canadian Business.* http://www.canadianbusiness.com/article/11403 — why-there-is-no- retirement-crisis.

McNally, D. (2010). *Global slump: the economics and politics of crisis and resistance.* San Fransisco: PM Press / Spectre.

McNish, J. et al (2009, October 16). Beyond the illusion of security. *Globe and Mail.* p. F3.

Minns, R. and Sexton, S. (2006). Too many grannies? Private pensions, corporate welfare and growing insecurity. London: The Corner House. http://www.thecornerhouse.org.uk/sites/thecornerhouse.org.uk/files/35grannies.p df.

Mintz, J. (2009, December 18). Summary report on retirement income adequacy research [prepared for he Research Working Group on Retirement Income Adequacy of Federal-Provincial-Territorial Ministers of Finance]. Retrieved from http://www.fin.gc.ca/activty/pubs/pension/riar-narr-eng.asp.

Morton, D. (1987). Resisting the pension evil: bureaucracy, democracy, and Canada's Board of Pension Commissioners, 1916-1933. *Canadian Historical Review*, 68(2),199-224.

National Advisory Council on the Status of Aging (NACA), Government of Canada. (2005). Seniors on the margins: aging and poverty in Canada. Retrieved from http://publications.gc.ca/collections/Collection/H88-5-3-2005E.pdf.

Organization of Economic Cooperation and Development (OECD). (2009, October). Pension markets in focus. Issue 6. Paris: OECD. Retrieved from http://www.oecd.org/dataoecd/30/40/43943964.pdf.

Palmer, R et al. (2008, October 7). Canada's Harper sees possible stock market bargains. *Reuters*. Retrieved from http://www.reuters.com/article/2008/10/07/financial-canada-opportunities-idUSN0747329620081007.

Scoffield, H. (2009, December 17). Cut standard of living now for comfortable pension later: Dodge. *The Canadian Press*. Retrieved from http://www.capebretonpost.com/Business/Personal-finance/2009-12-18/article- 777748/Cut-standard-of-living-now-for-comfortable-pension-later%3A-Dodge/1.

Scoffield, H. (2010, November 17). PRPP: Ottawa launches new pooled registered pension plans to boost retirement savings. *The Canadian Press*. http://www.huffingtonpost.ca/2011/11/17/prpp-pooled-registered-pension- plans_n_1099456.html.

Stanford, J. (2008) *Economics for everyone: a short guide to the economics of capitalism*. Toronto: Fernwood.

Stanford, J. (2001). *Paper boom: why real prosperity requires a new approach to Canada's economy*. Toronto: Lorimer.

Statistics Canada. (2006). Survey of financial security. Ottawa: Government of Canada.

Statistics Canada. (2005). *Pension plans in Canada*. Ottawa: Government of Canada.

Tomas, A. (2006). Recent trends in corporate finance. *Canadian Economic Observer*. Ottawa: Statistics Canada.

Townson, M. (2001). *Pensions under attack: what's behind the push to privatize pensions.* Ottawa: Canadian Centre for Policy Alternatives.

— — — (2009). *What can we do about pensions?* Ottawa: Canadian Centre for Policy Alternatives.

Van Riesen, G. (2007, February 12). Oral remarks made to the Government of Ontario Expert Roundtable on Pensions.

Wallace, L. (2009, April 16). Oral remarks made to the Department of Finance, Government of Canada, on "Federal regulation of private pension plans, Ottawa, ON, Canada.

Wilson, F. (2011, May 27). How the NDP gave unions a new opportunity to organize. Rabble.ca. http://rabble.ca/blogs/bloggers/fwilson/2011/05/how-ndp-gave- canadas-unions-new-opportunity-organize.

What is Trade Union Bureaucracy? A Theoretical Account

— David Camfield[1]

'Union bureaucracy' is an important yet vexed term in the study of trade unions and in radical politics. At worst, it can be a label pinned by left-wing activists on those union officers whose actions or beliefs are seen as repugnant. This usage confers the label of 'bureaucrat' on some union officials but not on those whose behaviour is seen as praiseworthy. The term is also used in a more serious way. Many critical analysts (and others) have drawn attention to the existence of a layer of full-time union officers and staff and argued that this group of people – 'the trade union bureaucracy' – plays a conservative role in unions. There are many versions of this kind of analysis of 'the bureaucracy,' some much more insightful than others. Yet there have been scarcely any recent attempts to refine and present a coherent theory of union bureaucracy.[2] Unfortunately, it remains the case that in the study of unions, as John Kelly (1988) argued over two decades ago, 'Rarely is the term "bureaucracy" defined or its use justified on any theoretical grounds, and it is normally unclear which of several different definitions is actually being employed' (p.155). More- over, theories of 'the trade union bureaucracy' understood as a group of people can function as blinkers to a critical understanding of the character of union activity itself. A focus on official leaderships can lead us to ignore or neglect how union activity happens, how the relations among members and between officials and members are organized. To put the same point

---

1   David Camfield teaches Labour Studies at the University of Manitoba and is the author of *Canadian Labour in Crisis: Reinventing the Workers' Movement* (2011). Thanks to David McNally, Charlie Post, Alan Sears and Sheila Wilmot for discussions about some of the ideas in this article, earlier versions of which were presented at the Annual Meetings of the *Society for Socialist Studies* in 2009 and at the 2010 Toronto *Historical Materialism* conference.
2   Brenner (1986), Leier (1991) and some of the essays collected in Hyman (1989) represent original contributions that attempt to clarify the character of union bureaucracy. The past two decades have seen very few theoretical contributions on this question. Darlington and Upchurch (2012) is a notable exception.

differently, bureaucratic forms of social practice in union organizations risk escaping examination when 'the bureaucracy' is the centre of our field of vision. When this happens, the result is a very partial understanding of unions as working-class movement organisations.

Consequently, this article proposes an alternative theoretical account of union bureaucracy and union officialdom (members who hold elected or appointed union office, and union staff). This account seeks to incorporate the best insights of the tradition of critical analysis of 'the trade union bureaucracy' (full-time union officials) into a theoretical framework founded on an original conceptualization of bureaucracy as a particular mode of existence of social relations, whose relevance is not limited to the study of unions.[3] The development of an explicit conceptualization of bureaucracy as a social phenomenon and, on that foundation, an account of union bureaucracy is intended to address the problem of theoretical unclarity identified by Kelly. Another reason for addressing the nature of bureaucracy itself is that Marxist writers on bureaucracy (e.g. Mandel, 1992) have tended to pay relatively little attention to theorizing the phenomenon at the most basic level, in contrast to the care paid to concepts such as class. The account proposed here attempts to grasp core processes of bureaucratization within unions in capitalist societies. It identifies the sources of bureaucracy in unions as wage-labour contracts, the separation of conception from execution in human practical activity, the political administration of unions by state power and union officialdom. The perspective advanced encourages analysis that combines attention to different manifestations of bureaucracy throughout union organizations with examination of the specific role of full-time officers and staff (rather than one or the other). The article concludes with a brief discussion of how this theory directs our attention in the analysis of contemporary unions, with specific reference to the US and Canada.

TRADE UNION BUREAUCRACY AS THE OFFICIALDOM

When the concept of union bureaucracy is used in a serious fashion (rather than as a superficial political criticism), it usually refers to a *group of people*. This is how the concept figures in classic sociological studies such as Robert Michels's oft-cited book of a century ago on

---

3   An anonymous reviewer pointed out that this theory could be used to scrutinize the "'NGOization' of social movements" and "the relationship between NGOs and social movements," but I am unable to address those issues here.

working-class movement organizations (1966)[4] and C Wright Mills's 1948 book on US union officials, *The New Men of Power* (2001, p.224). Union bureaucracy is equated with a group of people by most Marxist writers. For Ernest Mandel (1992), it is a layer of full-time officials that has carried out 'the usurpation of decision-making power' within the union organisation; a stratum of full-timers who have not accomplished this are 'an incipient bureaucracy' (p.68). For Alex Callinicos (1995), the union bureaucracy is 'a social layer made up of full time officials with a material interest in confining the class struggle to the search for reforms within a capitalist framework' (p.16). Robert Brenner (1985) uses the term in a similar manner, and many more examples of this kind could be cited. This usage is also common among non-Marxist radicals. For example, historian Mark Leier (1991) advances a perspective on union bureaucracy influenced by the anarchist Mikhail Bakunin. Leier argues that the bureaucracy is made up of leaders whose 'offices are protected from immediate and effective control by the membership' (p.420). By including shop stewards as part of the bureaucracy (p.424), Leier differs with the previously-mentioned writers, but he shares with them the idea that the term 'union bureaucracy' refers to a group of people.

In identifying the widespread use of the term trade union bureaucracy in this sense, I do not want to imply that all those who use it in this manner theorize union bureaucracy in the same way or equally well. For example, Callinicos (1995) argues that union struggle within capitalist society inevitably requires compromises with capital, which must be negotiated by workers' representatives. Some of these representatives become full-time officials and 'the effect, whatever the beliefs of the officials, is to isolate them from those they represent.' Removed from the paid workplace and no longer employed by capital, they 'come to see negotiation, compromise, the reconciliation of capital and labour as the very stuff of trade unionism' (p.17) and oppose struggle because it threatens negotiations and union funds. Mandel (1992)'s theory is different in important respects. In *Power and Money*, he sees the 'cultural underdevelopment' of the working class (the normal 'status of the proletariat under the rule of capital') as the basis of union bureaucracy (p.60). At the same time, he identifies an inexorable organizational logic that creates a bureaucracy: 'the development of mass political or trade-union organisations is incon-

---

4   While Michels's focus is on political parties and he does not use the exact term 'union bureau-cracy,' his work considers unions as well as parties and his discussion of party bureaucracy equates it with a group of people. See the comments on Michels by Perusek (1995).

ceivable without an apparatus of full-timers and functionaries. At the most basic level, it is impossible to collect, centralise and administer the dues of a million members through purely voluntary labour' (p.59). Leier (1991)'s notion of bureaucracy is different again, as he argues that the bureaucracy's 'distinguishing characteristic...is their power over the membership' (p.420). My point is simply that these writers share a certain understanding: union bureaucracy means the labour officialdom.

The strengths and weaknesses of these specific accounts is not my concern here, though it is worth pointing out that they are all more sound theoretical efforts than Michels's belief in an iron law of oligarchy rooted in the allegedly universal incompetence of 'the masses' and the inherent nature of organization itself (Michels, 1966; Barker, 2001; Perusek, 1995) or Lenin's influential but deeply flawed idea that union officials are conservative because they are part of a 'labour aristocracy' bribed with imperialist super-profits (Lenin, 1920; Post, 2011). These theories highlight the significance of the existence of layers of union officials, particularly full-time officers and staff, and nothing that follows should be interpreted as dismissing the importance of this social phenomenon, to which I will return.

The most important problem common to such accounts is that their focus on full-time union officials is conducive to neglecting how union activity is socially organized more broadly. At worst, it can lead to a depiction of union officialdom as a rotten crust beneath which lies a pure, untainted organization and membership. Another pitfall is that in situations where there are few or no full-time officials – as is the case in many smaller union locals in the US and Canada – the theory implies by definition that bureaucracy is not a significant issue, since there are few or no bureaucrats present. Above all, focusing on the head can, so to speak, lead to neglect of the body. For example, Callinicos (1995) devotes most of a chapter on 'Capitalism, the unions and union leaders' to 'the union bureaucracy.' It says very little about how relations between officers (whether lay, to use the British term for workers holding union office who remain on the job, or full-time) and other members are organized in the country whose unions are at the centre of the book, the UK. It also pays scant attention to the nature of collective bargaining relations or how the regulation of unions by state power (the political administration [Neocleous, 1996] of unions) influences UK unions, including the officialdom. Questions about the condition of union organization in paid workplaces and in branches (union locals), levels of member participation and control, the relationship between unionized workers and the non-unionized majority of the working class and the gender and racial order within British unions are raised barely or not at all. This kind of critical analysis leaves many important dimensions of a union movement unexamined or treats them as of little importance. The elaboration and defence by Ralph Darlington and Martin Upchurch (2012) of the same theoretical perspective on full-time union officials for which Callinicos argues is less narrow in scope. However, it has little to say about unions as bureaucratic organizations, rather than the character of the stratum of officials at their head.

This suggests that to identify bureaucracy with 'the bureaucracy' is too limited a notion. We need a theoretical approach that embraces other phenomena too, not just full-time officials. If union bureaucracy is not to be equated with the officialdom, what is it? Richard Hyman (1989) has proposed that bureaucracy in unions is 'a corrosive pattern of *internal social relations* manifest in a differential distribution of expertise and activism; in a dependence of the mass of union members on the initiative and experience of a relatively small group of leaders – both official *and* 'unofficial'' (p.246). To distinguish bureaucracy as a social relation from union officers and staff as a group, one can use the term 'labour officialdom' to refer to the latter. From this perspective, to the degree that the relationship between members and the officers and staff is one of dependence, then what we have is a bureaucratic officialdom.

This approach has the advantage of conceptually distinguishing the phenomenon of bureaucracy from that of the officialdom as a social layer. It allows us to understand many contemporary unions as *bureaucratic mass organizations* headed by particular *bureaucratic officialdoms.* Unfortunately, it also creates new problems: it severs bureaucracy from any notion of regulations that constrain agents, and its emphasis on dependence on leaders blurs the line between the problematic of bureaucracy and the broader problematic of subaltern agency, self-activity and leadership. The latter is relevant in situations where bureaucracy is absent or insignificant. For these and perhaps other reasons,[5] Hyman's approach, while a thoughtful attempt to move beyond the limitations of a conventional Marxist theory of union bureaucracy, is flawed and unsatisfactory.

---

5   See Darlington and Upchurch (2012) and the rejoinder by Hyman (2012).

WHAT IS BUREAUCRACY?

To raise the level of theoretical reflection on union bureaucracy to a higher level in a way that allows us to understand many unions as bureaucratic mass organizations, it is helpful to pose the question directly: what is bureaucracy? I suggest that bureaucracy is best understood as *a mode of existence of social relations in which people's activity (labour) is organized through formal rules that limit their ability to determine its character and goals, and which they themselves are not able to alter with ease.* Although informal rules may also affect people's activity in similar ways, one of the distinguishing features of bureaucracy as a social phenomenon is the formal character of rules, as recognized by Max Weber (1952).[6] It should also be noted that the understanding of bureaucracy suggested here does not claim that all social organization involving formal rules is bureaucratic (as might be argued by supporters of an extremely individualistic version of anarchism); rules are bureaucratic only when they limit people's ability to determine the character and goals of their own activity and cannot be easily changed by those affected.

This form of organizing social relations, while commonplace in contemporary capitalist societies, does not originate with capitalism. Bureaucracy can be found in societies that long pre-date capitalism. Anthropologist David Graeber (2006) argues that bureaucracy occurs where 'social situations...founded on structural violence' (by which he means 'forms of pervasive social inequality that are ultimately backed up by the threat of physical harm') are being managed (pp. 4-5). The development and geographical expansion of capitalism is associated with the spread of bureaucracy; as Georg Lukács (1971) noted, the concern for prediction and calculability in the capitalist enterprise observed by Weber is part of a broader drive to subject different aspects of social life to 'an increasingly *formal* and standardised treatment...in which there is an ever-increasing remoteness from the qualitative and material essence of the "things" to which bureaucratic activity pertains' (p.99).

One of the 'forms of pervasive social inequality' most relevant to bureaucracy is the separation of intellectual from manual labour and the monopolization of the former by a small number of people. Alfred Sohn-Rethel (1978) argues that intellectual labour, as distinct from manual labour, is defined by 'the use of non-empirical form-abstractions which may be represented by nothing other than non-empirical, "pure"

---

6   The conceptualization of bureaucracy being proposed here is obviously not Weber's. My point is simply that Weber was right to recognize the significance of formal rules to the phenomenon of bureaucracy.

concepts' (p.66). Intellectual labour in this sense, he contends, first arose with the emergence of philosophy in Greece, a development made possible by the 'non-empirical real abstraction' (p.66) involved in a 'social synthesis' – Sohn-Rethel's term for 'the network of relations by which society forms a coherent whole' (p.4) – that is 'in strict spatio-temporal separation from all acts of man's [sic] material interchange with nature' (p.67). Thus intellectual labour was made possible by 'the generalisation intrinsic in the monetary commensuration of commodity values promoted by coinage' (p.102). The first occurrence of coinage he dates to 'about 680 BC on the Ionian side of the Aegean, in Lydia or Phrygia' (p.59).[7] A number of questions can be raised about Sohn-Rethel's account.[8] However, for present purposes, what matters is that intellectual labour has been a source of bureaucracy to the extent that it has been monopolized by privileged social groups with the power to impose restrictive formal rules that organize the life activity of other people. Examples of such groups include priests and other office-holders in religious institutions and scientists in the service of state power.

A related but distinct form of domination giving rise to bureaucracy is the separation of the activity of conceptualizing the goals and methods of human activity from its execution.[9] We can see rudimentary examples of this before the development of capitalism, for instance in rule-books of military organisation and state administration and in patriarchal laws that authorize men's control over women's labour. But it is under capitalism that the separation of conception (thinking) from execution (doing) becomes pervasive. As Cornelius Castoriadis (1988a) observed

---

7   According to Seaford (2012, p. 82), "opinion has now shifted to a date towards the end of the seventh century."

8   To contemporary readers Sohn-Rethel (1978)'s historical argument as presented in compressed summary here may appear as simply an example of the kind of Hellenocentrism that was so marked in Eurocentric German culture in the 1800s. For discussion of Egypt (where he locates the earliest initial manifestation of the separation of intellectual labour), Asia and Greece, see pp. 86-103. An assessment of his theoretical account would require an interrogation of both his general claim about the social conditions required for the emergence of intellectual labour and the specific geographical and historical coordinates he posits for its emergence, bearing in mind the critique of Western European Hellenocentrism raised by authors such as Goody (2006). Kapferer (1980) raises a number of questions about Sohn-Rethel's argument, including about his claim that social synthesis in ancient Greek societies was based on commodity exchange. Seaford (2012) defends Sohn-Rethel's analysis.

9   I distinguish the separation of conception from execution from the split between intellectual and manual labour in order to help us recognize examples of the former that do not involve the use of what Sohn-Rethel calls 'non-empirical form-abstractions which may be represented by nothing other than non-empirical, 'pure' concepts' and to grasp that in contemporary capitalist societies intellectual labour *itself* is subjected to the separation of conception from execution. For a brief discussion of this in the case of physics see Schmidt (2000, p. 140). Schmidt (2000) deserves to be read by anyone concerned with bureaucracy in contemporary society.

in 1960, the 'arbitrary end' of 'maximum production' 'is accomplished through the ever-heightened separation of direction and execution, by reducing workers to the status of mere executants, and by transferring the functions of management *outside* the labor process' of producing goods and services (p. 273). As Harry Braverman (1998)'s better-known and slightly later version of such an analysis argues, capitalist development fuels an 'incessant breakdown of labor processes into simplified operations taught to workers as tasks,' creating more 'labor from which all conceptual elements have been removed and along with them most of the skill, knowledge and understanding' (p.319). Even Paul Thompson (1989), who does not argue that the separation of conception from execution is a necessary feature of capitalism's organization of labour processes, recognises that competitive accumulation drives capital to reorganize production in order to reduce costs, and that this 'sets limits to the use of workers' creative capacities and constrains attempts to dispense with hierarchical relations' (p.243). Whether one accepts the stronger or the weaker claim (or an intermediate position), it is evident that the separation of conception from execution takes place on a large scale in the sphere of paid work in capitalist societies. This is a feature of labour processes in capitalist societies in all but their earliest phases, and is often enforced through formal rules. Although capitalist development creates new productive forces and patterns of workplace organisation that generate novel kinds of conceptual work, employers have historically proceeded to attempt to separate conception from execution within such new types of labour. The example of computer programming work illustrates this trend (p. 111-112).

Importantly, the process of separating conception from execution is not limited to the sphere of paid work.[10] This separation is also basic to public political life in capitalist societies. In capitalist states with liberal democratic systems of government the contours of the political administration of society are decided by small numbers of elected officials and unelected high-ranking civil servants; other citizens are left to execute what is decided for them. Whether in the relations between employers

---

10 A merit of Castoriadis's work is his sensitivity to this, but he errs in going so far as to claim that 'the fundamental social relationship of modern capitalism' is that 'between directors and executants' (1988b, p. 201). Writing in 1963, Castoriadis displaced the relationship between capital and labour from the core of capitalist society: for classical Marxism, 'Society was seen as dominated by the abstract power of impersonal capital. Today, we see it as dominated by a hierarchical bureaucratic structure' (1993, p. 31). He contrasts 'the market' to 'bureaucratic-hierarchical organisation' as 'the central structuring moment of contemporary society' (p. 31). In so doing he wrongly conflates market with capital (value). Such a perspective is extremely ill-equipped to understand the rise of neoliberal capitalism and its current crisis.

and wage-workers or between state power and the governed, this separation is frequently accomplished by organizing people's life activity through the restrictive regulations of bureaucracy.

In the understanding proposed here, then, bureaucracy refers to a form of social relations, a way of organising social activity, rather than a group of people. This conceptualization is quite open, but also delimits the concept clearly. Bureaucracy does not encompass all situations in which people's ability to determine their own objectives and how to act are constrained. It is present when such constraint is associated with formal rules that people cannot easily change themselves. For example, a small business run in an utterly arbitrary and despotic fashion by an owner who 'micro-manages' a workforce of people carrying out extremely deskilled work and who goes to great lengths to prevent workers from having access to information about the enterprise's affairs is not a case of bureaucracy. Instead, it is a classic case of the employer control strategy that Richard Edwards (1979) dubs simple control.

This conceptualization also recognises that bureaucracy is not the only phenomenon that can impede subaltern self-activity. The phenomenon of *substitutionism* needs to be distinguished from bureaucracy. Substitutionism involves one or more persons substituting their own actions for those of a larger number of people. To put it differently, substitutionist actions are those which do not raise the level of self-activity among members of a given group. Bureaucratic methods are often substitutionist – as in the case of union rules which allow rank-and-file members little or no way to be involved in union affairs and which assign all important tasks to officers and staff, thereby substituting executive members and staff for an active membership – but not all substitutionism is bureaucratic. For example, a militant local union president who preaches 'leave it to me' to members and attempts to squelch or take control of any initiative that does not emanate from himself is undoubtedly a barrier to workers' self-activity. However, his behaviour should only be considered bureaucratic if (or to the extent that) it involves the use of formal rules that limit workers' ability to determine their own goals and actions.[11]

The conceptualization developed here can help us to understand how bureaucracy can pervade the practice of unionism. It is broad enough to cover a range of practices found in contemporary labour movements, including some phenomena excluded by the 'bureaucracy

---

11 My use of substitutionism is influenced by but not identical to that in Cliff (1960), which discusses it as a problem in the relationship between workers and a political party 'act[ing] as proxy in their name and on their behalf, regardless of what the workers thought or wanted.'

as officialdom' approach. For example, it alerts us to the fact that basic distinguishing features of how unions are politically administered by state power in Canada and the US – the legal and contractual prohibition of mid-contract strikes and sympathy strikes, and the requirement to resolve mid-contract disputes through grievance and arbitration procedures – are sources of union bureaucracy. These legal impositions take complaints about the employer out of the hands of unionized workers and channel them into a formal process. Once a grievance enters the process, it is 'owned' by union officials, not the workers affected. Another example of bureaucracy in the labour movement is when union rules sanction the monopolization of access to important information by a union executive or negotiating team. Members deprived of such information are less able to act independently. A union organizational structure that allows few or no opportunities for democratic decision-making by members during a strike is also an example of bureaucracy; even if the members have democratically set the goals of the strike, their inability to direct its course means that only a few people can determine how it is conducted. A union whose constitution gives members who hold no union office few or even no ways to participate in its affairs on an ongoing basis – for example, because general membership meetings are rare – is also bureaucratic. In such unions a few people conceive and execute union work, leaving most members with literally no way to get involved. When rules of order for the running of union meetings impede members' influence, this too is a case of bureaucracy. These examples, which are simply meant to give a sense of some of the ways that bureaucracy can be manifested within union organizations, suggest just how much is missed when a theory of union bureaucracy focuses solely or mainly on union full-time officers and staff.

THE SOCIAL ROOTS OF UNION BUREAUCRACY

What gives rise to union bureaucracy? It is arguably still true, as Alvin Gouldner (1955) claimed, that the root causes of bureaucracy are most often seen as human nature and the complexity and size of organizations such as unions (p.498-500). Even Darlington (2010), a Marxist, has written that 'a hierarchical and bureaucratic structure... is inherent in the requirement that unions are administratively efficient' (p.9). As Gouldner (1955) argues, such explanations, found in the work of theorists including Weber, Michels and Talcott Parsons, are shot through with 'pessimism and fatalism' (p. 498). A few years after Gouldner published his challenge to the dominant sociological theories of bureaucracy of the day, Castoriadis responded to the claim that large organizations must inevitably be bureaucratic by arguing that the need to organize centralization in organizations is indeed an inevitable and objective problem. However, it is a problem that can be resolved either through bureaucracy or direct democracy. 'A general meeting of strikers, an elected strike committee, the commune, the soviet, the factory council – that's centralisation' (Castoriadis, 1988b, p.207) or, more precisely, these are anti-bureaucratic responses created by self-organized workers in struggle to the problem of centralization. Castoriadis's demonstration that there are alternatives to bureaucratic organization suggests that theories which deduce union bureaucracy as simply the inevitable outcome of organizational scale are flawed. Instead of adopting an empty fatalism, we need to explore the determinate social conditions out of which union bureaucracy arises.

Arguably the most important cause of union bureaucracy is the practice at the centre of unionism itself: negotiating the price of labour power. The subordination of wageearners to capital in the paid workplace sphere leads organized workers to seek to regulate aspects of their working lives through collective agreements with their employers. The unequal balance of power between capital and labour is the reason why workers tend to try to codify wage levels and conditions of work in contracts. Only when workers' collective power and willingness to confront employers is so strong that they find it unnecessary or even undesirable to fix wages or conditions will wage-earners not try to lock in such matters in contracts. The 'episodic and discontinuous character of working-class struggle under capitalism' (Post, 1999, p.122) means that circumstances in which wage-earners enjoy such a highly favourable relationship of forces are both uncommon and generally short-lived. These rare situations have given rise to unions that refuse to sign contracts, such as the Industrial Workers of the World in the early 20th century and some early locals of the Committee for Industrial Organisation/ Congress of Industrial Organisations (CIO).[12]

Once contracts are in place, employers, who are concerned with the uninterrupted production of goods and services, have strong incentives to insist that there be no strikes for the duration of the agreement. Similarly, they have an incentive to assert their control over how their employees work. Since it is rare for the balance of class power in the paid workplace sphere in capitalist societies to be decisively in workers' favour – after all, this is the fundamental reason why workers fight for collective agreements in the first place – unions face pressures to accept

12 See Brissenden (1957), p.115, 324, 330, 371; Lynd (1996), p.5.

limits on strikes and to recognize managerial authority. Such concessions arise directly out of the relations between capital and labour in
the labour market and the labour process. When formalized, they are
bureaucratic: they limit workers' ability to determine the character and
goals of their activity. This, then, is the source of union bureaucracy at
the very core of unionism, probably its most important source.

Although the rule-governed separation of intellectual from manual
labour is an important source of bureaucracy in contemporary capitalist
societies, above all in matters related to the natural sciences and society, it
is not especially important in the case of union bureaucracy. If we follow
Sohn-Rethel (1978) and understand intellectual labour as involving 'the
use of non-empirical form-abstractions which may be represented by
nothing other than non-empirical, 'pure' concepts' (p.66) – for example,
abstract time, space and motion – then it is difficult to see them as important to unionism.

A far more important source of union bureaucracy is the separation
of conception from execution. This is a key element of the alienation of
labour – the structural lack of control by workers over the labour process,
workplace organization and production in general – that is a hallmark
of capitalist societies after their earliest phases (Rinehart, 2006). In societies in which the separation of conception from execution has become
normalized, or even just common, it is little surprise that workers tend to
organize unions in ways that bureaucratically reflect and reproduce this
separation. Organizing in this way is consistent with how many aspects
of their social lives are structured, including schooling, paid work,
state-citizen relations and, often, voluntary associations. The separation
between conception and execution can be seen in, for example, union
rules that give enormous decision-making power to staff and elected officers, treating the membership as passive executants. This corresponds to
how many employers treat employees, state officials treat citizens and
religious authorities treat members of their congregations.

Nevertheless, it is also noteworthy that the tendency for workers to
organize unions in ways that embody this dominant feature of capitalist
society coexists with a countertendency: workers can and do organize in
directly democratic ways. This democratic impulse arises out of experiences of workers' self-activity and self-organization, and disrupts the
separation between conception and execution. It can be observed most
clearly in the most democratic contemporary unions, such as the fledg-
ling National Union of Healthcare Workers in the US (Early, 2011); the
unions affiliated with France's Union syndicale Solidaires federation

(Coupé, 2007); and in forms of collective action such as strikes in which workers make important decisions in mass meetings and elect recallable strike committees.[13] Many unions bear, to some extent, the imprint of both this democratic countertendency and the tendency to reproduce the separation of conception from execution. The relative strength of the two in a particular case is the product of a concrete history.

Capitalist state power is also a significant root of union bureaucracy. States often impose formal rules that influence the social organization of unions. Such rules are examples of what Mark Neocleous (1996) dubs political administration, his term for the legal and administrative activity of capitalist state power in civil society. Political administration constitutes legal persons as both subjects of rights and objects of administration and regulates the working class through mechanisms that respond to workers' struggles but in ways that aim to extinguish their subversive potential (p. 88-92, 110-116). It is very common for capitalist states, once they legally recognize unions, to use their legal and regulatory powers to compel unions to structure themselves in ways that limit members' ability to determine the goals and methods of action. Bans on strikes or restrictions on the timing and nature of strikes are perhaps the most frequently imposed restrictions. In the US, the 'gradual metamorphosis of grievance arbitration from a voluntary and private mode of dispute resolution into a semicompulsory, institutional system for the management of complex enterprises' (Klare, 1978, p.377) was driven in large part by a series of judicial decisions, and the Taft-Hartley Act of 1947 imposed important restrictions on strike action (Green, 1980, p.198). In Canada, legislation passed in the 1940s prohibited all strikes during the term of a contract and made grievance arbitration compulsory (Fudge and Tucker, 2001). However, we should not forget that bureaucratic rules concerning such matters need not be imposed by state power, since they also arise from within capital-labour relations in the labour process and the labour market, as argued above. For example, in the US the initial 1937 contract between General Motors and the United Auto Workers 'established a grievance procedure designed to circumvent the shop steward systems and prevent wildcat strikes' and the 1940 contract stipulated that the grievance procedure would be the only way that the union would challenge management actions (Edsforth, 1987, p.177, 193). The new bureaucratic state mechanisms for the political administration of labour that were instituted in Canada in the 1940s amplified and generalized developments such as management rights clauses and grievance procedures

---

13 For example, the wildcat construction strikes in Britain in February 2009 (Gall, 2010).

that had already begun to emerge in collective bargaining (while also drawing on the US Wagner Act model of industrial legality and elements of pre-war Canadian legislation) (Camfield, 2002, p. 318).

Having argued that fatalist theories which simply deduce union bureaucracy from the existence of large-scale organisation are unconvincing, this article has discussed three social roots of union bureaucracy: contracts arising out of the wage relation, the separation of conception from execution and the political administration of unions by capitalist state power. It is now time to return to our starting point, the union officialdom. In addition to being a fourth source of union bureaucracy, it deserves some examination as a specific phenomenon.

WHAT ABOUT THE OFFICIALDOM?

So far this alternative account of union bureaucracy has said almost nothing about union officials. Some readers may be inclined to think that this is a theory of bureaucracy that gives bureaucrats an alibi. My concern, however, has simply been to foreground what is so often neglected or ignored in discussions of 'the trade union bureaucracy,' namely bureaucracy as a form of social relations. To use an imperfect analogy, this is no more an alibi for union officials than Marx's theory of the capitalist mode of production is an alibi for capitalists. The more bureaucratic a union is, the more bureaucratic its officialdom. But we should be more careful about making sweeping generalizations about union officialdoms than some radical theorists have been.

That said, there is plenty of historical evidence that as collective bargaining relations become more established, giving rise to or strengthening union bureaucracy as discussed above, unions tend to acquire (more) full-time officers and staff. Three examples will illustrate the pattern. As local contracts between craft unions and employers spread in the US and Canada at the end of the nineteenth century these unions began to hire full-time 'business agents' to administer their contracts. As Craig Heron (1996) puts it, these staff, along with the top officers and organisers of the craft unions, developed into an officialdom which began to develop a concern with protecting the union organization, its assets, its procedures, and its contractual obligations, as well as their own status and salaries. By denying access to central strike funds or ordering strikers back to work, these full-time officials sometimes put brakes on workers' anger and resentment (p.32).[14]

---

14 See also Heron (1999) and Green (1980, p.35-40).

Half a century later, the stabilization in the US and Canada of collective bargaining between employers and industrial unions that had recently become more bureaucratic also brought with it an expansion of union officialdom; the need to process grievances within the new mandatory grievance and arbitration systems was an important reason for this growth (Heron, 1996, p.80; Green, 1980, p.187). In South Africa, after the passage of the 1995 Labour Relations Act, which established a new mode of industrial legality, the officialdom of the Congress of South African Trade Unions swelled with the development of a layer of full-time shop stewards (Appolis and Sikwebu, 2003).

Many more similar cases could be cited.

The development of an extensive union officialdom is significant for a union movement. Regardless of their ideological outlooks or personal commitments, full-time officials (whether officers or union staff) have material conditions that are objectively different from those of the members they are supposed to serve.[15] They do not share workers' working conditions. They are often more highly-paid than rank-and-file members and lay officials. Full-time officials are only indirectly affected by employer attacks on wages and working conditions. Full-time officials who deal with management on a regular basis are particularly subject to employer efforts to enlist them in efforts to limit work stoppages, get workers to accept managerial control on the job, motivate workers to work harder, and the like. These material conditions create a real tendency for full-time officials to be less sensitive to the realities of workers' lives on the job and more attuned to management's desires than are rank-and-file workers. This is true even when a union is an insecure organization with very few full-time officials and meagre funds.

To the degree that serving as a full-time official actually becomes an occupation rather than a temporary commitment, this existence cultivates a different outlook. As the Welsh radical pamphlet *The Miners' Next Step* observes, full-time officers become '"trade unionists by trade" and their profession demands certain privileges' (Anonymous, 1912, p.3), or at least tends to. For full-time officials who can contemplate remaining full-timers for years, the union 'constitutes...a whole way of life – their day to day function, formative social relationships with peers and superiors on the organisational ladder, a potential career, and, on many occasions, a social meaning, a raison d'être.' Preserving this existence imposes its own imperatives:

---

15 This is also true for part-time officers (and other union members who are allowed time away from work for union activity), though obviously to a much lesser extent.

To maintain themselves as they are, the whole layer of officials must, first and above all, maintain their organizations. It is thus easy to understand how an irresistible tendency emerges on the part of the trade union officials... to treat their organizations as ends in themselves, rather than as the means to defend their memberships – to come to conflate the interests of the organizations upon which they depend with the interests of those they ostensibly represent (Brenner, 1985, p.45).

The material need to preserve the union in order to continue as a full-time official, which gives rise to the tendency to treat the union institution as an end in itself, is just as significant for a radical who takes office because of a sincere desire to further the fight for workers' rights as it is for someone who becomes a full-timer as a way to boost their income and status and escape from highly alienated labour.

An individual official may, of course, remain personally more committed to the workers she serves than to defending the union as an institution. The case of National Union of Mineworkers' leader Arthur Scargill in the 1984-1985 miners' strike in Britain springs to mind.[16] Brenner's point is not that all full-time officials are always more concerned with the institutional fate of unions than they are with workers' interests. Rather, it is that the officialdom as a whole cannot reproduce itself without preserving union institutions. There is more than one way to do this. An orientation to preserving union institutions is often accompanied with overtly class-collaborationist ideology, but need not be. It does not necessarily translate into a refusal by full-time officials to mobilize workers in struggles that defy the law to some extent – consider the political strikes organized by leaders of the Canadian Auto Workers (CAW) and most public sector unions during the Days of Action in province of Ontario in the second half of the 1990s (Camfield, 2000) and the efforts by leaders of the British Columbia division of CUPE to organize sympathy strikes to support striking teachers in 2005 (Camfield, 2009). The central issue is that when union officialdoms become consolidated social layers their continued existence depends on the security of union institutions. Consequently, the actions of full-time officials as a group will be influenced – and, in the last instance, determined by – the goal of preserving these institutions.

This allows us to pinpoint why union officialdom as a social layer is a fourth source of union bureaucracy. Motivated by the need to preserve union institutions in order to reproduce themselves as an officialdom,

---

16 See Callinicos and Simons (1985), which combines an appreciation of Scargill's strengths with observations about his political weaknesses.

full-time officials tend to organize union activity in ways that reflect their distinct interests as a group. Officials tend to favour ways of functioning that give themselves a great deal of decision-making power, at the expense of democratic rank-and-file control. As *The Miners' Next Step* puts it, of the privileges demanded by '"trade unionists by trade"...the greatest of all these are plenary powers...every inroad the rank and file make on this privilege lessens the power and prestige' (Anonymous, 1912, p.3-4) of full-time officials, who for this reason have an interest in opposing such democratizing moves. In short, full-time officials tend to organize union activity in ways that enhance their own sway. These are bureaucratic when they involve formal rules that limit the ability of members to determine the methods and goals of union action. This is a general tendency of the behaviour of full-time officials where union officialdom has become consolidated as a social layer; obviously there are individual exceptions.

When this kind of practice does arise, it can be challenged by the influence of active members firmly committed to democratic methods designed to limit the power of full-timers, such as the radical Welsh workers who a century ago proposed *The Miners' Next Step*. There are undoubtedly full-time officials who are so deeply committed to membership control that they seek to develop rather than curtail it. Nevertheless, full-time officials do generally tend to promote bureaucratic functioning rooted in their distinct interests as a social layer.

Contrary to a common assumption, the sway of the officialdom is not always exercised against militancy or radicalism. Full-time officials may try to advance one or both within unions within a bureaucratic framework. This can be seen, for example, in the militancy of the Justice for Janitors campaign initiated by leaders of the Service Employees International Union (Tait, 2005, p.188-189, 200-202) and the CAW's left turn in the second half of the 1990s.[17] However, as a theoretical generalization, we can say that once a union officialdom has crystallized as a social layer it will tend to display institutional conservatism. The strength of this conservatism varies enormously, and is influenced by a range of factors including the extent of union bureaucratization, the degree of unions' institutional security, the intensity of class struggle and the ideology of the union in question. The conservatism of union officials is not found only in stable contemporary unions in advanced capitalist countries; it

---

17 This turn and the CAW's subsequent evolution have not yet received adequate study, but see Gindin (1995) and Allen (2006). Recognizing the possibility of bureaucratic militancy implies a questioning of the notion (present in Voss and Sherman [2000]) that militant mobilization is evidence of a challenge to bureaucratic unionism.

has manifested itself in *far* more fragile and less bureaucratic organizations. For example, late nineteenth-century US and Canadian craft unions had weak legal rights, few officials and small bank accounts. Yet, as discussed above, their full-time officials were increasingly preoccupied with the defence of union institutions as well as contract obligations and their own perks. In addition to noting the tendency to a conservatism based on the preservation of union institutions, we can also conclude that full-time officials tend to favour their own control within union organizations, thereby promoting bureaucracy.

ANALYZING UNIONS TODAY

Where does this theory direct our attention in the analysis of unions? First, by highlighting the importance of formal rules that limit workers' ability to determine the character and goals of their actions and which they themselves are not easily able to change, this approach directs our attention *to the double-sided nature of collective agreements and labour law.* Both are often sources of union rights as well as restrictions on collective action.

For example, many basic features of US and Canadian labour law qualify as bureaucratic. In the US, the law prohibits sympathy ('secondary') strikes (Lynd and Gross, 2008). It also bans 'bargaining over managerial decisions "which lie at the core of entrepreneurial control"' and makes grievance arbitration 'semicompulsory' (Klare, 1978, p.337). Canadian law goes even further in its imposition of bureaucracy. It makes labour board certification the only permissible route to union recognition, bans recognition strikes, requires grievance arbitration procedures and (in most jurisdictions) a pre-strike compulsory conciliation process, contains a blanket prohibition of mid-contract, political and sympathy strikes, makes management rights clauses in contracts mandatory and requires the Rand Formula for union security (Fudge and Tucker, 2001, p.302-315). Such instances of bureaucracy are widely accepted by unionists, precisely because they are mandated by law. As Philip Corrigan and Derek Sayer (1981) have argued, 'Integral to the law is a moral topography, a mapping of the social world which normalises its preferred contours – and, equally importantly, suppresses or at best marginalises other ways of seeing and being' (p.33) and, I would add, doing. Although many instances of bureaucracy stemming from law and contract have the straightforward effect of making it difficult for workers to engage in collective action against employers and governments, some – such as exclusive representation rights and the Rand

Formula's requirement that all workers covered by a union contract pay union dues – have effects on workers' power that are more complicated.

Second, this theoretical perspective underscores the significance of others kinds of formal rules restricting the activity of unionized workers, chiefly those found in *union constitutions* and other union rules. In both the US and Canada, bureaucracy is widespread in the form of organizational structures and practices at all levels – from locals all the way up to the top labour centrals – that make it difficult or impossible for unionized workers to determine what their organizations will do and how they will do it. In these countries, this kind of bureaucracy is not the result of the political administration of labour by state power. US laws in fact guarantee many union members a number of basic democratic rights (Benson, 1979) while Canadian law and administration impose very few requirements on the internal organization of unions (Lynk, 2002). Much more significant as an influence on union organizational structures in the US and Canada is the pervasiveness of the separation of conception from execution in social life. The working-class movement is affected by the norms of societies in which organizations are generally understood to be properly run by small numbers of managers and 'experts,' with little or no popular participation. This approach has been unchallenged in the most influential political traditions within US and Canadian unions. What Heron (1996) writes of the politics of Canadian union officials in the years after the Second World War was also true of the outlook of many of their US counterparts (Mills, 2001): they 'had always emphasized the importance of expertise and centralized bureaucratic administration, rather than direct rank-and-file initiative' (p.80). Following the legal entrenchment of unions and collective bargaining in the US in the 1930s and in Canada in the following decade, newly-consolidated labour officialdoms put a stronger bureaucratic stamp on union organization.

The perspective advanced in this article broadens our understanding of what union bureaucracy is. Bureaucracy is not a group of leaders. Nor is it an external cage in which unions are trapped. Rather, as a mode of existence of social relations, it is, to varying degrees, a significant quality of unionism itself – to be precise, of particular forms of union praxis in specific times and places. Where union bureaucracy exists, it is usually deeply internal to unions as working-class movement organizations. For this reason, 'resolutionary radicalism' at union meetings and conferences and the denunciation of bureaucrats offer no escape from bureaucracy, which can only be

weakened through the promotion of forms of action whose character and goals are determined by workers themselves. Self-activity,
self-organization and democratic control from below are central to
anti-bureaucratic unionism, in which the conception and execution
of union activity are brought together through workers' active participation in and control over their organisations. Conditions which
are conducive to this kind of unionism and practices that foster its
development deserve study.

REFERENCES

Allen, B. (2006). Inside the CAW jacket. *New Socialist, 57,* 18-20

Anonymous (1912). *The miners' next step. Being a suggested scheme for
the reorganisation of the Federation.* Tonypandy: Unofficial Reform
Committee. Retrieved from http://www.llgc.org.uk/ymgyrchu/
Llafur/1926/MNS.pdf

Appolis, J. & Sikwebu, D. (2003). Pressing challenges facing the South
African labour movement: an interview with John Appolis and Dinga
Sikwebu. In T. Bramble & F. Barchiesi (Eds.), *Rethinking the labour
movement in the 'New South Africa.'* (p. 205-225). Aldershot: Ashgate.

Barker, C. (2001). Robert Michels and the 'cruel game.' In C. Barker, A.
Johnson & M. Lavalette (Eds.), *Leadership and social movements* (p.
24-43). Manchester: Manchester University Press.

Benson, H. (1979). *Democratic rights for union members.* New York:
Association for Union Democracy.

Braverman, H. (1998). *Labor and monopoly capital.* New York: Monthly
Review.

Brenner, R. (1985). The paradox of social democracy: The American case.
In M. Davis, F. Pfeil & M. Sprinker (Eds.), *The year left: An American
socialist yearbook* (p. 32-86). London: Verso.

Brissenden, P.F. (1957). *The IWW: A study of American syndicalism.* 2nd ed.
New York: Russell and Russell.

Callinicos, A. (1995). Socialists in the trade unions. London: Bookmarks.

Callinicos, A. & Simons, M. (1985). The Great Strike: the miners' strike of
1984-5 and its lessons. London: Socialist Worker.

Camfield, D. (2000). Assessing resistance in Harris's Ontario, 19951999. In
M. Burke, C. Mooers & J. Shields (Eds), Restructuring and resistance:
Canadian public policy in an age of global capitalism (p. 306-317).
Halifax: Fernwood.

— — — (2002). Class, politics and social change: the remaking of the
working class in 1940s Canada. Unpublished doctoral dissertation,
York University, Toronto.

——— (2009). Sympathy for the teacher: labour law and transgressive workers' collective action in British Columbia, 2005. Capital and Class, 33 (3), 81-107.

Castoriadis, C. (1988a). Modern capitalism and revolution. In D.A. Curtis (Ed.), Political and social writings (Vol. 2, p. 225-315). Minneapolis: University of Minnesota Press.

——— (1988b). Proletariat and organization, I. In D.A. Curtis (Ed.), Political and social writings (Vol. 2, p. 193-222). Minneapolis: University of Minnesota Press.

——— (1993). Recommencing the revolution. In D.A. Curtis (Ed.), Political and social writings (Vol. 3, p. 27-55). Minneapolis: University of Minnesota Press.

Cliff, T. (1960). Trotsky on substitutionism. Retrieved from http://www.marxists.org/archive/cliff/works/1960/xx/trotsub.htm

Corrigan, P. & Sayer, D. (1981) How the law rules: variations on some themes in Karl Marx. In B. Fryer, A. Hunt, D. McBarnet & B. Moorhouse (Eds.), Law, state and society (p. 21-53). London: Croom Helm.

Coupé, A. (Ed.). (2007). Qu'est-ce que l'Union syndicale Solidaires? Paris: Éditions de l'Archipel. Retrieved from http://solidaires.org/IMG/pdf/Union_syndicale_solidaires.pdf

Darlington, R. (2010). The rank-and-file versus bureaucracy analysis of intra-union relations. Unpublished paper presented at the European Social Science History Conference, Ghent.

Darlington, R. & Upchurch, M. (2012). A reappraisal of the rank-and-file versus bureaucracy debate. Capital and Class, 36 (1), 77-95.

Early, S. (2011). The civil wars in US labor: Birth of a new workers' movement or death throes of the old? Chicago: Haymarket.

Edsforth, R. (1987). Class conflict and cultural consensus: The making of a mass consumer society in Flint, Michigan. New Brunswick: Rutgers University Press.

Edwards, R. (1979). Contested terrain: The transformation of the workplace in the twentieth century. New York: Basic Books.

Fudge, J. & Tucker, E. (2001). Labour before the law: The regulation of workers' collective action in Canada, 1900-1948. Don Mills: Oxford University Press.

Gall, G. (2010, February 10). The engineering construction workers' strike. New Socialist Webzine. Retrieved from http://www.newsocialist.org

Gindin, S. (1995). The Canadian Auto Workers: The birth and transformation of a union. Toronto: James Lorimer.

Goody, J. (2006). The theft of history. Cambridge: Cambridge University Press.

Gouldner, A. (1955). Metaphysical pathos and the theory of bureaucracy. American Political Science Review, 49, 496-507.

Graeber, D. (2006). Beyond power/knowledge: an exploration of the relation of power, ignorance and stupidity. Retrieved from

http://www.lse.ac.uk/collections/LSEPublicLecturesAndEvents/ pdf/20060525Gra eber.pdf

Green, J. (1980). The world of the worker: Labor in twentieth-century America. New York: Hill and Wang.

Heron, C. (1996). The Canadian labour movement: A short history. Toronto: James Lorimer.

Heron, C. (1999). Review of the book Red flags and red tape: The making of a labour bureaucracy, by M. Leier. Labor History, 40, 410-412.

Hyman, R. (1989). The political economy of industrial relations: Theory and practice in a cold climate. Basingstoke: Macmillan.

Hyman, R. (2012). Will the real Richard Hyman please stand up? Capital and Class, 36 (1), 151-164.

Kapferer, N. (1980). Commodity, science and technology: A critique of Sohn-Rethel. In P. Slater (Ed.), Outlines of a critique of technology (p. 74-95). London: Ink Links.

Kelly, J. (1988). Trade unions and socialist politics. London: Verso.

Klare, K.E. (1978). Judicial deradicalization of the Wagner Act and the origins of modern legal consciousness, 1937-1941. Minnesota Law Review, 62, 265-339.

Leier, M. (1991). Which side are they on? Some suggestions for the labour bureaucracy debate. International Review of Social History, 36, 412-427.

Lenin, V.I. (1920). Preface to the French and German editions. Imperialism, the highest stage of capitalism. Retrieved from www.marxists.org/ archive/lenin/works/1916/imphsc/pref02.htm

Lukács, G. (1971). History and class consciousness: Studies in Marxist dialectics. London: Merlin

Lynd, S. (1996). Introduction. In S. Lynd (Ed.), 'We are all leaders': The alternative unionism of the early 1930s (p. 1-26). Urbana: University of Illinois Press.

Lynd, S. & Gross, D. (2008). Labor law for the rank and filer: Building solidarity while staying clear of the law. Oakland: PM Press.

Lynk, M. (2002). Union democracy and the law in Canada. Just Labour, 1, 16-30.

Mandel, E. (1992). Power and money: A Marxist theory of bureaucracy. London: Verso.

Michels, R. (1966). Political parties: A sociological study of the oligarchical tendencies of modern democracy. New York: The Free Press.

Mills, C.W. (2001). The new men of power: America's labor leaders. Urbana: University of Illinois Press.

Neocleous, M. (1996). Administering civil society: Towards a theory of state power. London and New York: Macmillan and St. Martin's.

Perusek, G. (1995). Classical political sociology and union behavior. In G. Perusek & K. Worcester (Eds), Trade union politics: American unions and economic change, 1960s-1990s (p. 57-76). New Jersey: Humanities.

Post, C. (1999). Ernest Mandel and the Marxian theory of bureaucracy. In G. Achcar (Ed.), The Legacy of Ernest Mandel (p. 119-151). Verso: London.

Post, C. (2011). Exploring working-class consciousness: A critique of the theory of the 'labour aristocracy.' Historical Materialism, 18 (4), 3-38.

Rinehart, J. (2006). The tyranny of work: Alienation and the labour process. 5th ed. Toronto: Thomson/Nelson.

Schmidt, J. (2000). Disciplined minds: A critical look at salaried professionals and the soul-battering system that shapes their lives. Lanham: Rowman and Littlefield.

Seaford, R. (2012). Monetisation and the genesis of the Western subject. Historical Materialism, 20 (1), 78-102.

Sohn-Rethel, A. (1978). Intellectual and manual labour: A critique of epistemology. Atlantic Highlands, NJ: Humanities.

Tait, V. (2005). Poor workers' unions: Rebuilding labor from below. Cambridge, MA: South End.

Thompson, P. (1989). The nature of work: An introduction to debates on the labour process. 2nd ed. Houndmills: Macmillan.

Voss, K. & Sherman, R. (2000). Breaking the iron law of oligarchy: union revitalization in the American labor movement. American Journal of Sociology, 106 (2), 303-349.

Weber, M. (1952). The essentials of bureaucratic organization: an ideal-type construction. In R.K. Merton (Ed.), Reader in bureaucracy (p. 18-27). Glencoe: The Free Press.

Interventions

Social Property Relations in the 21st Century: An interview with Ellen Meiksins Wood

— *Jordy Cummings*

Jordy Cummings[1] (JC): Let's start with Canada. What do you make of the current context of the Canadian state? Is it exceptionally right wing in comparison with earlier governments, for example, on issues like Palestine or the environment? Or are current policies continuous with past policy trajectories?

Ellen Meiksins Wood[2] (EMW): I don't think the two options here are mutually exclusive. Yes, this government is distinctively right-wing, not least on matters like Palestine and the environment. But, like everything else, it has a history. The simple continuity, of course, is that Canada was and remains a capitalist economy, with all this entails: the imperatives of profit-maximization imposed by the capitalist market, the necessity of constant capital accumulation, the constant need to reduce the costs of labour, the subordination of all social goods including ecological sustainability to the requirements of profit, the inequities and social injustices these imperatives inevitably engender, and the limitations placed on states as long as the economy is regulated by capitalist requirements. But let's be more specific. For

---

1 Jordy Cummings is a Ph.D. candidate in Political Science at York University, Toronto, Canada. He has written for *Counter Punch, The Bullet* and *Socialist Studies*. His main research area is classical Marxist political theory and is working on a dissertation examining the significance of the French Revolution for the socialist project in light of the rethinking of the concept of Bourgeois Revolution.

2 Ellen Meiksins Wood, who for many years taught at York University, Toronto, Canada, is the author of, among other books, *The Pristine Culture of Capitalism, The Origin of Capitalism, Democracy Against Capitalism, Empire of Capital,* and most recently two volumes of a social history of western political thought: *Citizens to Lords* and *Liberty and Property*. She was an editor of *New Left Review* from 1984 to 1993 and co-editor of *Monthly Review* from 1997 to 2000.

instance, inequality in Canada today is growing at a faster pace than in most OECD countries, and we have to acknowledge that this isn't entirely Harper's doing.

A previous Liberal government in the 1990s did more than its share in bringing about the current conditions: massive cuts in public spending which have made Paul Martin—who boasted that he had brought public spending back to 1950s standards—a model often cited by the current austerity maniacs. But this doesn't mean that Harper isn't a particularly malevolent development in Canadian history, devoted to reversing as much as he can of what has been best about Canada. It hasn't even been enough for him to undermine the social functions of the state and to do everything he can to create a new culture in Canada which treats the state not as an instrument of social responsibility but as the source of our problems. He has also been conducting a lethal attack on civil society and its independent institutions, undermining everything from sources of public information like Stats Canada to various autonomous human rights and environmental organizations – to say nothing of the ongoing attack on trade union rights. It's all very well to attack other governments as instruments of capital, but this government is undermining Canadian democracy in wholly new ways.

JC: The new buzzword is "austerity." Like neoliberalism (and sometimes used in combination), to what extent is austerity the specific manner in which the capitalist state is dealing with the current slowdown of capitalist accumulation? In other words, is there a risk that when we talk too much about austerity or neoliberalism and corporations that we risk softening our critique of capitalism?

EMW: That's a good point. We have to be careful that by stressing adjectives like 'neoliberal', or for that matter 'globalized', in the characterization of capitalism (to say nothing of 'market capitalism', as if there were any other kind) we don't obscure as much as we reveal, at least when we're trying to explain capitalist crisis or the damage done by capitalism. Of course we have to understand the differences among various kinds or phases of capitalism. But we also have to acknowledge the problems endemic to capitalism in all its forms. The imperatives of capital inevitably create periods of crisis. We don't have to underestimate the importance of, say, neoliberal ideology in creating the mess we're in today in order to understand that this ideology itself was a response to an already existing problem in the profitability especially of US capital. The decline started with the end of the long postwar boom, some time after American capital had been challenged by competition from Germany and Japan.

That economic decline was generated by the systemic mechanisms of capitalism, and neoliberalism, set in motion by Reagan and Thatcher, was in large measure an ideological response to that decline. This brought with it attacks on the labour movement, extracting huge concessions from workers, the deregulation of markets, and so on. But the ultimate effect wasn't to correct the problem. On the contrary, it was to make matters worse by reducing aggregate demand, which would be countered by what Robert Brenner has called 'asset-price Keynesianism', the stock market bubble, the encouragement of increasing indebtedness, and so on. Instead of genuine growth in the 'real' economy, there was a kind of 'bubblenomics'. In other words, this 'privatized Keynesianism' and the encouragement of private debt by means of reckless financial practices were designed to enhance capitalist profit without social spending, while, of course, reducing taxes for the rich. So the neoliberal 'solution', like current austerity programs, was an ideologically driven response to an unavoidable structural problem.

I think it would be safe to argue that the solution hasn't worked, to put it mildly, and it has never worked. There are no doubt insurmountable problems in any growth-stimulating alternative, and we will eventually have to confront the whole difficult question of 'growth'—how sustainable it is to have an economy driven by a constant need to accumulate capital and maximize profit. But we'd certainly be entitled to say that even an imperfect kind of Keynesian demand management would work better even now as a mode of crisis management. At the same time, there's no use pretending that even the most democratic and humane mode of state intervention could avoid the recurrence of crisis. That leaves us, as ever, with a political conundrum: it's always tempting to say that, capitalism is capitalism is capitalism, and that since, no matter what we do, capitalism inevitably produces crisis— to say nothing of endemic problems like social injustices and gross inequality—we should maintain our political purity by not settling for imperfect solutions. But the simple truth is that, for most people, imperfect solutions like increased social spending and the raising of taxes on the rich are a far better option than neoliberalism and austerity—which, however driven by big financial interests, don't even seem to work on their own terms.

JC: You have always accepted the label "Political Marxist", as originally a riposte by Guy Bois to Robert Brenner. Recently, Charlie
Post claimed a preference for "capital-centric" Marxist. In any case,
whichever way we label it, what is it about political or capital-centric
Marxism that so arouses, even to the point of vituperation, such
polemical disagreement and criticism?

EMW: I've always had my doubts about that label 'political Marxism',
though I have to take some responsibility for starting it. But I've come
to accept it, more or less reluctantly, to identify what has become a
very fruitful approach to the study of history and social reality. When
Guy Bois accused Brenner of this heresy, it was on the grounds that
Brenner had adopted a voluntarist kind of Marxism, which placed too
much emphasis on 'social factors', in particular class struggle, while
neglecting 'the most operative concept of historical materialism' (the
mode of production) and abandoning 'the field of economic realities'.
In my article on 'The Separation of the Economic and the Political in
Capitalism' I argued that this criticism was based on a false dichotomy,
because there was no such thing as a 'mode of production' in opposition
to 'social factors'. In fact, Marx's most radical innovation was precisely
to define the mode of production and economic laws themselves in
terms of 'social factors'. Political Marxism', as I understood it, believed
in the importance of material factors and the mode of production just
as much as economistic Marxism did, and it certainly didn't involve
some kind of voluntarist denial of historical causality. But it took seriously the proposition that production is a social phenomenon.

So, the first premise of this approach is that economic relations
are social relations, and its primary organizing principle is what Bob
Brenner called 'social property relations'. One of the main points
that follows from this is that each specific system of social property
relations has its own dynamics, its own 'rules for reproduction', and,
of course, this is true of capitalism in particular. The old forms of
Marxist technological determinism tended to read back into all history capitalism's laws of motion as if the drive constantly to improve
the forces of production by technical means were a universal, transh-
istorical law. Political Marxism is far more conscious of the specificities of capitalism, and so it can shed more light on how capitalism
operates today, why it does what it does, why its crises take the form
that they do, and what the possibilities are for the future – though
I'd hesitate to call the approach 'capital-centric', if only because of its

usefulness in identifying the specificity of other social forms too, not just capitalism. The whole point is that it seeks to be a truly historical approach, as distinct, say, from the teleological tendencies of certain kinds of Marxism.

I'm not really sure why this approach has provoked hostility in certain quarters – though I don't think this should be exaggerated, given the growing number of impressive scholars it has attracted, and the very fruitful and wide-ranging research agenda it has produced. Some of the hostility is probably just the old bad habit of the left, the so-called narcissism of small difference and the kind of sectarianism that tends to be most antagonistic to those outside one's sect but closest to it. But there's no denying that our approach to history represents a significant challenge to certain old orthodoxies, not just the old technological determinism but specific notions like 'bourgeois revolution', an idea that some people regard as sacrosanct even if it no longer serves any useful purpose, theoretical or political. There has also been another kind of criticism, which simply misunderstands 'Political Marxism' in the most fundamental way. One such criticism responds to my arguments about capitalist social property relations and how they generate the specific market imperatives of profit-maximization, constant capital accumulation, increasing labour-productivity, etc., by claiming that this emphasis on market ('economic') imperatives fails to acknowledge the persistence of 'extra-economic' coercion in capitalism, in particular in capitalism's exploitation not only of free wage labour but of unfree labour, and that my analysis of the 'economic' as formally separate from the 'political' in capitalism makes such an approach incapable of recognizing the political implications of 'economic' relations and of dealing with 'extra-economic' factors like race or gender.

This criticism seems to me completely, and astonishingly, off-base for a whole variety of reasons: because the whole point of my argument about the distinctive relation between the 'economic' and the 'political' in capitalism is to insist that the 'economic' is a social, and indeed a fundamentally political, relation; because I, like others who have adopted this approach, have said quite a bit about capitalism's exploitation of unfree labour, to say nothing of my writings on the interactions between capitalism and 'extra-economic' identities like race and gender; because one of the first premises of Political Marxism is Brenner's important observation that the market-dependence of economic actors, which creates its characteristic imperatives, long predates the generalization of wage labour and that its original imperatives were not generated by a relation between capital and wage labour; because

I have elaborated at great length my views on the 'extra-economic' power of the state, which, I argue, has always been essential to capitalism and even – in some ways even more – to neoliberal 'globalized' capital; and so on and so on. There's no space to go into this here, so let me just say this: it's one thing to acknowledge the persistence of 'extra-economic' relations and coercion in capitalism; it's quite another to understand the very specific social property relations that create capitalism's specific imperatives.

If you want to understand the relations between capitalism and, say, race, gender, or slavery, you obviously need to understand what makes capitalism distinct from other social forms, what generates its very specific operating principles and the distinctive historical dynamic that it has set in motion. Of course it's important to recognize the 'extra-economic' realities of race, gender, or unfree labour. But to say, for instance, that capitalism continued to exploit slave labour, not just wage labour, gets you nowhere in explaining capitalism and why it operates the way it does, which means you can't even explain how capitalism interacted with, how it affected and was affected by, slavery itself in ways distinct from other slave societies. I've said a few things about this in my own work, but, of course, the specialist on this is Charlie Post. Nor can we explain how race and gender operate in capitalist societies, as distinct from other social forms, without understanding the specific dynamics of capitalism.

JC: In relation to criticism of political Marxism, at a recent *Left Forum* panel, one of Post's critics claimed that political Marxism was fundamentally in error, more than anything else, over its rejection of Leninist and other "classical" theories of imperialism. Speaking personally, one of the things that made the most sense to me when I first read your work was your continuing argument that the early theories of Imperialism presupposed a world in which capitalism was not yet universal, yet today for all intents and purposes, capitalism has penetrated social relations everywhere, it has indeed "created a world in its own image"? What kind of theory of imperialism do we now need?

EMW: I'm not sure who exactly has rejected Leninist and other 'classical' theories of imperialism, but at any rate, my own argument has always been that those classical theories, as powerful as they were and remain, belong precisely to, and are most illuminating about, the 'classic' age of imperialism, in which major colonial powers were engaged in inter-imperialist rivalries to divide and redivide the territories of a largely non-capitalist world. This simply isn't true today, and I've suggested that what we've been lacking is a theory of today's capitalist imperialism, when, among other things, conflicts among capitalist powers take a very different form. I've argued in various places that, for all their strengths, neither Lenin's nor Luxemburg's theories were intended to deal with a new historical reality in which the economic imperatives of capitalism have overtaken old forms of colonial domination and inter-imperialist rivalries. I've also explained, for instance, why I think Lenin's idea of finance capital and his prediction of its growing dominance, however prophetic they may seem, were dealing with a form of financial dominance quite different from what's on display today: when, for example, he adopted Hilferding's notion of finance capital, he had in mind the very particular role of German banks in consolidating industrial production into 'cartels' and thus, in the process, fusing with industrial capital, not detaching speculation from the 'real' economy in the disastrous ways finance capital has been doing, or seeking to do, in our most recent crises.

In any case, his ideas don't, and couldn't have been intended to, offer an explanation of imperialism in our own time, especially given the ways in which the imperialism of his day was still significantly shaped by non-capitalist relations and forces. If we're going to cite Lenin, the least we have to do is apprehend not only what binds the capitalism of his day to our own but also what differentiates one from the other. And what this means above all is that any theory of imperialism today has to deal with the very specific forms of domination made possible by capitalism, not simply capitalism's continuing use of 'extra-economic' forms of colonial domination but its elaboration and universalization of its own specific forms of purely 'economic' coercion, the expansion and manipulation of market dependence and market imperatives, which have really come into their own in barely more than the last half-century.

JC: You have written with cautious optimism about the strength of the Occupy movement that has developed in the last year. What is it about this movement, its ideas, its rhetoric, that gives you this sense of optimism, in comparison, for example, with the global justice movement of the late 90s?

EMW: I guess the most heartening thing about the Occupy movement is how it has started to change the conversation. One of the things that has always struck me about the earlier movements you mention is how they tended to blame *global* capitalism often less because it was capitalist than because it was global. The principal target of many 'anti-capitalists' was less capitalism than 'globalization', at least in its present form, and particularly transnational corporations, together with the international organizations like the IMF, World Bank, WTO, and G8 that help to organize the world for global capital. There's still a lot of that emphasis today, and it certainly has its place. But I think we're beginning to see more directly anti-*capitalist* sentiment.

I don't want to exaggerate this shift to a focus on capitalism as capitalism. There's probably still too much focus on the greed of bankers rather than on the systemic imperatives of capitalism, which compel even the most socially responsible and least personally greedy capitalist to pursue profit-maximization and subordinate social goods like equity or environmental sustainability. But we may now be seeing something different – for instance, in the growing concern about inequality as endemic to the system, or in an increasing recognition of the ways the capitalist market restricts our choices and our individual freedoms. It's encouraging, too, that at least in some places there are signs of collaboration between Occupy groups and the labour movement. And it's certainly encouraging to see the concerns of the Occupy movement expressed in the most mainstream media, who have clearly been compelled to take notice. We've yet to see the movement take a truly political form with a capacity for organized action, and I'm not entirely convinced that it's well suited to producing that kind of effect. But I'd never underestimate the importance of changing the conversation in – eventually – giving rise to something more.

One thing that may be encouraging in this respect is that the new movements seem more inclined to see the point of national struggles. The old global justice movement certainly had room for very local struggles, but with its focus on global institutions it seemed to suggest that any truly effective political action would have to occur on the global stage, and this in the end may have proved politically disabling. After all, 'global' power is rather hard to target and in the end seems beyond the practical reach of any effective political action, in contrast to national states, which represent more visible, less daunting targets, more susceptible to local struggles and some kind of democratic accountability.

It's not insignificant that globalization theories on the left have tended to emphasize the uselessness of national struggles in globalized capitalism, or even, as in the case of Hardt and Negri, the absence of any identifiable locus of power at which we can aim some kind of organized counter-power. What we may be seeing now is a different perception of where the targets lie. I don't want to stretch this point too much, but the Occupy movement, while certainly aware of globalization and open to international solidarity, may be more inclined to look closer to home, not just to meetings of the G20 but, say, to Wall Street and Washington, not just as symbols but as identifiable centers of power.

This applies in various ways to other instances of turbulence you talk about, in the Arab Spring or the Eurozone crisis. I can't say much with any confidence about the Arab Spring, given the setbacks we've been witnessing, which are likely to continue – except that it's hard not to be moved by the passionate and courageous demands for freedom and dignity we were hearing at the height of the revolutions, and it's hard not to believe that they have changed the world for good, in both senses of the word. The crisis in the Eurozone may have more immediate implications for the kinds of working class and popular struggles you seem to have in mind. This is a crisis that, like no other in the recent past, has forced a confrontation with the realities of capitalism. The tensions between the purveyors of austerity and their vicitms can't help but draw the lines more sharply along class lines than we've seen, or been willing to see, for a while.

But there's also something else: as, say, the Greek state takes on the job of doing the dirty work for German banks, there's no mistaking the role played by local states as the primary instruments of capital, however 'global' – or at least regional – capital may be. It is, after all, national states that have been putting more and more of our lives outside the reach of democratic accountability by subjecting us more and more to market imperatives, by privatizing and commodifying ever more aspects of life. What greater 'democratic deficit' is there than the one effected by increasing marketization? And how can this be resisted without directing struggles at the local state? What other struggle is there that can offer Greeks – or Spaniards or Italians – any better hope than a struggle directed at the power concentrated in their own national states? We have to see those struggles as not only a challenge to this or that austerity program but as an effort to restore and expand democracy – and also as a challenge to the long prevailing wisdom that the state has become an irrelevance, not worthy of targetting in struggle.

JC: One aspect of the current Left conversation is an interest in horizontalism, as it is called, and a skepticism towards engaging with state power. What do you make of the continued resilience of this phenomenon?

EMW: If you're asking me why many on the Left are disinclined to regard the state as a useful target of struggle, or the achievement of state power as a useful objective, I think there are several different kinds of reasons. There are what we might call general structural reasons having to do with the nature of capitalism, which appears to make the state a less relevant player in everday struggles than the daily struggles of the workplace or the tensions between employers and workers. Then there are historical reasons, not least the dark record of the state in 'actually existing socialism' or the disappointments of social democracy. There's also something specific to the current generation of young people, which distinguishes them sharply from their parents and grandparents.

The generation that went through the Great Depression and World War II and lived to see the golden age of welfare state capitalism had a very particular experience of the state as a source of social goods, from housing to health care to universal education. This was particularly true of Canada. The next generation, the so-called 'baby boomers', may have taken these things for granted, but that's no longer true of the current generation of young people. They are hard pressed to think of any positive example of state action that has emerged in their own life-time, as their grandparents may have experienced the rise of the health service and other public goods. On the contrary, young people today have witnessed deteriorating public services. Long after the decline of postwar capitalism and the end of the postwar boom, they have grown up with both the ideology and the consequences of neoliberalism. I don't think it's too much to say that the objective of neoliberalism has been to destroy the state as an instrument of social solidarity and democratic responsibility. It has left the state bereft of both resources and positive objectives, deliberately destroying, in large part simply by means of cuts in funding, much that has been good about state services. So it's no wonder that this generation finds it hard to think of the state as a positive force in the way that their grandparents did.

Meanwhile, as I suggested before, we're constantly inundated by what's become an almost unchallenged convention: that globalization has rendered the state pretty much irrelevant, a spent force that – for better or worse – can't keep up with global capital. This kind of thing, which we get from the Left no less than the Right, has long seemed to me a particularly disabling idea and, as it happens, not even close to the truth. I've argued endlessly that global capital needs the state, in many ways more than before, and that it remains a very relevant target of struggle, so I won't go on about it here again But, again, I think it's worth considering how the current crisis might dramatically bear out the view that struggles at the level of national states may be the most effective counter to the current depradations of global capital. I certainly wouldn't dismiss the importance of popular efforts to challenge transnational organizations like the G20, but in the EU, for example, take Greece. It's hard to imagine any popular action on the international stage that could have anything like the effects, however limited so far, brought about by the the upsurge of popular opinion that led to the rise of Syriza. Even without an electoral victory for that radical party, the rules of the game have changed, not only for the Greek government itself but for the politics of Europe.

JC: Your new book *Liberty and Property*, a companion to *Citizens to Lords* has as an underlying theme the contestation over the meaning of freedom as we currently understand it. What is the significance of this contestation - I'm thinking in particular about the Putney Debates, but stretching from Hobbes and Locke to the Diggers, the original "occupy movement"? In relation to this, can - and should, as recently suggested by Corey Robin – the Left reclaim "freedom" as an animating principle, in our rhetoric, in our organizing strategies, in our guiding principles?

EMW: Of course the Left should 'reclaim' freedom as an animating principle –though I'm not really clear on what it means to suggest that 'the left' has ever abandoned it or what particular left we're talking about. The kind of socialism I've always believed in – and I'm hardly alone in this – has always regarded freedom as a central guiding principle. I might be tempted to add that various postmodernist trends have in their own ways tended to undermine such 'universalistic' principles. But I've said enough about all this too often, so let me try to answer the question as you posed it. For Corey Robin, if I understand him correctly, the issue really has to do with US politics and how the left can challenge the monopoly claimed by the Right on the traditional American ideology of individual freedom and mobilize that ideology in favour of progressive causes. Progressives in the US, he suggests, tend to invoke security or equality as their animating principles, which has the effect of treating people not as free and active citizens but as passive beneficiaries of state intervention, social welfare, redistributive policies, and so on. This may be a useful comment on US political discourse; but Robin's argument may beg the essential question by conceding too much to rightwing conceptions of rights and liberties, which, in a classically American way, define freedom in opposition to equality and collective solidarity. For me, any convincing idea of freedom has to recognize from the start, for example, that liberty and equality are anything but antithetical and that for vast numbers of people the growing inequality we have today is a restriction, not an enhancement, of individual freedom.

One of the points I make in Liberty and Property is that Western conceptions of freedom have long been distorted and constrained by the fact that they owe so much to ideas of 'liberty' conceived not as a defence of democratic freedoms but as an assertion of class privilege and the autonomy of dominant property classes in their conflicts with monarchical states or other claimants to superior jurisdiction. Of course there have been more democratic ideas too, like those of the Levellers and the Diggers whom you mention, and they are more likely to recognize the mutual reinforcement of liberty and equality, individual and collective. But we shouldn't underestimate the influence of the dominant tradition and the ways in which our own ideas are still restricted by it.

The other essential point I make in *Liberty and Property*, as elsewhere in my work, is that our contemporary ideas of freedom haven't adequately acknowledged the new forms of power and coercion created by capitalism. It's not enough to defend our liberties against the power of the state. We also have to consider the compulsions imposed on us by distinctively capitalist forms of coercion – and here I mean not just the excessive power of money in politics, nor even just the power of capital in the workplace, but also the compulsions of the market, its imperatives of profit-maximization and constant capital accumulation. We're so used to thinking of the market as a realm of choice and freedom that we tend to overlook the degree to which it's a form of coercion and domination, which compels us to subordinate all other considerations –fairness, social justice, human dignity, ecological sustainability, and, yes, the freedom of the individual – to the demands of profit.

Twenty-First Century Socialism and the Global Financial Meltdown: In Conversation with Michael Lebowitz

— Rebekah Wetmore and Ryan Romard

Rebekah Wetmore and Ryan Romard[1] (RW/RR): The crisis of world capitalism starting in 2007 was the most severe crisis of capitalism since the Great Depression and thus far the recovery, both globally and within Canada, has been weak at best. With this mind, to what extent is the current crisis cyclical and in what ways is this related to a broader, systemic crisis of the capitalist system?

Michael Lebowitz[2] (ML): This is not a question for which there is a quick answer. What do we mean by a crisis of capitalism? I distinguish between a crisis *in* capitalism and a crisis *of* capitalism. For me, there is only a crisis of capitalism when there is an organized and conscious subject prepared to put an end to capitalism.

There are always crises, though, *within* capitalism. Understanding this distinguishes a Marxian perspective from the perspective of mainstream neoclassical economists for whom the normal state of capitalism is equilibrium and crises are aberrations. For Marx and Marxists, crises are inherent in capital's tendency toward overaccumulation. It is inherent in the nature of capital that its orientation is to grow, to expand — to accumulate, accumulate! In a crisis, though, that process of accumulation is checked.

All crises take the form initially of the inability of capital to realise the

1 Rebekah Wetmore is an independent researcher and community organizer. She has an MA in Sociology from Acadia University in Wolfville, Nova Scotia. Ryan Romard is a MA Candidate in Sociology at Acadia University. He studies the Sociology of Agriculture in Cuba.
2 Michael A. Lebowitz is Professor emeritus of Economics at Simon Fraser University in Vancouver, Canada, and the author of, most recently, *The Socialist Alternative: Real Human Development*, and *The Contradictions of "Real Socialism": The Conductor and the Conducted*. He was the Director of the Program in Transformative Practice and Human Development, Centro Internacional Miranda, in Caracas, Venezuela, from 2006-11.

surplus value extracted from workers through exploitation in the process of production. If capital is unable to realise the surplus value which is contained within commodities through sale of those commodities, it will cut back on their production. And, the result is unemployment as well as reduced demand for investment—- in other words, reduced demand for the sector producing means of production. Growing unemployment in both the consumer goods sector and the sector producing means of production means that there will be greater difficulties in selling commodities. Thus, the initial emergence of the inability to sell commodities brings with it a deepening crisis within capitalism.

Part of that deepening of the crisis involves a significant reduction in the values of capital — in the value of raw material stocks, for example, but especially what is called fictitious capital. By fictitious capital, we mean the capital invested in various vehicles which, while linked ultimately to the fortunes of real capital within the spheres of production and circulation, takes on a life of its own. For example, the values of shares in corporations (which have their real basis in the profitability of those corporations) expand significantly in the period of a boom. Presumably, these values are related to expectations of that profitability but those stock values are determined instead by prospects of money to be made in the stock market. Until the moment of truth, there comes a point as a crisis within the real economy emerges in which there is an enormous destruction of those values contained in this particular form of fictitious capital—- i.e., a crisis of the stock market. And this is not the only form of fictitious capital. We've seen a great destruction of fictitious capital in the form of various financial instruments such as derivatives, etc. as well as real estate values. All of this has its impact and feeds back on the real, underlying economy to deepen a crisis.

None of this explains *why* crises occur, though—- why capital's drive to expand comes up against barriers. In Marx's *CAPITAL*, he indicated that capital develops an ability to grow by leaps and bounds and comes up against no barriers except those presented by the availability of raw materials and the extent of sales outlets. Both those barriers are the result of capital's tendency for overaccumulation. In the case of the first, Marx described how overaccumulation tends to be manifested in lagging production of raw materials and other products whose source is nature. Agriculture and extractive industries such as mining, Marx noted, are modes of production *sui generis* — they cannot be expanded in the same way as spheres of production which are users of raw materials. Precisely for this reason, then, in an extended period of accumulation, capital often comes up against the problem of the rising value of raw materials with the result that a greater proportion of capital outlays must be for what is called constant capital. These will be periods in which the rate of profit tends to fall because overaccumulation in industry has as its counterpart underaccumulation in the production of raw materials. You can see my discussion of Marx's argument in 'The General and the Specific in Marx's Theory of Crisis', which is reprinted in my book, *Following Marx: Method, Critique and Crisis*.

The second barrier that Marx identified is rooted in the antagonistic conditions within which capital functions — in other words, in the nature of capitalist relations of production themselves (recall that Marx stressed that the real barrier of capital is capital itself). Capital's drive to increase the rate of exploitation brings with it a tendency for its ability to produce more and more articles of consumption to come up against a barrier in terms of its ability to realise the surplus value contained in those commodities; this tendency for overproduction of capital often takes the form of intensification of capitalist competition. The begged question, though, is if a rising rate of exploitation is significant, why doesn't the relatively increased share of income for capital lead to increased capitalist expenditures (investment and consumption)? The answer is that capitalists are not likely to expand productive capacity if there is already unused capacity in the productive sector (because of overaccumulation) and falling profit rates because of the burden of the high costs of raw materials. The situation is one in which *workers can't spend and capitalists won't*. It's a situation when capitalists choose to place their funds elsewhere—in securities, real estate, etc.

I have been describing a crisis which is essentially a cyclical crisis. Cyclical crises, though, by definition don't last. For one, the process of destruction of values can restore the conditions for resumption of profitable production. But crises can be more than cyclical; they can also be structural. When we talk about the overaccumulation of capital, it is essential to recognise that capital does not expand in unison. There is an inherent tendency toward unevenness: some capitals will be the major contributors to the growth and accumulation of capital while others may bear the brunt of the effects of overaccumulation. In particular, there are periods in which capital expands in new areas, new geographical regions, more rapidly than in the old regions of capitalist expansion. This process may reflect new, advanced productive forces (thus, better means of securing relative surplus value) or very high rates of exploitation based upon low real wages and a high length and intensity of work—and sometimes it may be *both* modern techniques and very low wages.

This emergence of new capitals and new forms of production provides a basis for a structural crisis — in other words, a crisis which is the result of the changing structure of capital. Although it does not occur with the periodicity of a cyclical crisis, this definitely has happened before—- in what was called the Great Depression in England in the latter part of the 19th century (as the result of the growth of production in Germany and elsewhere on the Continent as well as the US) and in the 1930s (after the growth of mass production in the US and the growth of the rate of exploitation in the 20s). Crises in capitalism which embody both cyclical elements but also significant structural elements will be deeper and longer than those which only involve cyclical swings. Further, structural crises may generate significant tensions because the change in the geographical locus of capital resulting from unevenness may lead to an attempt to redivide spheres of influence and power (and thus inter-imperialist rivalry). Finally, their resolution may require a process of restructuring of capitalist institutions in order to incorporate the new elements and manage these new relations—- the obvious case being the restructuring which occurred with the Bretton Woods agreements after the depression of the 30s and World War II.

I have been stressing this question of restructuring because it is obvious that the current crisis within capitalism is both cyclical and also structural in this sense. There's been a very significant growth in productive capacity, an accumulation of capital, in centres such as China, South Korea, India, Brazil, etc. A significant part of the explanation of this process has been the enormous reserve armies of labour in the countryside which could be drawn upon for the expansion of wage labour within industry at wage rates well below the levels in the old capitalist centres. As a result, this has been a period marked by a rising rate of exploitation on a world scale and at the same time a rising demand for raw materials from these new expanding centres of capitalist accumulation (reflected in prosperity in raw material producing centres).

Both these characteristics tend to generate a crisis within world capitalism; however, within that general crisis, the unevenness is obvious. In the old centres of capital, we see that rather than the expansion of productive capital, money has flowed into finance and real estate; thus, one can speak accurately about the separation of finance capital from productive capital there (much like England's shift toward rentier capitalism in the late 19th century). But there is more: in the context of capitalist competition and pressures upon profits we see that capital in these old centres has managed to insulate itself somewhat because of its success in shifting the tax burden to the working class—- reducing taxes upon corporations and upon those with high income (who are described as the 'job creators'). Capital has been able to do this because the defeat of the working class in these centres.

To describe, though, the growth of finance capital at the expense of productive capital as characteristic of this crisis in capitalism (and especially to see this as a sign of the crisis *of* capitalism) is an example of one-sidedness (which happens to coincide with the location of those who come to this conclusion). It doesn't look at all like a crisis of capitalism in China, Vietnam, India, Brazil etc. In short, what we are seeing is a change in the structure of world capitalism, and the attempt to manage the change in that structure is reflected in such developments as the shift from the G7 to the G20. Will that restructuring of capital succeed? I suggest that, in the absence of the ability of the working class throughout the world to prevent it, capital will succeed in this as it has in the past.

Let me turn, though, to a question which you didn't ask explicitly: is there anything in this existing situation which points to the ultimate, final crisis of capitalism? Although there are many Marxist economists who are predicting the end of capitalism (something Marxist economists are prone to do), my perspective is somewhat different. It is obvious that there is a very serious problem of an emerging ecological crisis to which capital is contributing substantially. However, that is a crisis of humanity — not a crisis of capital. How and if this crisis of humanity can be prevented depends upon a serious movement of working people to put an end to capitalism by all means possible and as soon as possible. And *that* will be the crisis of capitalism.

RW/RR: Canada's Prime Minister Stephan Harper has unashamedly promoted the myth that the financial crisis did not greatly affect Canada. Is this notion of Canadian exceptionalism warranted? If not, what might the next couple of years be like for Canadians, particularly in light of the recent austerity measures?

ML: It is true that Canada has not been as affected by the financial crisis as the United States. But that has really little to do with the actions of the Harper government. In part, it reflects the difference in the nature of the banking system and the traditions of finance in Canada. In part, too, it also reflects the difference in the risk orientation of Canadians. But this is not a case of Canadian exceptionalism at all. Not unless you forget about all those other exceptions like Chile, Ecuador, Venezuela, Brazil, and indeed all countries exporting raw materials to China and experiencing a boom based upon this.

There have been two distinct tendencies affecting the Canadian economy. One is the tendency related to the depression in the United States, given Canada's long-term dependence upon that market. The other tendency reflects the resource boom based upon exports to China and other Asian countries. Those two tendencies reflect the changing structure of world capitalism, and the geographical division involved is reproduced within Canada itself. Thus, provinces like Québec and Ontario, which have focused upon manufacturing, are suffering significantly whereas Prairie provinces like Alberta, Saskatchewan and Manitoba in particular have been benefiting from their resources.

The Harper government has thrown its lot in with the latter group of provinces and with the emerging new centres of capital. In its so-called budget bill, its determination to push through pipelines to serve China, its interest in Chinese foreign investment, its removal of environmental protection measures, etc, we can see that it is placing a wager on the structural changes in capital. This strategy has major implications for the Canadian economy. Thomas Mulcair of the NDP has raised the question of the 'Dutch disease' — i.e., the blow to Canadian manufacturing as a result of a rising value of the Canadian dollar linked to resource exports. I think that's a bit premature because we cannot say at this point how much of this particular decline is cyclical and how much is structural. However, over a long time period, I think it is correct to talk about the spectre of the Dutch disease. The Harper government strategy points in the direction of a new model — actually a return to the *old* model, that of the hewers of wood and drawers of water (i.e., to a hollowing-out of the economy similar to what happened to Venezuela over a number of years as the result of its oil wealth).

In this period, the two tendencies interact. Budget deficits reflect the fate of the old capitals—- in particular, the problems in the U.S. economy and the pattern of tax cuts for corporations and high income earners that have occurred here. As in the case of the United States, the defeat of the working class and the weakness of working class institutions has meant the successful imposition of capital's austerity plan which is an attack on the working class. To this can be added the effect of resource exports which have significantly elevated the value of the Canadian dollar relative to that of the US and seriously affected manufacturing exports as well as those of sectors such as the forest industry (and thus employment in these sectors).

Of course, it is essential to recognise that these two tendencies are not occurring in two separate worlds. The rapid accumulation of capital in China and other emerging capitalist countries has itself been based on the existence of markets in the developed North. To the extent that the latter continue to slump, it can not help but affect the accumulation of capital in the former and thus their demand for resources. When that happens (and I think the only thing in question will be its extent), Canada faces the real prospect of a serious decline. All other things equal, this will accelerate and intensify the capitalist austerity project.

So, when you ask the question as to what may the next couple of years be like for Canadians, it is difficult to provide a definite answer. It depends. All other things are not necessarily equal. If the working class continues to be defeated, we can look forward to one defeat after another—- one attack after another on social services, health and safety, education, everything that people have made sacrifices and struggled to achieve in the past. It's not, of course, inevitable. Nothing is inevitable when it comes to the question of class struggle.

RW/RR: In The Socialist Alternative, you argue that "given the heterogeneity of the collective worker (and its various forms of immiseration) and capital's use of differences to divide the working class in order to defeat it, a political instrument is needed to mediate among the parts of the collective worker, provide the welcoming space where popular movements can learn from each other and develop the unity necessary to defeat capital.." Is the anti-capitalist left in Canada ready to form such a party? If not, what can be done to foster the development of this type of party?

ML: My immediate response is no, the anti-capitalist left in Canada is definitely not ready to form a party which can defeat capital. But there is also the question as to whether an anti-capitalist left as such can ever defeat capital. I doubt that. When I was involved in *Rebuilding the Left* in Vancouver, I argued that we needed to go beyond organising on the basis of anti-capitalism and instead to stress explicitly the necessity for a socialist alternative. Anti-capitalism means something different for everyone. For some people, it is opposition to big corporations; for others, it is opposition to the banks or the capitalist state or money or large-scale industry, international capital or inequality in income and wealth. Accordingly, the perceived alternative can range from breaking up the corporations to developing alternative currencies to supporting cooperatives and credit unions to putting an end to private ownership of the means of production and to returning simply to the good old days when people could anticipate a good job, a home of their own and all the amenities that their parents had. The multiplicity of views about what we don't like about capitalism (ie., anti-capitalism) was apparent in the Occupy movement.

Of course people should struggle against every assault by capital and every violation of our conceptions of justice. Marx made the point well: without the struggles of workers over wages, workers would be a 'heartbroken, a weak-minded, a worn-out, unresisting mass' and would be incapable of any larger struggles. Of course, too, it is essential to try to link these struggles. However, in the absence of a positive vision, capital can and will separate and defeat those who oppose it. Trade unions under attack and facing capital's demand for concessions, for example, can look at issues outside their immediate concerns and say, 'what's this got to do with our members?'

Sometimes, though, capital and the capitalist state make it easier to connect issues. In 1983, a simultaneous blanket assault by the Social Credit government in BC created conditions in which it was possible to unify teachers, hospital workers, renters, poverty movements and private sector trade unions who were injured by the proposed legislation in a movement toward a general strike. Similarly, when capital is in a crisis period and moves to administer its affairs through a general programme of capitalist austerity, it is possible to bring together those under attack—both those suffering from the crisis itself and those under attack by the capitalist state. That is what Occupy, the Enraged and the Middle East Spring demonstrate. And, right now that potential is there as the result of the Harper Government's so-called Budget Bill.

But, as the disintegration of the General Strike movement in BC demonstrated, many 'No's' do not make a big 'Yes'. At the present time, people are fighting against reductions in social services, against measures which make universities and education inaccessible for many, against the removal of measures protecting against the destruction of the environment, against the removal of support for our current health-care system — against, indeed, many characteristics of what is viewed as our entitlement, an entitlement which didn't drop from the sky but which was the result of years of struggle. In short, people are struggling out of a sense of fairness. But there's a difference between struggling over questions of fairness (sometimes identified as characteristic of moral economy) and being able to understand why all this is occurring — enough so to be able to put an end to such attacks. If you don't understand the underlying factors, you are likely to look upon what you're fighting for as the restoration of the good old days.

Marx made this point in talking about the limits of wage struggles. 99% of those struggles, he said, were reactions against capital's previous actions to drive down wages. They were attempts to restore the traditional standard of life and occurred under the conservative banner of a fair day's pay for a fair day's work. And, it was accurate to describe this as a conservative slogan because workers fighting under that banner were seeking to conserve or preserve the pre-existing conditions. While though those struggles were essential for developing their collective strength and dignity, Marx stressed the necessity for workers to go beyond those guerrilla wars against capital and its state and to struggle under the revolutionary banner of putting an end to capitalist relations.

We need to understand the nature of capitalism, and we need a vision of a socialist alternative if we are to defeat capital. This is my point in *The Socialist Alternative: Real Human Development*, where I argue for a vision of socialism which involves social ownership of the means of production, worker and community decision-making and production for social needs rather than exchange. A focus upon human development unifies these elements and, indeed, has the potential to unify all our separate struggles. This vision of a society in which all human beings are able to develop their capacities and realize their potential is the vision contained in The Communist Manifesto—- a society in which 'the free development of each is the condition for the free development of all'. We need to communicate and struggle for the realization of that vision.

Defeating capital won't happen spontaneously through some kind of collective epiphany. It requires conscious effort. But any attempt to create at this point a party to defeat capital would be viewed correctly as just another vanguard sect promising to deliver socialism. It is important to start from people's conception of fairness and to understand why they are moved to struggle. However, we need to recognise the limits of guerrilla wars against capital and to learn to work together in practice to build an understanding about the nature of capitalism and the need for a socialist vision. That means finding ways to create spaces where popular movements can learn from each other—- spaces and new forms like people's assemblies at every level. We need but we're not ready to form a socialist party that can defeat capital. But we can develop a socialist project, one which listens, educates and helps to create the basis for a new type of party which is integral to and does not stand over and above social movements.

RW/RR: Drawing on your work in Venezuela, Cuba and the former Soviet Union what might a socialistic response to the ongoing economic crisis look like? What has been Venezuela's response to the economic crisis? What can socialists in Canada and elsewhere learn from these experiences about how to respond to the crises of capitalism?

ML: I've just completed a new book, *Contradictions of 'Real Socialism': the Conductor and the Conducted*, which stressed, among other things, the importance of building upon aspects of the 'moral economy' of the working class in the former Soviet Union in order to move forward to socialism. As we know, however, what did happen was precisely the opposite—- an attack on the concepts of fairness and justice of workers as part of the process of moving to capitalism. Unfortunately, too, there are many signs in Cuba that the response to their current crisis is to move in the same direction although it is still too soon to rule out the possibility that there can be a return to the ideas of Che Guevara about the importance of building socialist human beings.

Venezuela, though, does offer some ideas that Canadians can draw upon—- precisely because it is a capitalist country with resource wealth, has the experience of suffering the Dutch disease and now has a government with the articulated goal of building a new socialism different from the experiences of the 20th Century. In particular, the government of Hugo Chavez has decided to use its resource wealth to expand enormously access to health services and education, to reclaim as state property the oil and other basic industries as well as telecommunications, electricity, steel, cement, airlines and a host of other sectors seen as important for satisfying the many needs of Venezuelans. By building up local industry, housing and agriculture with oil revenues, it is explicitly attempting to demonstrate that there is nothing inevitable about the Dutch disease if you have a government committed to food sovereignty and to creating opportunities for jobs that can serve the needs of people.

There are many problems in Venezuela, and not the least is the inherited culture of clientalism and corruption (as well as a tendency to populism) to which the Chavez government is not at all immune. But there are elements that can inspire many people within Canada who don't think of themselves as part of an anti-capitalist or socialist Left. The idea of neighbourhood government where people can work together with their neighbours to solve local problems and to plan (something embodied in the communal councils and communes in Venezuela) and the idea of workers councils (without which, Chavez has said, you can't build socialism)—- these are ideas which don't need oil revenues or major state-directed programmes. This concept of protagonistic democracy, a concept of democracy as practice through which people can develop their potential, can appeal to people precisely because of their sense of their powerlessness in modern capitalist society.

Are there ideas here for Canadian socialists to draw upon in the context of the current crisis and the capitalist austerity programme under way? Think about it. Taking resource wealth away from private corporations to be used for fostering the education and health of the people and building new socially-owned industry, creating new institutions which allow for the development of the capacities of people through their own practices, i.e., developing the ultimate productive forces—- wouldn't these be elements with which to counter capital's austerity programme and to substitute for it a socialist austerity programme (i.e., austerity for capital)?

Consider how different would be the situation in the current crisis in Canada if resource revenues were poured back into the economy for education and health and for building and modernising economic activity—- investments for the future as well as a means of mitigating (instead of exacerbating) the current crisis. Capitalism, as Chavez has said, is a perverse system—- one which doesn't care about human beings. We can use the opportunity of the current crisis to demonstrate how it is a system that we need to go beyond.

Neoliberalization and the Matrix of Action: In Conversation with Neil Brenner, Jamie Peck, and Nik Theodore

— *Peter Brogan*

Peter Brogan[1] (PB): There's been tons of ink spilled in the last few years in efforts to try to understand different formations neoliberalism has taken and the meaning of the capitalist crisis that broke in 2008 and what that has morphed into. In that context you guys have continued to refine and rethink your theorization of neoliberalization, part of which has been a consistent argument for the need to hold onto the concept of neoliberalism/neoliberalization. Can you give me an outline about why you've made this argument for the continued relevance of understanding the contemporary period through a conceptualization of neoliberalism or neoliberalization and what's different or unique about your understanding of neoliberalism?

Jamie Peck[2] (JP): There's no point in holding onto the concept of neoliberalism for its own sake. Clearly it has to be doing some work. I think the work that it does is to force you to think through connections across different geographical sites and historical time periods. It's that impetus that it gives you to think through *connections* that is important, connections between neoliberal projects in one place and another, their family resemblances and structural features. It also provides a spur to think about opposition to neoliberalism in a more-than-local way. Neoliberalism becomes one of the

---

1   Peter Brogan is a Ph.D. candidate in the Department of Geography at York University, Toronto, Canada. His research focuses on the geopolitical economy of contemporary capitalism, urbanization, education and teachers' unions. In May 2012 Neil Brenner, Nik Theodore and Jamie Peck sat down with Peter Brogan in Chicago to discuss their scholarship and the present political and economic conjuncture. The following interview is an edited transcript of this dialogue. In the past 10 years they have collaboratively and individually published widely on the changing dynamics of neoliberalism, urbanization and labour market change.

2   Jamie Peck is the Canada Research Chair in Urban and Regional Political Economy, and Professor of Geography at the University of British Colombia.

points of reference—even if it's an extremely problematic, unloved, rascal concept—which we have to be prepared to reconstruct. It at least places all of these developments in a wider frame.

Recently, we can see how it has provided a frame through which the global financial crisis has been understood and, as it turns out, responded to. And we can see that the character of neoliberalism post-crisis is not quite the same as it was before. It has gone through another of its mutations. At the same time, it is still recognizably neoliberal, even as it is being actively reproduced at such moments. The work it does as an ideological formation is an important part of understanding the present crisis, and the extremely ideologically constrained responses to that crisis that we've witnessed. Of course, it was not absolutely predictable and necessary that the ideological and political responses have been constrained. The neoliberal frame will not hold forever. But that's the way things have worked out, at least so far. We need to try and understand the limitations of the responses to neoliberalism and why it's been possible to resuscitate a form of market rule on the back of a crisis manifestly created by the excesses of monetization and deregulation; how a kind of Houdini escape has been fashioned once again.

But I don't think it offers you any pat, easy answers to this question. And certainly it's not an excuse for saying; ah, it's just neoliberalism again, end of story! That isn't an explanation. Invoking neoliberalism is the beginning of an explanation, not the end. You've actually got to get in and amongst the processes of institutional transformation, which I think is one of the reasons we argue for working at different levels of analysis, rather than just having an entirely macro-level understanding of neoliberalism. This is why we insist on exploring how neoliberalization is reproduced through all these domains—the institutional, the ideational, the ideological, the social and so on—as a contradictory process. And so that's why we've argued for a fairly refined and complex notion of how this process works.

Neil Brenner[3] (NB): I would just add a couple of things to Jamie's arguments. First, we agree with the tradition of Neo-Gramscian political economy that there is a world-historical, epochal struggle under capitalism over the form and extent of commodification. Throughout the history of capitalism there has been an ongoing political and institutional struggle to determine how far commodification processes can be extended into the fabric of society. Obviously both the classical liberalism

---

3   Neil Brenner is a Professor of Urban Theory at the Harvard Graduate School of Design.

of the late 19th century and neoliberalism of the post-1970s period represent internally distinct sets of approaches to this problem that involve creating specific types of regulatory infrastructure designed to intensify the extension of commodification across society and across space. And the kind of Keynesian interlude that, broadly construed, obtained after World War Two can be construed as an attempt, albeit unevenly developed, to insulate the fabric of society from processes of commodification.

So in this sense, our own use of the term neoliberalization is a way of trying to demarcate the historical and geographical specificity of the post-1970s regulatory reorganization of capitalism—it is not simply an ideological movement or a political alliance, but a pathway and trajectory of regulatory reorganization. This reorganization has involved a renewed attempt, as Jamie has said, to intensify market rule at every spatial scale. But having said that—and I now turn to the latter part of your question—we are equally interested in uneven regulatory development. What this means is that the process of extending and intensifying market rule in the post-1970s period has been deeply unevenly developed, both spatially and temporally: it does not simply unfold in state-by-state or city-by-city, but involves regulatory recalibrations that crystallize a kind of wave like process in which inherited institutional infrastructures, including those inherited from postwar Keynesianism undergo processes of institutional creative destruction, generating new institutional landscapes in which markets are promoted and commodification is extended. This is not simply a unilinear succession, along the lines of a total dismantling of Keynesianism followed by the rise of a new, neoliberalized regulatory formation.

In effect, our usage of the term neoliberalization is a first-cut attempt to demarcate the broadly developed force field of strategies and struggle in and around market rule in the wake of the collapse of the Keynesian compromise. Our arguments about the uneven development of regulation and the regulation of uneven development are an attempt to understand the different ways in which this process of regulatory restructuring unfolds, without embracing a traditional phase model of capitalist regulation in which one fully formed phase disappears and another fully formed model emerges. For us, neoliberalism is not a model at all—it is an unevenly developed process of market-oriented regulatory reorganization.

JP: Because we have to remember that absolute market rule is impossible. So the process of neoliberalization not trending towards some complete or fully articulated condition. That's why we think of neoliberalization as a transformative process, not as a label for this or that economic system or phase of development; it shapes a paradigm of restructuring. It's a process of continuing to intensify, displace, and reschedule contradictions which are endemic to the prevailing regime of market-oriented development, corporate rule, and social discipline. But while neoliberalization is strategically focused in this way, it's also repeatedly failing.

So, in a sense that's why we're interested both in perpetual restructuring, crisis-driven experimentation, and what are often improvised, zigzagging responses to failure—which is inevitable because there is no historical trend towards absolute market rule. Yet that's the unattainable destination, the conservative-neoliberal utopia which remains the inspiration of these projects, but must not be seen as a prediction of where they are leading. Hence the necessity for critical work on actually existing transformations of neoliberal rule, neoliberal policy failures, new forms of experimentation, and so on. You can't just read The Road to Serfdom and conclude, "Ah-ha, this is the plan!" Actually, it works out very differently—always unpredictably, and always reshaping the political terrain.

Nik Theodore[4] (NT): So then the analytical and the political are linked by a shared concern to understand the terrain across which neoliberal projects are being prosecuted, as well as the processes through which they occur and of course their material effects. I really do believe the analytical and the political are firmly bound together with a set of shared concerns to understand the contours and limitations of neoliberalization.

PB: I want to bring in the urban dimensions of all this because I think this is where you guys have been pushing the theoretical and political envelope in your work on neoliberalization. In what ways have cities played central and strategic roles in not just the extension of neoliberalism in the post-2008 crisis period, but the entrenchment or resurgence as you put it? Conversely, how should we understand cities as sites for the renewal of organized resistance to neoliberalism?

NB: One simple way to start in explaining our position on this is through a distinction we made a long time ago between the neoliberalization of urbanization and the urbanization of neoliberalism. This is a kind of short-

---

4   Nik Theodore is an Associate Professor at the University of Illinois at Chicago (UIC), and former Director of the Center for Urban and Economic Development (CUED) at UIC.

hand, but it's simply a way of saying two things. On the one hand, if you're interested in looking at urban governance during the last thirty years, you can see a tendential reorganization of local institutional arrangements in ways that promote, intensify and extend market rule as opposed to earlier, managerial and distributionist orientations. As David Harvey argued back in 1989, reorientation has been transformed since the 1970s from postwar concerns with social reproduction and redistribution, towards the priorities of economic development, place promotion and territorial competitiveness.

Of course, this realignment has been documented extensively in the literature on urban entrepreneurialism and local economic development; it's a pretty well-established argument. To some degree Jamie's more recent work criticizing Richard Florida and the idea of the creative city is a further development of that discussion—economic development is now connected to broader questions of culture and place identity. But, on the other hand, if you flip that idea around, it is also possible to observe various ways in which projects of neoliberalization around the world are now increasingly contingent upon the reorganization of urban built environments themselves. So it's not just that cities and urban governance systems get neoliberalized, but that the broader, global project of neoliberalization is increasingly anchored in specific places—it doesn't just involve reorganizing wide rule-regimes governing, say, financial transactions, trade and capital investment, but hinges massively upon investments in built environments to facilitate a kind of neoliberal societal project. To some degree some of David Harvey's recent work interpreting the global financial crisis as an urban crisis provides a very useful entry point into that idea—it goes beyond his earlier concept of urban entrepreneurialism to suggest that neoliberalism is today itself being urbanized in important ways.

JP: And I'm just remembering one of the conversations that we had 10 years ago when we we're setting up the workshop that Nik and Neil put on here. It's the anniversary of this event that we've been marking this weekend. There was an early preamble to the original meeting, I remember, that raised the question of whether we should understand the urban and the city as a privileged scale where these processes work out, where the politics are played out, or a vital scale? And as a result of this conversation, we decided that we didn't want to say that it was privileged in a straightforward way, but rather that it is vital; you need a multiscalar reading of these processes to really make sense of them. So we don't sequester key processes or certain kinds of politics to one scale; we don't say that neoliberalization is a process that operates primarily at this scale or it is a creature of this scale, because it clearly operates across scales. But perhaps one of the more neglected scales—until relatively recently—has been the urban.

The Neo-Gramscian strand of political economy talks very powerfully about the global. And we have a whole literature about national transitions to different forms of neoliberalism, say in Britain and Chile, and the politics of Thatcher and Pinochet. What didn't exist 10 years ago was thinking about how the urban scale was connected to these wider transformations, and how cities had become a vital scale both for the projects' reproduction and its contestation. So the city becomes a kind of crossroads, where you find some of its most excessive forms of neoliberal politics and the strongest forms of resistance, but it's not only that scale that matters. We wanted to place an understanding of urban political economy in this broader context. And we can all see now how the most recent financial crisis as partly incubated in the American housing market, but was constituted globally at the same time. We can also see how speculative dynamics, financialization, and capital switching have driven an epic city-building across China in the last 20 years, but as Harvey has argued that's a development of world-historical significance, not just an urban thing. It's simultaneously a global phenomenon. So we would argue against the privileging of one scale or another. Yet, we also argue that the urban needs to be taken seriously, alongside those other scales which in many respects are well documented in political-economic work. The urban really needed to be integrated into these accounts, far more effectively than it was 10 years ago. There has been a lot of progress on this front in recent years.

NB: Just a couple other things on this. First, a really important point for us hinges on the concept of the secondary circuit of capital which was developed in the 1970s by Lefebvre and Harvey. According to this idea, in a time of crisis, capital floods into the built environment as a potentially safe refuge – so urban property markets may experience particularly intense investment pressures precisely under conditions of industrial decline. This insight certainly provides some purchase on contemporary neoliberalization patterns in cities—but insofar as such property markets are also, today, tightly connected to global financial markets and instabilities, they certainly no longer provide the kind of "safe haven" from crisis tendencies that they appeared to offer during previous rounds of economic crisis. This dimension of neoliberalization has been very productively explored by Manuel Aalbers and others in their recent work on the financialization of urban land markets.

Second, equally important to our interest in cities is that cities are sites of important forms of ideological work: they are represented, in media and policy discourse, as sites of crisis and policy failure, and simultaneously, they are situated rhetorically and practically as the target zones for increasingly punitive, repressive and exclusionary "solutions" to those issues. In this ideological trope, which is repeated in various ways across the global urban landscape, the city thus becomes the arena for both problem and solution—regulatory failure and market-based pathway out of the crisis. Now that the failures of these market-based "solutions" to earlier regulatory failures are also becoming blatantly apparent within urban built environments around the world, can new or revamped forms of neoliberalized regulation be layered on to already deeply crisis-stricken, tendentially marketized regulatory environments? Or will this situation provide an opening for alternative mobilizations, urban and otherwise, that challenge the illogics of market authoritarianism and hypercommodification?

PB: That's the thing I want to push on, because in an earlier interview Nik and I discussed new organizational forces like the Right to the City (RTTC) Alliance and other non-traditional urban struggles and movements that have emerged to contest neoliberalism in the United States.[5] I want to ask where you think some of these struggles have moved in the past few years. In particular could you talk about different efforts to scale up or to build interurban networks like the Right to the City Alliance and amongst domestic workers and so on? Occupy is another kind of movement which is very place-based but also has this kind of urban, translocal dimension to it. What's going on with these struggles?

NT: One of the important aspects of the RTTC Alliance is that it establishes a framework for local action but one that connects those actions across different localities. And so a national framework was in place to respond to the very financialization crises that Neil was just mentioning. So when the housing market tanked and the bubble burst and the wave of foreclosures began to hit low-income, predominantly African American and Latino communities, you had a set of organizations that had

---

5   Hugill, D. and P. Brogan. (2011). The Everyday Violence of Urban Neoliberalism: An Interview with Nik Theodore. *MRzine.* http://mrzine.monthlyreview.org/2011/theo-dore050411.html

aligned both to engage in struggle in their local communities but also to scale up that struggle to target what they viewed as some of the principle actors in that hardship, the banks. And so next week [early May 2012] you'll see the RTTC Alliance ally with other networks like the National Day Laborers Network and the National Domestic Workers Alliance to descend on Charlotte, North Carolina - the home of Bank of America.

This is similar to the alliance that formed about a year ago in Boston where a number of social movement organizations went to the streets to target Bank of America and other financial leaders to call attention to the foreclosure crises, which is disproportionately being wrought on low-income African American and Latino communities. And so it's through those types of social movement formations that you're able to do two things: deal with the local specificities of the crisis, but then scale up the struggle to go after financialized capital which operates not just locally but transnationally.

JP: I believe that this is also a case where political responses to neoliberalism, even though they may begin at the local scale, and in many ways may need to, they do not stop at this scale. While resources and capacities can be built at the local level, experiments can gain traction at the local level, it's crucial that the horizons of action and imagination exceed the local. The local is invariably where organizing starts, where mobilization begins. The logic, rationale, and the power structures of neoliberalizing regimes always exceed the local, however. So political responses—counter-neoliberal actions—have got to attack those targets, as well as taking on immediate issues at the local scale. The living wage movement is a good example, a movement which begins local and specific but which builds up and out as it develops.

NT: And what these networks do is create spaces within which to develop a shared analysis. They are spaces to communicate that analysis to a wider public and they are spaces, crucially, to link up local resistance into something larger—something regional, national or international. So they are a strategic response to the globalizing, destablizing and displacing effects of neoliberalization. They are a way to try to project beyond the local and try to reveal at least some of the root causes of social suffering. Usually when we think of "roots" we think of them as being local. But the root causes primarily are extralocal. This it requires resistance to move to a position of extralocal resistance, to something beyond the local. You can see this notion contained in the World Social

Forum, for example. The creation of those types of formations show that, even 20 years ago, activists worldwide were starting to think in this way.

PB: I want to push on this question of resistance a bit further. It seems to me rather important to interrogate the fact that rather than coming out of one the worst crises periods in capitalism since 1929, arguably, with a more revitalized and fighting spirit movement of the left, both in North America and globally, to push for an alternative global rule regime or even more local alternatives to neoliberalism, what we have instead are working class and oppressed people on the defensive everywhere. In city after city the working class is being hit with massive austerity and from a progressive perspective we should have been able to take better advantage of this crisis, as people fighting for social justice. So, as your work has argued instead of taking advantage of the crisis to push forward socially just alternative we have this entrenchment of neoliberalism rather than a development of real alternatives. Why?

JP: One way of addressing this question is to first ask how neoliberalization works. It actually works as a kind of refraction and displacement machine. So a fiscal crisis which was germinated by the banks is refracted into a state crisis and projected onto marginalized populations. And so we get this period of austerity politics. It's in this hall of mirrors that neoliberalization does its work, making sure that others pay for the cost of crisis. It also has a kind of shape-shifting character, exhibiting different forms, inhabiting different political shells. This means that it's extremely elusive and intractable politically. It can leave many of its opponents flat footed as a result. And because we've gone through 30 years or so of neoliberalization, which has targeted organized labor and other sources of potential opposition, the foundations from which counter-responses might be constructed have been eroded. That gradual incapacitation has not been accidental, it's been an explicit goal of the project.

The current crisis has morphed into an attack on public-sector unions, now that something like half the remaining union members in the United States are in the public sector. In a sense neoliberalism is always going to take the fight to you, to the remaining sources of resistance. What the left I supposed needs to do is figure out a sort of jiu-jitsu move that would enable different kinds of responses to be imagined, to exploit the weight of the opponent. Because clearly just relying on the old structures which have just been under relentless attack for decades is not going to be sufficient. It may be a place to start but it's never going to be enough on its own. So that's why you need different kinds of coalitions, you need to think across scales in different ways and connect struggles in different locations.

NT: In addition to that, many of the recent counter-neoliberalization moves that we have seen remain, in our terms, "disarticulated" in this time of crisis. They are disarticulated in the sense that explicit extralocal linkages—nationally, continentally and globally—are still, in most cases, only emergent. They may be gathering steam now, but at the onset of the crisis they were not capable of offering a plan that could avoid the false choices and politically rigged tradeoffs that have been presented by centrist and right-wing politicians. So the progressive response—in terms of offering alternatives to neoliberalism, to austerity politics, and to the goal of restoring corporate profits above all else—was not up to the task. I would add that from a political standpoint, the state of our public intellectuals is likewise not up to the task. There are not enough progressive public intellectuals who can clearly articulate an alternative vision and program, and seize upon the strategic openings that are created during times of crisis. But in defense of grassroots social movements let's be clear that the social violence of the crash was visited most severely on marginalized communities, and while we may have wished or hoped for a more coherent and comprehensive response, the reality was they had to deal with the crisis first and foremost. In times of upheaval, sometimes you have to take care of the more immediate needs of your community, which makes it difficult to articulate the grand alternative.

PB: You gotta put the fires out.

NT: You must put the fire out; to stop the house from burning. And that was a major challenge. So our position would be to not judge social movements, and even public intellectuals, too harshly. We understand the constraints imposed during a time of crisis, but let's remember for the future that you've got to strike when the moment presents itself. Progressive alternatives need to be put forward precisely at the moment when upheaval is greatest, since it is in those moments that public attention is most fixated on social problems and the search for potential solutions.

NB: I would add to that one specific point: it is very important to transpose the fight for redistribution into broader critiques of the capitalist character of production in the world today. Obviously, the distribution of wealth, the surplus, matters a lot, and the Occupy movement has very effectively problematized this. But that shouldn't distract us from a broader discussion about how economic life is organized—for instance, about the ramifications of private ownership and control over investment decisions that affect the entire world (socially and environmentally); about the endless reinvestment of socially produced surpluses in pursuit of privately appropriated profits; and about the financialization of huge dimensions of everyday life and public resources (including, in a neoliberal era, not only housing and food but, in many contexts, water and clean air).

In other words, there's a broader question here about social and political control over the surplus, at any spatial scale, and in my view this needs to be debated and to remain on the agenda for the Left. Such concerns do not displace the issue of redistribution; they are tightly connected and reinforce one another in powerful, productive ways. It may be useful, in other words, to re-appropriate and update some of the ideas about economic democracy that were mobilized by European communist and socialist movements during the interwar period and, later on, within the certain strands of Euro-communism and the New Left in the wake of '68.

PB: I want to push on this a little bit and get all you guys to chime in because I was going to ask this question before you made these comments, Neil. Should progressive forces be trying to build counter hegemonic strategies to neoliberalism or counter hegemonic strategies and alternatives to capitalism? And what's the difference between the two? I think in some ways Neil put it squarely when he said we need to raise critical questions about what the economy is for and how we make decisions about production and not just redistribution. Because I feel like this has been a common critique of regulation theory, and it can be leveled at some of your work, which is that if we're going to focus so much on neoliberalism/neoliberalization as a mode of regulation we don't necessarily see or put the priority on the underlying system of capitalist production.

JP: I wouldn't see those as mutually exclusive choices. Neoliberalism can be seen as the current historical form of capitalism, its contemporary expression if you like. This is the kind of institutional, ideological shape that capitalism has taken and this is also the landscape from which alternatives will have to be mobilized and articulated. So understanding this terrain is going to be important for how you can develop transformative responses to the present reality. But clearly you would never want to just stop at the institutional level; you can't expect to achieve much simply by switching neoliberal institutions for, say, retro-Keynesian ones. These are both essentially liberal responses to regulating capitalism, and need to be understood as that. The agendas of anti-capitalist struggles and visions are clearly much more expansive than that. This said, I think one of the worst misrepresentations of regulation theory, one that is still out there, is that it's a kind of nostalgic yearning for a return to Fordism and Keynesianism, those thirty golden years after the Second World War, and if you could just get that system going again everything would be fine!

Clearly this is not possible in the world we live in now, neither would it address the racial and gender inequities, ecological problems, and such like, of the Fordist-Keynesian regime. We need something different than that. It's kind of interesting though that the vacuum created in the financial crisis and the Wall Street crash, just about all that was sucked into that vacuum was a kind of retro-Keynesianism, which seemed to last for a couple months before we found ourselves back with some rebooted version of the neoliberal program. And the public intellectuals that were calling for this were the likes of Stiglitz and Krugman. There was no other story in the mainstream debate around the crisis. There was clearly a vacuum there. But that was all there was to fill the void in that moment. At least in terms of the mainstream conversation about what the meaning of the crisis was and what appropriate responses were. So clearly you've got to transcend that. The inadequacy of that is self-evident.

PB: I think that's a really important clarification. I don't know if you guys want to come in on that.

N.B.: I agree with what Jamie just said. Many of the major disagreements in those classic debates between Bob Jessop and the British journal Capital and Class related less to matters of substance – the interpretation of what capitalism is and how to change it – but rather to questions of method – the question of which level of abstraction was most relevant to particular types of analytical and political concerns. One side emphasized the CMP (the capitalist mode of production) on a very high level of abstraction, whereas Jessop built upon such arguments and – much like we do in our present work – emphasized a meso-level of abstraction connected to the regulation of that mode of production and its associated contradictions.

Jessop's then-claim, and our claim now, is not that capitalism can be reduced simply to the institutions of regulation –this is not an institutional ontology but a stratified ontology in which different layers of reality are expressed in different ways at each level of abstraction. One payoff of this stratified conceptualization of reality is that it permits analysis of the concrete institutional and regulatory forms in which broader, systemic features of capitalism are expressed. This in turn permits consideration of path-dependencies—whether of Keynesianism, of first-wave neoliberalizations or of second-wave neoliberalizations – through which institutions may demonstrate resilience even in the face of systemic pressures associated with accumulation processes and crisis tendencies. If you're only operating with abstract models, looking for "pure" expressions of capital's dynamics, it is difficult to explain the variegated institutional and regulatory geographies that we have tried to explore in our work—they are often quite dysfunctional from the point of view of capital, but they are also not easy to dismantle or creatively destroy for a whole range of contingent political reasons. But, more generally, I think that many arguments from structuralist variants of Marxism are quite compatible with—and can very usefully inform—the institution-centric and regulationist analyses that we and others have been developing.

JP: It's important to note that one of the ways in which neoliberalism works is through the downscaling and outsourcing social risk. That also explains why the contradictions tend to pile up in cities. Because essentially everybody's passed the buck down until it can't be passed any further. In many ways this is quite specific to neoliberalization, or at least there is a particular nexus between neoliberalization and urbanization. I think if you paid some attention to that it will help give you a sense of the structure of the present terrain and what it means to try and respond to the challenges of neoliberalization, financialization, and the extension of corporate power in this historical moment. So the broader questions about capitalist transformation are always there, but you have to get at them by understanding some of these ideological and institutional realms that create the kind of matrix for action in the present time.

PB: What do you think are the biggest challenges – politically, strategically and theoretically – for mobilizing a counter hegemonic alternative to this resurgent neoliberal capitalist world that we're confronted with and embedded in?

NB: We might want to break this question down and start with some of the problems with social-scientific analyses of neoliberalization. A lot of social-scientific research on neoliberalization, for example, might not have an immediate payoff for the practical question of what is to be done, but we would argue that it still is really important, especially insofar as it contributes to theoretical conceptualizations of contemporary institutional and spatial transformations. From my point of view, a big part of what theory does is to illuminate the essential properties of structures and processes that exist in the world, and thus to clarify the parameters of necessity and possibility given current institutional arrangements. While such arguments may not have immediate consequences or payoffs for questions of political strategy, I believe that they can inform activism and the work of social movements by helping them understand what they are dealing with—systemically, institutionally, politically and so forth.

This kind of argument is sometimes met with frustration by colleagues and friends who want theory to offer direct insights into the strategic questions that are of such urgent concern to the Left. This is not an unreasonable demand, but I also would strongly defend the moment of abstraction, as distinct from immediate questions of practice, as also being hugely relevant to the work of the Left. Simply put, sometimes you have to wrestle with a theoretical problem in a focused way, as a basis for illuminating the dynamics and tendencies that obtain in the world, before you can even begin to figure out how that analysis might morph, on a more concrete level, into arguments about strategies and tactics. This position resonates a bit with the one Theodore Adorno took, very defensively, at the end of his life in relation to the activists of '68 who viewed his work as too theoretically distant. While I would not necessarily stand by that particularly austere conception of theory I do think that Adorno's position continues to have relevance for us today.

Part of the freedom which theory offers is precisely connected to the fact it's not an immediate handmaiden to instrumental, practical concerns—that is how I understand Adorno's position in relation to the '68ers. In other words, it is precisely the autonomy of theory from the question of what is to be done that gives it a certain power to engender utopian and radical thinking about possibilities that might barely be visible in the everyday world. That's of course not the only function of theory, and here I would not go as far as Adorno did in distancing himself almost totally from the realm of practice. But I do believe in that moment of theory as a pulse of freedom, as a projection beyond the present into a realm of the possible.

JP: Something that is both a near-term and a strategic challenge is how to escape the localist trap. If, in a strategic sense, one of the consequences of the way in which neoliberalization has worked is that it has backed the

Left into local enclaves. In a practical sense, Left responses to neoliberalism may therefore have to begin with local action, but the local enclave cannot be the limit of the Left's imagination or ambition. But to get out of the trap, and to start to think much more translocally about political strategies, is a real challenge. There's a huge challenge in figuring out how you move from those local responses to something that is more organized across scales and internationally. I'd say so far the kinds of networking that we have seen is suggestive, but it remains relatively frail. And certainly it is not enough to carry the project of countering neoliberalism to its next stage. Globalizing resistance networks have been around for a couple of decades but in a sense we're still trying to figure out how to take that next step, to move from these loosely networked global responses to something more generalized, which actually starts to tackle the rules of the game and turn around the rules of the game, which are still being organized according to the logic of finance capital and the logic of competition. The dominant rules of the neoliberal game also undermine local forms of resistance and counter-politics, not coincidentally, both in strongholds and in other places. Working extra-locally is the next step.

NT: We come from a tradition that values both action and thoughtful reflection. I think one of the positive developments, when you look at formations like the Right to the City Alliance, is that they act, they use that activity as a way to generate an analysis, they then reflect on that analysis and action, and they act again. So it's not an approach that says there's a distinct time for thinking and then you act. Instead, you see an approach to social struggle that may turn to abstract analysis and theoretical reasoning, but then merges these with an on-the-ground analysis of contemporary conditions, and sees this as an ongoing process of action and reflection. This praxis can propel social struggle forward in ways that you may not have predicted at the outset of an action. It is both trying to forge a path towards social justice while reacting to the everyday realities and the obstacles that are put in that path. And you can only do that by simultaneously acting and reflecting, making the road as you walk, so to speak. I think we're deeply sympathetic with that approach, and to the extent that our work has informed progressive social movements, even in a small way, we feel gratified and, I dare say, honored.

Austerity is Bad for Our Health: Gender and Distributional Impacts of Ontario's 2012 Budget

— *Sheila Block*[1]

There are many questions to be asked and answered about the shifts in fiscal policy stance and discourse from the start of the 2008 financial crisis to the present. The policy consensus on the need for concerted international government intervention and the need for constraints and regulation of markets has vanished from the mainstream policy discussion. It has been replaced by an austerity agenda that suffers from short-term amnesia about the causes of government deficits and debt, and is focused instead on a further reduction in the role of the state. This paper will, however, limit itself to an analysis of the 2012 Ontario budget, and its gender and distributional impacts. The agreement reached between the NDP and the Liberal government resulted in the first progressive change in Canadian income tax rates in more than a decade (Benzie & Ferguson, 2012). The agreement included a temporary increase in taxes for Ontarians earning more than $500,000 per year and a 1 percent increase in rates for people who are surviving on social assistance. These were small, but important, first steps in addressing the record levels of income inequality in Ontario.

These adjustments around the edges, however, will not change the fundamental impact of this budget. The Budget document boasted that for every dollar in new revenues, there were four dollars of savings and cost containment measures. Even after the agreement with the NDP, average annual growth in program spending will be held to 1.0 percent between 2011–12 and 2014–15 (Ontario Ministry of Finance, 2012). This means that there will be real, per capita decreases in government spending in Ontario. A program of reductions in government services to this size and scale will increase inequality. Research by Mackenzie and

---

1   Sheila Block is the Director of Economic Analysis at the Wellesley Institute, an independent research and policy institute focused on advancing population health.

Shillington (2009) shows the progressivity of government expenditures. These reductions will have the most detrimental impact on low-income Ontarians, but will also reach far beyond them. Some Ontarians will have to do without the public services they have relied on because they will not be able to afford to purchase them privately. For others, life will become far more expensive when they have to start paying privately for services their tax dollars used to pay for. Only those whose resources are so large that they rarely need to rely on public services will be unaffected by the impact of such a shift in the landscape of Ontario public services. Given their higher incidence of low income, racialized and immigrant communities will be disproportionately affected by these cutbacks.

An example of the distributional impact of cutbacks in services is the changes to education funding (People for Education, 2012). These changes will include cuts to programs that support math acquisition in schools. Some children, who need this assistance, will go without it because their families will not be able to afford to purchase these services privately. For other families, life will become more expensive when they have to privately purchase this help for their children, previously paid for by their tax dollars. Only those parents who were already privately purchasing these services for their children will be unaffected. The impact of the loss of public services will be compounded for the thousands of families who have members with public sector jobs. Many of these families will face unemployment, reduced access to public services, reduced family incomes, and increased economic uncertainty. Again, the impact of these changes will be felt more acutely by lower-income Ontarians. Workers in lower-paid occupations — such as cleaning, food preparation, and clerks — are generally better paid in the public sector than in the private sector. A cook working in the public sector was paid an average of $26,216 a year in 2006, which is 24 percent more than the $21,089 average received by private sector cooks.

On the other hand, higher-paid occupations — such as managers, lawyers and accountants — tend to be paid considerably less in the public sector than in the private sector. For example, engineering managers in the public sector were paid an average of $93,514 in 2006, which is 27 percent below the average of $128,886 in the private sector (Sanger, 2011). As a result, higher-income public sector workers who lose their jobs have better prospects in the private sector than lower-income workers who lose theirs. These cutbacks in services and loss of public sector jobs will come at a time when income inequality in Canada is at levels that have not been seen since the 1920s (Yalnizyan, 2010).

HEALTH IMPACTS OF AUSTERITY

The government's austerity agenda poses substantial risks to the health and well-being of Ontarians. A recent report from Statistics Canada provides a stark example of the impact of income and income inequality on health. The difference in life expectancy at age 25 between the highest and lowest income groups was 7.1 years for men and 4.9 years for women (Tjepkema & Wilkins, 2011). While these differences are striking, an equally important finding is that life expectancy increases with each and every step in the income scale. This research found that the gaps are even greater in health-related quality of life, where once again, there was an improvement in health at every step up the income scale. As this research shows, the health impacts of government actions that improve social conditions are not limited to low-income individuals and families. This is supported by international research that shows that inequality has an impact on our health and well-being (Wilkinson & Pickett, 2009). In more equal countries, people are healthier, live longer, and commit fewer crimes. These relationships hold among all income groups. Even for the highest income segment of the population, people are safer, healthier and live longer when they live in a more equal society.

There are many ways that austerity programs have an impact on health. The link between unemployment and ill-health has been clearly established. Research on the aggregate level has shown that high levels of unemployment in society and in neighbourhoods are correlated with poor health and increased mortality (Block, 2010). A recent IMF report, based on international evidence, shows that austerity programs increase unemployment and long-term unemployment in particular (Ball, Leigh, & Loungani, 2011). The report also shows that the burden of austerity is disproportionately borne by wage earners rather than those who rely on profits or rents for their incomes. Increased unemployment, lower job quality, decreased levels of/access to social benefits, and reduced access to services that support social inclusion will all have a negative impact on Ontarians' health. And these impacts will fall disproportionately on Ontarians from marginalized communities – particularly those who are low-income, racialized, and new immigrants.

GENDER IMPACTS OF AUSTERITY

The burden of reductions in public services, loss of public sector employment, and privatization of public sector employment falls more heavily on women than on men. The slowdown in spending proposed in the budget cannot be accomplished without reduced employment in the public sector, and a shift of employment within the public sector from better paid unionized jobs with pensions and benefits to more precarious work. These changes will have a differential impact by gender. Women comprise just over 60 percent of Ontario public sector employees, and about 47 percent of private sector employees (Statistics Canada, n.d.). The impact of layoffs will be compounded by the differences in wages for women in the public and private sectors. On average, women employed in public sector jobs are paid 4.5 percent more than women in comparable occupations in the private sector: $45,821 compared to $43,841. Women who are laid off from the public sector will likely have difficulty finding employment with similar remuneration, Men in the public sector are paid an average of 5.3 percent less: $57,318 compared to $60,531 (Sanger, 2011). As a result, a decrease in public sector employment will tend to widen the gap between men and women's wages. The impact on women's remuneration is not limited only to job losses. Shifts in the method of public service delivery will also have a disproportionate impact. Private delivery of services and a shift to community–based health care delivery will move women to more precarious employment situations, where they are less likely to be unionized and typically have lower compensation.

Caregiving makes up a substantial portion of public services. When these services are reduced, the responsibility falls on disproportionately on women to pick up the slack. For example, 21 percent of women in Ontario provide unpaid caregiving to seniors as compared to 16 percent of men. Women also provided more hours of caregiving, with 9 percent spending more than 5 hours a week as compared to 5.7 percent of men (Statistics Canada, 2008). The loss of public services will increase unpaid work for women while reducing their remuneration and opportunities for paid work. Reducing women's employment and wages has an impact on their families and their communities. The table below shows the increasing importance of women's contributions to family incomes. The increase in the share of families where women contribute more than 50 percent of income has been sharpest in areas of the province that have been particularly hard hit by the downturn in manufacturing. These families and areas will be particularly disadvantaged by this year's budget.

SHARE OF TOTAL NUMBER OF FAMILIES WITH THE WIFE CONTRIBUTING OVER 50% TO HUSBAND-WIFE EMPLOYMENT INCOME

	2000	2001	2002	2003	2004	2005	2006	2007	2008	2009
Toronto	27.7%	28.2%	28.7%	29.2%	29.5%	29.7%	30.1%	30.5%	31.2%	32.8%
London	26.2%	26.3%	26.8%	27.2%	27.4%	27.8%	28.0%	28.8%	30.0%	32.4%
Windsor	20.4%	21.5%	22.5%	22.7%	23.7%	24.2%	25.2%	26.5%	27.9%	31.6%
Hamilton	22.8%	23.7%	24.4%	24.7%	25.1%	25.9%	26.7%	27.5%	28.3%	30.4%
Ontario	25.8%	26.1%	26.8%	27.3%	27.7%	28.0%	28.5%	29.0%	29.7%	31.6%

Source: Statistics Canada. Table 111-0021 - Family characteristics, husband-wife families, by wife's contribution to husband-wife employment income, annual (number unless otherwise noted)

CONCLUSION

The changes to the 2012 Ontario Budget that resulted from the agreement between the Liberal government and the NDP were a welcome departure from the austerity agenda. They increased the progressivity of the tax system, and mitigated the erosion of purchasing power of inadequate social assistance rates. However, the overall impact of this budget is to increase inequality in Ontario. By relying much more heavily on cutback on expenditures than increasing tax revenues, it will have a disproportionate impact on lower income Ontarians. Because of the role of public sector employment in women's working lives; it will also erode gender equity in the province. Increased inequality, unemployment, and low income resulting from this budget will have negative health impacts for Ontarians.

REFERENCES

Ball, L. Leigh, D. and Loungani, P. (2011). *Painful Medicine: The International Monetary Fund Finance and Development*, 48(3), 20-24. www.imf.org/external/pubs/ft/fandd/2011/09/PDF/ball.pdf

Benzie, R. and Ferguson, R. (2012, April 23). Ontario Budget: McGuinty Agrees to Horvath's Tax the Rich Scheme *Toronto Star*. http://www.thestar.com/news/canada/politics/article/1166296—ontario-budget-mcguintyandhorwath-in-last-ditch-talks-to-prevent-election

Block, S. (2010). Work and health: Exploring the impact of employment on health disparities. *The Wellesley Institute*. http://www.wellesleyinstitute.com/publication/our-working lives-affect-our-health/

Mackenzie, H., & Shillington, R. (2009). Canada's Quiet Bargain The Benefits of Public Spending

Canadian Centre for Policy Alternatives. http://www.policyalternatives.ca/sites/default/files/uploads/publications/National_Office_Pubs/2009/Benefits_From_Public_Spending.pdf

Ontario Ministry of Finance. (2012). *Balancing the Budget*. Toronto: Queen's Printer. http://www.fin.gov.on.ca/en/budget/ontariobudgets/2012/bk3.html

People for Education. (2012). *Education Funding Cuts in 2012 Budget*. http://www.peopleforeducation.ca/pfe-news/ontario-budget-includes-cuts-to-education-funding/

Sanger, T. (2011). Battle of the Wages: Who gets paid more, public or private sector workers? Ottawa:

Canadian Union of Public Employees.

Statistics Canada. (n.d.).Table 282 0012 - Labour force survey estimates (LFS), employment by class of worker, North American Industry Classification System (NAICS) and sex, annually (persons).

CANSIM (database). Last updated January 4, 2012. http://www5.statcan. gc.ca/cansim/pick-choisir?lang=eng&p2=33&id=2820012

Statistics Canada. (2008). *2006 Census*. Unpaid work, age groups and sex for the population 15 Years and over of Canada, Provinces, Territories, Census Divisions and Census Subdivisions. Catalogue Number 97-559-XCB2006015.Last Updated July 4, 2011. http://goo.gl/HokXY

Statistics Canada. (n.d.). Table 111-0021 - Family characteristics, husband-wife families, by wife's contribution to husband-wife employment income, annual (number). CANSIM (database). Last updated June 26, 2012. http://www5.statcan.gc.ca/cansim/pickchoisir?lang=eng&p2=3 3&id=1110021

Tjepkema, M. & Wilkins, R. (2011). Remaining life expectancy at age 25 and probability of survival to age 75, by socio-economic status and Aboriginal ancestry. *Statistics Canada Health Reports.* 22(4), 2-7. http://www.statcan.gc.ca/pub/82-003-x/2011004/article/11560-eng.pdf

Wilkinson, R. & Pickett, K. (2009). *The Spirit Level: Why More Equal Societies Always Do Better.* London: Allen Lane.

Yalnizyan, A. (2010). The rise of Canada's richest 1%. *Canadian Centre for Policy Alternatives.* http://www.policyalternatives.ca/sites/default/files/uploads/publications/National%20Office/20 10/12/Richest%201%20Percent.pdf

Austerity and Aboriginal Communities: An Interview with David Newhouse

— Carlo Fanelli

Carlo Fanelli[1] (CF): The Public Service Alliance of Canada (PSAC) has suggested that the 2012 Canadian Federal budget "is true to Conservative governments course of assimilating the Aboriginal population by making life in Aboriginal Communities unbearable."[2] PSAC points to the fact that the budget has done little if nothing to address housing issues faced by Indigenous peoples and is subsequently continuing a trend of inequality thereby subtly forcing Indigenous communities to assimilate in attempts to escape impoverished conditions. To what extent would you agree with such a proposition? If so, in what ways is the current budget a continuation of past attempts to assimilate Indigenous communities in Canada?

David Newhouse[3] (DN): The 2012 budget provides limited funding for services such as education and community infrastructure, primarily improvements to reserve water systems. There are no additional funds to address the chronic housing problems nor to assist those who wish to pursue post secondary education. As we all know, one of the keys to effective labour market participation is a high level of education. Without adequate support for primary and secondary education, the graduation

---

1   Carlo Fanelli is a Ph.D. candidate at the Department of Sociology & Anthropology, Carleton University, with interests in critical political economy, labour studies, Canadian public policy, social movements, urban sociology and education. In addition to serving as editor *of Alternate Routes: A Journal of Critical Social Research*, his work has appeared in *Socialist Studies, Journal of Critical Education Policy Studies, New Proposals: Journal of Marxism and Inter-disciplinary Inquiry*, as well as *The Bullet, MRzine* and *Labor Notes*.
2   Public Service Alliance of Canada. (2012). *Impact of the 2012 Budget on Aboriginal Peoples.* http://www.psac-afpc.com/news/2012/issues/20120417-e.shtml
3   David Newhouse is Chair of the Indigenous Studies Department, and Associate Professor of Business Administration at Trent University. His works include *Improving the Aboriginal Quality of Life: Changing the Public Policy Paradigm, From Woundedness to Resilience: Urban Aboriginal Health, Hidden in Plain Sight: Aboriginal Contributions to Canada, Not Strangers in these Parts: Urban Aboriginal Peoples and Well-Being in the Urban Aboriginal Community.*

rate will not improve and without increased support for those who make it to post secondary education, fewer will be able to continue. The lack of adequate funding makes it difficult to break from the cycle of poverty that exists in many aboriginal communities. Despite land claim agreements and other types of agreement, most researchers and policy analysts agree that the current level of funding is considerably below what is needed to close the gap in social and economic conditions between Aboriginal peoples and Canadians.

The cuts to the Aboriginal health organizations removes an important set of actors from the policy advice circle. At a time when all of the indicators tell us that increased attention to Aboriginal health services are important, it doesn't make sense to remove the source of advice that can assist in the effective and efficient spending of funding on Aboriginal health. The removal of an independent Aboriginal voice, effective to a modern Canadian democracy, means that Aboriginal people lose the ability to affect government policy and participate effectively in the design and delivery of their own programs in this extremely important area.

As to the issue of assimilation, I think that this process is more complex. Certainly governments can require certain types of organizational behaviours and structures from their funding partners but that doesn't mean that Aboriginal people are assimilated if they adhere to them. There is an incredible movement within Aboriginal communities to use ideas, practices, theories, etc from our own intellectual heritage as the basis for everyday life, including organizational and community lives. What is important is that the thinking of organizational actors is Aboriginal and that thought is translated into appropriate action.

Two of the foundational ideas of Indigenous thought are transformation and adaptability. The truth test for Indigenous Knowledge is whether or not it works in real life; does it help one to survive? This allows for change and adaptation while remaining Aboriginal. We see this in the remarkable resurgence of traditional ideas being brought back into everyday life. Assimilation occurs when one stops thinking in Aboriginal terms.

I'll tell you a story from one of my first year classes a decade ago. We were reading a paper on the introduction of iron pots into Mi'kmaq culture in the 16th and 17th centuries. Some of the non-Indigenous students argued that the Mi'kmaq should not have used the pots since it changed their way of life and was not 'traditional.' A Mi'kmaq student in the class spoke up, after a lengthy debate: But we liked the pots. They made life easier for us. Using the pots didn't make us any less Mi'kmaq. They strengthened us by enabling us to do more things easier. My views on assimilation and that of the students were challenged and changed in this instant.

The history of Aboriginal people is filled with similar adaptations and yet we remain Aboriginal (of all types). Yes, life has changed and we have adapted, just like other cultures around the world. The real problem around assimilation is the homogenization that is occurring as a result of the dominance of North American modernity and the market, which are proving to be remarkably powerful forces.

CF: Recent focus on Attawapiskat has caused much of the Canadian public to become aware of the impoverished conditions apparent on a number of reserves and has highlighted the significant disparities in wealth and income between Indigenous and non-Indigenous communities. To some extent, this renewed interest in Attawapiskat and elsewhere has compelled the Canadian government to develop new strategies for tackling poverty amongst Indigenous peoples both on and off the reserve. To what extent are these challenges rooted in the failure of earlier policies and have there been any major shifts in policy orientation?

DN: The conditions that created Attawapiskat-like situations are myriad and are rooted in Canada's colonial history, the Indian Act and government paternalism, the establishment of Indian reserves outside the economic space of Canada, the continued racism towards Aboriginal peoples, and a lack of adequate funding for local government services including education and job training. In addition, the funding regulations for Indian bands did not provide for much local discretion in shifting funds to meet local needs as they emerged and changed over the course of a funding cycle. While First Nations Councils now have some increases in flexibility and a higher modicum of local control, in reality, demands for higher level of accountability from governments (both federal and provincial) effectively remove this control and the cycle of colonial administration continues, albeit in a different guise. In the economic area, the focus is now on success and helping those who are most likely to be successful. The new Aboriginal economic development framework is based on neo-liberal principles, providing assistance to those who need it least and leaving those who need it the most behind.

We seem to be moving towards a policy that emphasizes the market as a primary vehicle for the way in which individuals participate in society. The emphasis on individual participation is at odds with the collectivist nature of much of Aboriginal society. It will be a challenge for Aboriginal communities to develop institutions that can effectively mediate between these two approaches. Without them, and lacking the high levels of education needed to effectively participate in the market, I have great fears that the economic and social divide will continue to widen. The playing field isn't level yet.

CF: Although the 2012 budget has been presented as being focused on providing more educational opportunities for Aboriginal children, the Canadian Coalition for the Rights of Children[4] (CCRC) has argued that the budget fails to recognize the importance of early education and is ignoring the needs of Canada's youngest generation. Although the government has assigned $275 million over three years for both literacy and for the building of new schools, do you think that they are failing to address the earlier educational needs of Indigenous children? Moreover, the funds have only been provided for elementary school education rather than high school or post-secondary education, so in addition to neglecting early educational needs it seems as if the government is also failing to encourage later educational opportunities. What might the consequences of this be both in the short and long term?

DN: What we fail to recognize is that education is a system of institutions that include more than schools and local education programs. For the system to function well, all aspects of it need to well designed and adequately funded. Funding for classroom teaching is important but also needs to be supplemented by other activities these days: local school boards/committees that bring local control and parents into governance activities of schools, breakfast and lunch programs for students who often come from low income families, academic assistance such as tutors, mentors and guidance counselors, important cultural elements such as elders, traditional teachers and language teachers which help to provide a sense of pride in one's own heritage and culture.

One also needs capital funding to ensure that schools are up to date and well maintained. Learning in outdated schools or poorly maintained ones doesn't do much to improve success. It is also important to have parents involved in meaningful ways in their children's education. The consequences of not adequately funding edu-

---

4   Canadian Coalition for the Rights of Children. (2012). *Right in Principle, Right in Practice.* http://rightsofchildren.ca/wp-content/uploads/CCRC-Report-to-UN-on-CRC.pdf

cation means lower graduation rates, lower labour force participation rates, lower incomes and an inability to contribute to Canada at ones potential. As the Aboriginal population grows, additional resources for social assistance are required, at funding levels higher than the cost of the initial educational investment.

CF: The CCRC has also raised concern that the budget has allocated no new funds or resources to address youth rehabilitation. To the contrary, among Prime Minister Stephen Harper's first tasks since gaining a majority government in 2011 has been to introduce Bill C-10 which among other things eliminates conditional sentences for minor and property offenders and instead mandates mandatory minimum sentences. A plethora of research has shown that such an approach is not only counter-productive but actually intensifies the very problems they allegedly seek to solve.[5] As a consequence, this has resulted in the Canadian Civil Liberties Association and Canadian Bar Association, among other groups, opposing the implementation of such legislation.[6] Given that Aboriginal youth make up only 5 percent of the overall Canadian youth population but are disproportionately represented in Canadian prisons at 28 percent of the population, what kind of impact will this lack of rehabilitative funds have on Indigenous communities? Does this threaten to further victimize the vulnerable?

DN: The budget changes and Bill C-10 make it likely that the level of incarceration of Aboriginal youth will continue at its same level and even more likely that it will grow. The mandatory minimum sentences mean that more aboriginal youth (and others) will serve time; the loss of rehabilitative funds increases the possibility of re-offending upon release. One could analyze the effects through two lenses: the first is a loss of community productive capacity as a disproportionate number of aboriginal youth are removed; the second is through the lens of community safety as the cycle continues as youth return to communities after custody. The loss of funding for rehabilitative services also means a shift in philosophy away from restoration and rehabilitation towards deterrence and punishment. Given the gains made over the last two decades in trying to bring Aboriginal ideas into the justice system and the move towards restorative justice practices, it appears that the system would

---

5   For an introductory overview see Barken, S.E. and G.J. Bryjak. (2011). *Fundamentals of Criminal Justice: A Sociological View*, 2nd edition. Toronto: Jones and Bartlett Learning.
6   The CCLA has called Bill C-10 "unwise, unjust, unconstitutional." See http://ccla.org/omnibus-crime-bill-c-10/

become less amicable to aboriginal peoples rather than more.

CF: One of the most contentious issues emerging from the 2012 federal budget has been to grant the Canada Revenue Agency and other federal departments the power to withdraw the tax-free status as well as government grants from charities that are involved in so-called political activities. Environmental groups, in particular, have been singled-out by federal Minister of the Environment, Peter Kent, for having been accused of money laundering, illegal activities and ubiquitous with radicals and terrorists. Given the intimate relationship between many Indigenous communities and Canadian charities, as well as efforts intent on, for instance, limiting the reckless development of the Alberta tar sands, destructive resources extraction on First Nations lands or broader issues related to climate change, how might such changes have potentially damaging affects for First Nations communities and issues related to social justice?

DN: As a society I think we have moved in a direction that criminalizes dissent. Dissent itself is defined quite broadly as any criticism or opposition to the government positions. This is dangerous territory and goes against the foundations of an liberal democratic society. It creates a climate of fear where groups of citizens are unwilling to speak their mind and advance their views as part of the public policy process. Since Aboriginal peoples have been subject to public debate restrictions in the past and have successfully found ways to advance their views, I would anticipate that aboriginal leaders and organizations will continue to advance their views, even at the risk of having their funding cut or affairs investigated. Threats of interrogation and the like have not been effective in the past at silencing Aboriginal voices. There has been much effort at building alliances with non-Aboriginal groups over the last few decades on social justice issues. I would forecast that the attempts at labeling criticism dissent would not be effective and might have the opposite effect of creating more alliance and more pointed criticism and action. The groups who might be most affected are those who have charitable status and who are engaged in advocacy work that is considered critical of government policy.

CF: In *From Wounded to Resilient*, you argue that the Indigenous community needs to become aware of the ongoing colonial discourse that constructs Indigenous people as 'wounded', causes them to remain reliant and restricts their ability to become aware of their own agency. If I understand you correctly, you argue that a collective consciousness needs to be developed in order for Indigenous communities to see themselves as resilient. Given the economic crisis and Harper's cuts to many social services that Aboriginal and non-Aboriginal communities often depend on in terms of health, welfare and so on, do you think that this process has been restricted? In your view has the economic crisis constrained this process of 'healing'? How might these cuts have continued this notion of 'woundedness' or prevented Indigenous communities from moving past this stereotype?

DN: Good question. Will the reduction or loss of government funding stop the healing process? It may slow certain aspects of it down but I don't think that it will be stopped as its essential core doesn't depend upon government funding. The developing resilience I think will be able to find new ways to address some of the problems. My major concern is for those who are the most vulnerable and the most wounded who need specialized supports and attention. We seem to have forgotten about them and it is clear that the institutional support will not be available. Aboriginal people have always lived in a polarized environment with sharp differences in economic and social conditions. Reducing this distance is a national challenge which the state has been reluctant to take up, except on its own terms. Aboriginal peoples have articulated over and over again what they believe needs to be done to reduce the economic and social distance as well as bring them into confederation. The best articulation of an Aboriginal vision of Canada is the final report of the Royal Commission on Aboriginal Peoples. It forms the foundation of contemporary Aboriginal political action on many fronts. It's aim is to reduce the polarization.

The question in my own mind is whether or not Canadians can deal with a 'healed' Indian. So much of our public policy effort is based upon the notion of woundedness. This is not to say that there is not genuine poverty and social dislocation that needs addressing. Can we support Aboriginal led efforts as I believe that healing comes also from doing things for oneself. I was struck by the results of the Environics Urban Aboriginal Peoples Study that indicated that 100 percent of those interviewed had experienced discrimination and racism in their lives and had to a large extent decided that there was nothing they could do about it and so were getting on with living with it.[7] It was an astounding finding for the year 2011 but it is illustrative of the complex environment that we live in. A recent IPSO-REID poll also showed that most Canadians

---

7   Environics. (2010). *Urban Aboriginal Peoples Study.* http://www.uaps.com

believe that Aboriginal peoples get too much from government.8 A part of the issue as I see it changing the attitudes of non-Aboriginal Canadians so that they can find a way to live comfortably with us.

CF: In an era of unprecedented austerity and continuing economic insecurity, what are some of the major challenges facing First Nations communities that have yet to garner the serious media, academic and popular attention that is warranted? In what ways are health care, housing and other social services at risk of deteriorating? And why is the continuing study of First Nations peoples central to improving the lives of both Indigenous and non-Indigenous communities?

DN: What always strikes me is the fragility of some of the gains over the last two decades. It is clear that government funding for services and institutional development is important and critical to continued improvement in health, education and economic participation. Without stable predictable funding for a set of societal institutions in these three areas it will be difficult to improve. The loss of National Aboriginal Health Organization and the First Nations Statistical Institute will be felt as they represent important sources of knowledge for policy makers in all foray. What many focus upon is only the delivery of services; what is missing is an understanding of the nature of the institutions that are necessary for direct support organizations to function. The issue of racism and its effects has been consistently ignored by researchers and governments as have urban issues (which are now slowly beginning to gain some attention). Policy makers have consistently ignored urban Aboriginal peoples until recently.

Research helps us to better understand the issues and to devise, hopefully, better policy and programming interventions. Aboriginal leaders complain that their communities have been researched to death and that their interest in more in action than more research. And to some extent this is true. Much of the research on Aboriginal peoples has been performed by outsiders and directed towards improving the knowledge of outsiders. What is needed is more research that is undertaken on issues identified by aboriginal communities as important to them, undertaken by researchers working with them rather than for someone external and which helps local communities understand their situations better. The likelihood of improved local effort is much improved.

---

8   Smith, Teresa. (2012, June 30). *Canadians think government is too generous with aboriginals: poll.*
    Global News. http://www.globalnews.ca/canadians+think+government+is+too+generous+w
    ith+aboriginals+poll/6442671478/story.html

Climate Change and Crisis: In Dialogue with Simon Dalby

— Jen Wyre

Jen Wyre[1] (JW): Since the economic collapse, spending on environmental programs has decreased around the globe. Can you comment on the similarities and differences in such reductions between Canada and the U.S. or Eurozone?

Simon Dalby[2] (SD): In general environmental programs may have suffered but clearly European states remain much more concerned about environmental matters than at least the federal governments in both the U.S., given Republican agendas, and Canada, given the Conservatives' agenda. However, that said, other jurisdictions do have a very varied response. California's climate change agenda is completely different from Washington's even if austerity is the order of the day there. If you count in such things as Obama's green jobs initiatives then things look rather different in the U.S.. Europeans, and even Ontario in the Canadian federation, are working on initiatives that, while not traditional environmental regulations, are nonetheless important in terms of the larger climate change issue in particular.

JW: How ideologically driven are cuts to environmental spending, Canada's abandonment of Kyoto commitments, etc.? Are the circumstances

---

1   Jen Wrye recently completed her Ph.D. at the Department of Sociology and Anthropology, Carleton University. She now teaches in the Humanities and Social Sciences Department at North Island College in Courtenay, British Columbia.
2   Simon Dalby holds the CIGI Chair in the Political Economy of Climate Change, and is Professor of Geography and Environmental Studies at Wilfrid Laurier University. His published research deals with climate change, political ecology, geopolitics, global security, environmental change, militarization and the spatial dimensions of governance. He is co-editor of *Rethinking Geopolitics*, *The Geopolitics Reader*, the journal *Geopolitics*, and author of *Creating the Second Cold War*, *Environmental Security*, and *Security and Environmental Change*.

a reflection of the Conservative government mainly or do you see these tendencies as part of broader transnational and neoliberal restructuring?

SD: The Canadian Conservative government is particularly clear that its agenda is ideologically driven. Yes, there is a certain structural dimension in the Canadian political economy as resource extraction is a key part of the national economy. Canada is also home, through both the Toronto and Vancouver stock exchanges, to many of the largest international mining companies. Some of these companies are more concerned about their environmental records than the Conservatives apparently are, and indeed if environmental standards are abandoned in Canada, exporting may actually get more complicated given international standards on many things such things as food safety standards.

Abandoning Kyoto is clearly ideologically driven, but in line with the anti-multilateralism of the Conservatives, expressed in foreign minister John Baird's formulations of enlightened sovereignty quite as much as its anti-environmental agenda. In the so called stimulus package the Federal government could have chosen to push hard on renewable energies, sensible public transit initiatives in Canadian cities and other projects, and fund these by removing subsidies to the petroleum sector, but they ignored these opportunities to shift investment to build green projects. Instead Canada is portrayed as an energy superpower given its Tar Sands, although how much of this oil will make its way to international markets remains unclear given the difficulties with various pipeline projects.

JW: Can you highlight some of the environmental consequences to austerity we might expect in Canada? For example, which communities might be impacted most?

SD: If austerity is about reducing environmental reviews of numerous proposed mines, pipeline and other resource extraction "developments" then clearly communities close to such developments obviously are most likely to have to deal directly with the disruption of developments and subsequent habitat disruption and pollution issues. In terms of forgone green building initiatives and modernization of infrastructure then the effects are likely to be widespread. The big unknown in the next few years is of course how much of the reduction of Federal activity will be taken up by the provinces. That depends on provincial politics in complicated ways. But clearly the gutting of Federal environmental science programs and environmental reviews isn't about austerity; that at least is clearly an ideologically driven agenda to silence the production of information that might challenge the priority of promoting the resource extraction sector as the key to Canadian prosperity.

JW: There seem to be conflict between an austerity agenda that diminishes environmental spending on one hand, and the need, as the frequency and scale of environmental catastrophes increases, to prioritize the environment politically on the other. What types of responses might we anticipate to these events if state spending is retracting?

SD: Gradually it is dawning on policy makers in municipalities and provinces that the Federal government can't be relied on to help in ways that it used to. Pretending that companies and contractors can step in to deal with floods or oil spills in the absence of resources and coordination from the Federal government is a very dangerous way to conduct public policy. The neoliberal ideology that markets can provide and that government should have no role in many aspects of public life leads to the reduction of facilities and capabilities in ways that may imperil people in coming years. Can municipalities and provinces agree to pool resources to compensate for the withdrawal of Federal support? That remains to be seen, but as all the predictions of climate change make clear, extreme events are becoming more frequent.

But some of the most important things that need to be done to prepare for what is coming are simple practical matters of sensible land use planning and building resilient emergency systems and infrastructure. If short-term market priorities continue to be the priority the prognosis isn't good, especially if self-regulation in the construction sector leads to shoddy construction and bad planning decisions. Marketizing risk in terms of catastrophe bonds, and relying on insurance for many things is logical if markets and adaptation are the policy priority. This leaves those without financial resources especially vulnerable when government programs are withdrawn.

JW: The United Nations anticipates that austerity will reduce environmental spending by up to $50 billion in the foreseeable future. What do you think this will mean for global human security, particularly in the global south?

SD: This issue has to be handled very carefully given that some of the projects, such as community forestry projects funded by various international development schemes, are dubious both in terms of their environmental and local community impacts. Forestry plantations that are claimed to be carbon sinks are not always helpful to local communities and indeed one might argue that canceling some of these might actually be beneficial in many parts of the South. If the cuts affect urban infrastructure, flood prevention measures and such things then the security of many poor people are further imperiled.

JW: How do you think ideas about a 'depressed' economy and austerity affect people's opinions about environmental problems? Does austerity shift public attention from environmental degradation and sustainability? For example, do we stop thinking in terms of reducing our dependency on non-renewable resources, curbing resource use, or funding green initiatives and more in terms of maintaining our current lifestyle as is?

SD: Constraints often have perverse consequences for the environment; reduced economic activity frequently reduces pollution and resource use. It may also prevent modernization projects that use cleaner technologies, meaning that old polluting technologies are used longer than might otherwise be the case. Traditionally hard times have meant environmental matters slip down the list of political priorities; environment being seen as a matter of a luxury for affluent times. But the relationships are never that simple; and efficiency responses often reduce resource consumption and hence pollution.

JW: Which strategies might you expect to be most successful in resisting cuts to environmental investments?

SD: In the Canadian context electing Tom Mulcair as Prime Minister might seem to be the most obvious strategy! But clearly some of the ecological modernization arguments are important. Efficiency matters in things like heating bills and electricity consumption for schools, hospitals and numerous parts of the public sector. Conservation in such matters helps in dealing with controlling costs in all aspects of economic activity. What seems to be happening across the globe is that numerous institutions are starting to think much more carefully about their fuel use in terms of travel budgets and the running costs of factories, housing and numerous other things. Here in fact neo-liberal mantras about efficiency do make environmental sense. But austerity will no doubt affect new innovative investments that might be cleaner alternatives to existing systems.

The key to all this remains the ability of the political left to articulate a clear vision of a more just future that is also one that uses less resources than the production systems of the past. In times of austerity unions are often politically boxed into fighting to protect existing jobs, even in "dirty" industries rather than trying to articulate a larger agenda of green jobs and public investments. This is what many green parties have tried to promote, but often ended up too close to the market ideologies of neo-liberalism, and too focused on the narrow technicalities of environment to produce a convincing alternative narrative that can challenge the ideologies of neoliberalism combined by the re-articulation of citizenship in terms of consumption and "life-style". Challenging this discourse of "entitlement" remains a key ideological task for those who think that a more just and less destructive mode of political economy is both necessary and possible.

The Electro-Motive Lockout and Non-Occupation: What Did We Lose? What Can Learn?

— Herman Rosenfeld[1]

In the months since the February 2012 settlement at the Caterpillar-owned Electro-Motive plant in London, Ontario, the already bleak context for unionized workers in Canada has deteriorated. Austerity budgets at all levels of government and political attacks have continued to target public sector unions. The Wall government in Saskatchewan issued a Consultation Paper, which, if implemented, could eliminate the Rand formula and attack union rights to engage in politics (CEP, 2012), while Ontario opposition Tory leader Tim Hudak went even further calling for the kinds of anti-union policies initiated in Wisconsin, Ohio and Indiana (Ontario PC Caucus, 2012). The ruling Ontario Liberals, with a minority government, have tabled a bill to freeze wages for teachers and plan to extend it to all provincial public sector workers.

Prime Minister Harper's government has virtually eliminated the right to strike in areas under federal jurisdiction, forcing postal workers, airport and rail workers back to work in the name of preventing disruption to the economy. The notorious omnibus budget law targeted Employment Insurance (recipients must agree to seek jobs that pay dramatically below their normal pay rates); temporary foreign workers and even refugees.

This has to be placed in the context of the dramatic pressure of restructuring, concessions bargaining and weak job demands in the private sector. While this has been an ongoing characteristic of the neoliberal period, a new phase began with the aftermath of the 2008 crisis, with the state-guided restructuring in auto, steel and other sectors (Albo

---

1   Herman Rosenfeld is a former educator in the Canadian Auto Workers' Education Department, and has taught Labour Studies at McMaster University and Political Science at York University.

et al, 2010). This process is still working itself through, as Detroit-Three auto bargaining recently ended with the union agreeing to extend a two-tier wage for new hires with a "grow-in" period of 10 years, starting at 60 percent of the regular wage, with a "hybrid" pension, combining defined benefit and defined contributions plans (Rosenfeld, 2012b). The high Canadian dollar exchange rate – itself tied to the dominance of oil, gas and other natural resource export-dependency – certainly contributes to the problem (CAW, 2012).

There have been notable efforts at resistance by the labour movement and the social movement Left. But these have been extremely weak, isolated and have, for the most part, ended in defeat. The larger labour centrals, such as the Canadian Labour Congress and provincial federations have also been unable to mount impressive or even consistent resistance (although the experience in the latter is admittedly more mixed). This is the context that has driven a number of recent conflicts in this country, most notable the Caterpillar-owned Electro-Motive lockout and closure. This experience is both particular to the changes in the larger transportation sector in North America, but also characteristic of the pressures facing the manufacturing industries, and therefore its unions and workers.

ELECTRO-MOTIVE: WHAT HAPPENED?

By now, many people have a certain familiarity with the events at Electro-Motive in London. Caterpillar, as part of its Progress Rail subsidiary, owns Electro-Motive.[2] It was bought from two vulture funds that had previously purchased it from General Motors in 2005 (Wells, 2012). The notorious anti-union employer paid $820 million for EMD, which also includes an electronic manufacturing facility in LaGrange,

---

2 Caterpillar is the world's largest manufacturer of construction and mining equipment. General Electric is its chief rival in locomotive production. Caterpillar is noted for breaking the UAW plant in Peoria, Illinois, in 1995 and the closure of the Brampton, Ontario plant and CAW occupation in 1993. In 2008, Prime Minister Stephen Harper visited the Electro-Motive Plant to show off a $5 million federal tax break for buyers of the locomotive-maker's products, and provided a further tax break on capital investment. In 2009, they set about a major expansion plan seeking to cut costs, laying off upward of 11,000 workers or 9 percent of its workforce. Even though it lost sales and revenue through the 2008-2010 recession, Caterpillars shares rose 64 percent on the Down Jones in 2010, reaching total sales of $43 billion in 2010, and profits rising 95 percent in the first 9 months of 2011. Outgoing CEO James Owens received $22.5 million for 6 months of work and a defined benefit pension plan worth $18.7 million. In the past year, Caterpillar has opened new locomotive plants in Brazil, Mexico and Muncie, Indiana, in order to take advantage of their low-paid and exploited workforces.

Illinois (Griffin, 2004; Moody, 1998).[3] EMD was the only manufacturer of locomotive engines in Canada and the sale brought control over key technologies to CAT. Four months after the EMD sale, CAT announced plans to convert a factory in Muncie, Indiana into a union-free locomotive assembly plant.

In December 2011, the company issued a final offer to its London workers that would cut hourly wages from $35 to $16.50 per hour, while slashing pensions and benefits, even though Caterpillar enjoyed record profits and a 20 percent boost to production over the previous year (MacDowell, 2012). The bargaining unit and local leadership refused and the company locked out its workers on New Year's Day.

The union local, with the support of the National CAW, began a campaign to challenge and isolate the employer, and demand that they bargain seriously and withdraw the demands. The OFL called a "Day of Action" for 2012 January 21, drawing attention to the failure of the Harper government to protect Canadian jobs and interests when domestic companies are acquired by foreign multi-nationals. The demonstration drew upwards of 5,000 people, but was little more than a rally.[4] The union did not occupy the plant. On February 3, after a month of campaigning, EMD publicly announced the impending closure, and after a tense period, the union bargained a decent severance and closure package that the membership ratified on February 23rd" (Grant and Keenan, 2012).[5]

The closure of this facility in the face of the bullying by Caterpillar is important – and will be addressed further in this article. But more important is the nature of the resistance – and the limitations of the strategic approaches used. The Electro-Motive/Caterpillar experience is an example of a gross attack by a ruthless employer on a group of union members. The ultimate goal was not to get a wage cut, but to set the stage for a workplace closure and in the process, humiliate and defeat the union, thereby contributing another setback to the larger union movement. The union, CAW Local 27 refused to accept these outrageous demands and waged a locally-based campaign of resistance, on terms that traditionally would have meant something powerful, but in the cur-

---

3 A six-year struggle in the 1990's defeated the UAW, one of a number of key defeats that the union suffered at the hands of this ruthless employer.

4 Participants simply listened to speeches – difficult to hear with a faulty PA system. Some went to the EMD site and talked with the workers on their protest line, but there was a great deal of frustration and disappointment from many of the protesters. The author was also there.

5 Later, at the CAW-Detroit-3 contract talks in September 2012, the CAW was able to bargain job openings for 160 former GM workers from EM at the auto assembly, at Oshawa and CAMI. Those working in Oshawa would be able to add to their pension time, and retire at a full rate, while CAMI has an independent pension plan (Grant and Keenan, 2012).

rent era, turned out to mean very little.[6]

The kind of resistance chosen was unsatisfactory and, although the worst did not happen – the ultimate outcome was a decent severance package – it signalled both a serious defeat and a major opportunity lost. There is little to celebrate out of this episode. It should be sobering, disheartening and a learning moment, about what *not* to do and what must be done to win in this era. In a union culture that is unable to deal with defeats and retreats and learn from them, where every challenge must end up appearing as a 'victory' of sorts, it is difficult to learn the proper lessons and use that learning to make change.

The union resistance was positive in a number of ways, but ultimately proved to be too limited. It resulted in a defeat that hurt the CAW, the rest of the labour movement and the Canadian working class. It helped contribute to the ongoing destruction of Canadian manufacturing capacities, and therefore our sovereign capacity to build a different kind of economy. It helped the capitalist class and its political allies move forward in their efforts to deepen the neoliberal defeat of the working class. We need to look at what was done right and wrong.

Finally, this is not something that is limited to the CAW. It is chronic throughout the Canadian labour movement and is reflected in the recent defeat of the CUPE municipal workers in Toronto[7] and the Steelworkers locals at Vale Inco and US Steel in Hamilton (all of which had very different leadership structures and even ideological orientations).[8]

LARGER ISSUES

As it was unfolding, it was clearly on the radar of labour and people around North America and the world, who correctly, saw this as a kind of private-sector Wisconsin, with all of the issues that this entails (Yates, 2010). The interest in CAT was, in a sense, a kind of culmination of the frustration that so many working class people have had to live with in this era of the re-constitution of neoliberalism. It touched a nerve with

---

6 Local 27 is an amalgamated local – meaning it includes a number of bargaining units, including auto parts, manufacturing, public sector workers and members for other sectors. It has a long history of activism in the community, politics, in the CAW and in the larger union movement. The current local president is also the president of the CAW Council (Russell, 2011).

7 With the notable exception of the public library workers unit of CUPE that waged a strike – after building public support – and came out rather successfully. (CUPE, 2012, March 30). Steelworkers at Rio Tinto in Quebec also staved-off defeat (Jamasmie, 2012)

8 Even the CAW, in its merger documents and at its major convention of August 2012, acknowledged the nature of these defeats and some of the underlying reasons for them (CAW-CEP 2012; Rosenfeld, 2012).

many people. Even mainstream pundits critiqued the larger phenomenon of blackmail against working people (and saw in it, the reality in most workplaces these days). It also linked up with the Occupy narrative – of the unfairness of income and wealth inequality, in the face of the crisis unleashed by the financial elite. This sense of outrage diffused across North America, and, as was clear to all who would listen, working class people across cultures and labour market segments embraced the theme of the 1% versus the 99% as their own.

It was a living example of the de-industrialization process and the loss of key manufacturing capacities; of large mega-corporations, moving capital investment at will just to pressure working class people to reduce living standards to accommodate private profit accumulation. It symbolized the threat to Canadian sovereignty and the survival of our communities that capitalism has become. It was clearly part of a new and dangerously aggressive round of attacks on the working class in both the private and public sectors. It reinforced some key defeats in the private sector. There were times where the unions simply gave up and accepted the logic of competitiveness. These included 2 tier wages in auto in the US, acceptance of concessions in the Canadian auto plants in recent bargaining rounds, situations where defeats were imposed by the state (e.g. auto concessions in 2008); and, even where the unions did mount a battle for resistance such as at Vale Inco, St. Mary's Cement and US Steel, where there were key defeats, anyway (Rosenfeld, 2009; 2012). The losses in these situations were aimed at particular targets, such as wages, defined-benefit pensions and benefits. The attacks that Electro-motive/CAT imposed on workers, took this to another level

The main thrust in the most recent period has been in the public sector, where these attacks have dovetailed with efforts to eliminate unionism completely (Wisconsin, Indiana, Ohio, etc). In Ontario, BC, and now through Ottawa, attacks on unions threaten their very survival. The terrain of the current attacks are different in many ways than the previous rounds. They take advantage of capital mobility made possible by free trade. They seem to be centred in employers that have been favoured by government, either through negotiated aid deals or other forms of support (and are usually related to larger, continent-wide restructuring strategies). The demands of the employer result in either the destruction or dramatic weakening of the union and a radical shift in the rights of the workers. They mark a new level of defeat for the labour movement and affect the willingness and capacity of workers to organize collective resistance. They undermine the rights of all working people – from those of us in the better paid jobs, to those of us out of work, on social assistance and in precarious jobs.

WHAT WAS WRONG WITH THE RESPONSE TO THE EM LOCKOUT AND CLOSURE?

There are many issues to raise with the response of the CAW. Both the national and the local leadership had very limited horizons and goals. They saw themselves as addressing the immediate needs of the workers in the EM unit: refusing to accept the threatened wage cuts, but planning for a plant closing that seemed inevitable. The plan was to build a base of community and labour support in the London area and the larger labour movement, get material support for the workers during the lockout period and then work to bargain severance and pension rights. Many of the political themes raised were the right ones: corporate greed, the need to maintain manufacturing capacity, how the attacks on the workers contrasted with the wealth of the corporate elite and the 1%, the role of Harper and efforts to have the rest of the Canadian Auto Workers and the Ontario Federation of Labour support them. Their tactics and strategy reflected those goals. Their local campaign built widespread support across the London community. They engaged the provincial government behind the scenes to pressure CAT for pension and severance. They blockaded the movement of goods in and out of the workplace and began a campaign to place information pickets outside CAT outlets in Southern Ontario.

But both their goals and their strategy were extremely limited and problematic. There was no move to occupy the workplace or extend and deepen the campaign to pressure Caterpillar, or raise *political* demands to pressure the Canadian government to stop an impending closure. They argued that "we didn't want to turn people in the community off", or threaten the possibility of bargaining a decent close-out agreement.[9] The situation required a dramatic tactical move to politicize the struggle. A plant occupation, rather than "turning people off" could have galvanized already-existing concerns of working people across the province and continent. It could have created an opening to call for state intervention – in the form of nationalizing EMD – as part of a larger project of building Canadian capacity

---

9   While some might argue that there were differences inside the union, between the local, national and bargaining unit, the public face of the union at all levels clearly looked to downplay any radical actions, such as an occupation. Any differences might be better explained with hindsight, but further research would be necessary.

to manufacture heavy transportation equipment, through the public sector. Certainly, Caterpillar is known as a ruthless employer, impervious to the claims of workers, unions or communities. No one seriously argued that actions could change their minds. But the struggle needed to be directed at the state – federal and provincial – to intervene to protect jobs and the manufacturing infrastructure that was clearly threatened.

Instead, the union's perspective was local and short-term. There was absolutely no interest in making this a larger, political battle. There was blindness to the opening and opportunity that this universally condemned action by capital represented. It was almost as if the union was basking in the sun of public pity. The idea of pressuring Harper for state intervention was seen as a pipe dream, beyond the pale of what and who the union is. An occupation could have concentrated interest and anger in London and created a platform to place nationalization on the public agenda, but this was the farthest thing from their sense of the possible. The tactic of occupation was portrayed as possibly threatening short-term interests of the workers at EMD. (Aside from the narrowness and strategic incompetence this represented, it made the positive links the union built with the Occupy movement, rather hypocritical and embarrassing – ignoring the tactical and strategic audacity and originality of Occupy).[10]

HOW MIGHT A DIFFERENT KIND OF CAMPAIGN PROCEEDED?

The union could have expanded the campaign in London to include challenging government offices, banks, larger industrial employers, all of whom suddenly became "allies" in the union's perspective. It could have built a campaign across Southern Ontario – that might have included new and exciting educational materials and challenges to employers. There could have been a boycott of CAT products around the Tar Sands and construction projects. There might have been a new educational effort with the members so that they are no longer afraid of "turning off the rest of the community". Education turned the tide during the Ontario Days of Action in the 1990's, which relied on the organizational and educational capacities of many of the same local activists in London today to win over workers who had voted for Tory Mike Harris, to a protest movement against him.

---

10 It is one thing to speak out against inequality and give material support to protesters occupying public spaces to challenge injustice, but it is quite another to take similar control over the private property of capital, to demand that it become the property of the community.

Where is the will and capacity to develop and build those mobilizational and educational resources today?[11]

The CAW has had experience with bold campaigns that challenge employers in the past. The 1997 contract bargained at GM successfully dealt with the issue of outsourcing. It was preceded by a strike and campaign waged by the union. In that campaign, the union was able to win over public opinion by appealing to common experiences in dealing with job insecurity. There were many workplace occupations in the early 1980's and late 1990's. True, they were mostly organized over demands for decent closeout agreements, but there is no reason that the tactic couldn't also be used to be the central sparkplug for a larger political campaign to keep a workplace open. The CAW has the institutional memory to carry out such a campaign. Certainly, the times and context are different today – but the CAW had no intention of considering an occupation for more than severance and a decent close-out.

Indeed, the current defeat of the labour movement and the working class as a whole – the strength and hegemony of employers and the entire, united, capitalist class – demands that bold actions and radical approaches be taken to help inspire an awakening in the labour movement. Certainly, there is no tactic or individual struggle that can magically transform the dismal situation the labour movement faces overnight. But a more ambitious plan could have possibly helped get the labour movement off dead centre, where it remains. Waiting until the political and economic balance of forces 'improves' is equally problematic – as if the stubborn power of capital can ever be challenged without an upsurge of some kind from below.[12]

This moment constituted "the" critical opening to deal with the unspoken issues and concerns of working people across the country. The moment was there to raise and answer questions like:

---

11 In the period preceding the hugely successful London Day of Action, local and national union activists and leaders came to London to engage with members, many of the latter whom were reluctant to oppose Harris, let along strike employers or picket. This was a major game-changing educational effort, which made the early one-day general strikes possible (La Botz, 2011). After a few minutes in conversation with workers at EMD in front of the locked-out plant, it wasn't difficult to see that the union could have quite easily convinced the membership to take part in an occupation.

12 Can one seriously claim that tightening labour markets could, by itself, miraculously produce a surge in militancy, or a growth in radicalism? It seems that every new concessionary agreement coming from unions like the CAW is couched in a discourse lamenting the unfavourable larger balance of forces, and claiming the "we will live to fight another day". The latter, like tomorrow, never seems to come.

- Why should we accept the constant threats to jobs in the name of cost-reduction and competitiveness?
- Why should CEO's receive massive incomes, when we have to accept wage and benefit cuts?
- Why must we and our children "get used" to the lack of good, secure, well-paying jobs, and instead, accept the normalization of part-time, low paid, precarious work? If workplaces like this are going to close without any alternative plan – what have we to look forward to?

But there are other political issues that could have and should have been raised as part of a fight to keep this workplace working:

- Why can't we defend our right to produce locomotives in this country? Isn't it central to our needs for political sovereignty? Isn't it important for efforts to create a transportation system that is environmentally sustainable? What about mass transit investment for urban areas?
- While Harper continues to negotiate new Free Trade agreements, doesn't the EMD closure create an opening for us to raise the call to challenge and ultimately abrogate existing agreements that allow the free movement of investment and capital unregulated by democratic institutions?
- Wasn't Harper vulnerable on all of these points? His government intervened with the postal workers and repeatedly did so at Air Canada to supposedly protect the national interest. He was also seen to be in cahoots with CAT in his praise of subsidies to the employer. While the P.M. claimed that the EMD closure was between a union and a private employer and a matter of provincial jurisdiction, the hypocrisy of all of this made the federal government a legitimate target.
- It poses the question of the role and limitations of the Investment Canada Act. The demands of the union movement (often echoing the limitations of social democracy) have been largely limited to soft nationalistic issues of foreign takeovers; getting tradeoffs for financial help to help foster investment and local, provincial or national procurement policies. Those are all important and positive. But, as in previous struggles, these are limited demands and will not address the larger issue of capitalist restructuring.

- Shouldn't Ontario Premier Dalton McGuinty's government be held to the fire, as well? Ongoing corporatist illusions seemed to colour union's comments about McGuinty's 2012 January 31 limited public condemnation of CAT. One can understand the union's concerns about pressuring the province about severance issues, but it is quite another issue to be satisfied with mealy-mouthed statements from bourgeois politicians. Corporatist relations with the Liberals should be publicly repudiated.
- Demands to have the state finance and run a secondary manufacturing capacity (and in this case, heavy machinery, locomotives and engines and mining equipment) practically beg to be raised in this instance.
- Won't the outcome of key private sector struggles such as this also affect the outcome of public sector struggles, such as the fight against cuts and privatization in Toronto, B.C. and elsewhere?
- Then, there are issues of the rights of unionization and the right of collective bargaining, both being undermined by this sort of activity;

This experience must be understood in the context of previous struggles, such as Vale Inco, US Steel (Hamilton) and St. Mary's Cement. In each, there was important support from surrounding communities and other locals and unions, but there were no efforts to organize collective forms of direct action, such as rotating work stoppages in other workplaces or occupations. The struggles remained centred in their individual communities, with support from across the country in the form of picket lines and solidarity messages, but no co-ordinated efforts to pressure employers and/or governments. Aside from the local unions involved, the campaigns were not transformed into large-scale movements, with educational components, geared towards reaching the entire working class. They were not tied to larger effects that working class and unionized workers have been experiencing – or to political strategies to shape the future of each of these sectors (steel, mining, cement, etc.)

CONCLUSION

There are two general areas that come to mind when summarizing the lessons of the EMD-CAT experience: one, relating to the strategic challenges it raises for the union movement and second, larger economic and political issues raised by the loss of the Electro-Motive facility itself. The broader labour movement – even in its strongest and most militant spaces – is still reeling from previous political defeats, the economic offensive of employers, the heritage of defensiveness and at times corporatist or concessionary tactical retreats, dependence on employers and the low-level of collective experience of political as well as industrial struggles that the neoliberal era has brought. In a seemingly never-ending series of responses to vicious attacks, they repeat the same limited strategies. At best, they include local-based campaigns to get support for jobs, investment and livelihoods, looking for sympathy ("feel sorry for me") and forms of solidarity, but never learning from mistakes and weaknesses of this strategy.

They call for defending collective bargaining rights and protecting against foreign corporate predators, but the larger political demands are very limited and don't challenge any of the rules of neoliberalism. There are no efforts to combine struggles with political demands that put capital on the defensive and plug into the real concerns of millions of Canadians and Americans. In order to address these weaknesses, the union movement must move in new directions and embrace the following strategies:

- Audacious industrial actions which challenge the power of the employer, and reinforce that challenge in the eye of other workers;
- Reliance on some of the more creative collective traditions of the respective unions;
- Seizing the moment to create political campaigns that tap into the almost universal revulsion with the attacks on living standards and jobs that come along with competitiveness requirements of neoliberalism;
- Putting forward demands for manufacturing investment and jobs, with a new and robust role for the state – including nationalization of manufacturing, finance and creation of new capacities, tied to industrial strategies linked to working peoples' needs (transportation, health care, environmental transformation). We need demands that argue for a logic other than competitiveness and open up space for challenging our dependence on competitive export regimes and private sector accumulation in a crowded field – or worse, resource extraction. Audacious demands need to be raised in the context of audacious actions, such as workplace occupations and strikes.
- Engaging members and working people in general on these themes.

- Developing a different relationship between unions and community-based organizations and needs. For example, what kinds of links COULD have been built with working class communities over this struggle – communities literally dying for decent-paying and secure jobs?
- Reflective and self-critical "renewal" projects – which, I believe requires a socialist politics outside and inside unions.

The consequences of not doing this have been unfolding right before our eyes. About two weeks after the ratification of the agreement at Electro-Motive, there was an announcement circulated in the local newspapers about a new collective agreement with the CAW at Lear Seating, in Kitchener. That contract was said to contain wage reductions of about 30 percent over the four years of the agreement and the workers are supposed to get a $40,000 transition payment to cushion the permanent wage cut. New hires would start at about half what the workers had been paid, allowing the company to bid on future work with a lower labour-cost base. (QMI Agency, 2012)

One wonders if this embarrassing agreement was in the works when the Electro-Motive struggle was going on. If it was, it certainly raises a number of questions about the way the lockout was handled. Even if not, it provides a sorry, but all too predictable lesson about the consequences of not stepping up to the challenges raised by Electro-Motive. Aside from the move into retirement for some of the 160 former GM workers laid off from EMD, bargained by the CAW in September 2012 (Grant and Keenan, 2012), others haven't been as fortunate.

A journalistic account in the *Globe and Mail* from October 5 2012, shows a story of financial and emotional strain: marriage breakups; low-paid, part-time work for most; severance running out; food bank usage and so forth (Grant 2012). But there is more. In the middle of August 2012 (as this essay underwent revision) Caterpillar and the International Association of Machinists local union in Joliet, Illinois, signed a six year collective agreement that settled a four month strike of 780 workers making hydraulic parts. The contract freezes the wages for all workers hired before May 2005, provides a 3 percent one-time wage increase for workers hired after that date and doubles the cost of health care premiums, eliminates pensions and reduces seniority rights. This settlement took place in the context of hugely successful sales and profits for the company (second quarter profits of $1.75 billion, up 67 percent from the previous year) (Cancino, 2012; Keenan and McFarland, 2012).

Numerous commentators around the U.S. noted that this Caterpillar settlement reflected a fundamental change in the balance of forces between labour and capital. The subtitle of the *Chicago Tribune* article cited above says it quite distinctly, "Manufacturer breaks link between profits, workers' pay; settlement raises wage issues for industry in general, labor experts say." In other words, corporate behaviour towards workers that used to be considered "egregious" or beyond the pale, has now become the norm. It doesn't take too much imagination to think about how this might have turned out differently, had the Electro-Motive struggle been expanded, deepened and fought to its potential conclusion.

Also in August of 2012, the merger talks between the Canadian Auto Workers and the Communications, Energy and Paperworkers of Canada culminated in a proposal for new union. The documents accompanying the project – some of which have been cited in this essay – are rife with references to shortcomings in the collective resistance mounted against attacks by government and employers. With the timetable set for the formation of a new union, whose mandate will include efforts to addressing these weaknesses, one hopes that the lessons of the Caterpillar experience will be critically evaluated – especially in the light of the other defeats that the labour movement has suffered in the past period (CAW-CEP, 2012; Rosenfeld, 2012).

Finally, the lack of any serious discussion about strategies to create environmentally sustainable manufacturing capacities (aside from mild nationalistic commentaries from progressive academics and the bourgeois press[13]) was critical. Militant resistance is absolutely essential, but it has to be tied to new sectoral strategies and approaches that challenge the neoliberal straightjacket that is dramatically weakening working class life and institutions. Put another way, fighting back makes a difference, but it must be paired with independent working class strategies for rebuilding and re-imagining industrial and sectoral capacities.

It should be clear that unions themselves are incapable of posing alternative industrial strategies that reject corporatism and dependence on progressive-sounding schemes for competitive private sector projects. This requires a larger socialist and anti-capitalist movement – left of social democracy – that could research, debate and place a range of alternatives into the large political arena. But even within the broader

---

13 Actually, some of the commentaries posed key questions and raised issues that the labour movement seemed unable to put forward. (Yates, 2012; MacDowel, 2012; Olive, 2012; Walkom, 2012ab).

left, this is not yet happening (although some of Jim Stanford's ideas for development of manufacturing industries tied to resource extraction is a legitimate contribution (Stanford, 2012). Changing this will require thinking through alternative plans for manufacturing and service job creation and political demands associated with them at local union and community levels, as well as through the creation of theoretical, organizational and political projects on larger national, provincial and municipal levels.

REFERENCES

Albo G., S. Gindin and L. Panitch. (2010), *In and Out of Crisis: The Global Financial Meltdown and Left Alternatives*. Oakland: PM Press.

Canadian Auto Workers (CAW), Re-thinking Canada's Auto Industry: A Policy Vision to Escape the Race to the Bottom. *Canadian Autoworkers Union*. https://d3n8a8pro7vhmx.cloudfront.net/caw/pages/29/attachments/original/13351 89435/554AutoPolicyDocumentweb.pdf?1335189435.

Canadian Union of Public Employees. (2012, March 30). *Toronto library workers ratify collective agreement*. http://cupe.ca/bargaining/toronto-library-workers-ratify.

Cancino, A. (2012, August 18). Caterpillar, union settle; Joliet contract sets new tone. *Chicago Tribune*. http://articles.chicagotribune.com/2012-08-18/business/ct-biz- 0818-cat-vote-20120818_1_labor-issues-contract-aerospace-workers-union

CAW President's report. (2012, August 20). Constitutional and Collective Bargaining Convention. http://www.caw.ca/en/11396.htm

CAW-CEP Discussion Paper. (n.d.). *Canadian Auto Workers Union, Moment of Truth for Canadian Unions*. http://www.caw.ca/assets/images/CAW_-_CEP_Discussion_Document-final.pdf;

CAW-CEP. (2012, August). *Towards a New Union: CAW-CEP Proposal Committee Final Report*. http://www.newunionproject.ca/wp- content/uploads/2012/08/Final.Report.pdf.

Communications, Energy and Paperworkers Union of Canada (CEP). (2012, July 24). *Submission to Saskatchewan's labour "consultation", International standards and the bid to turn the clock back on workers' rights*. http://www.cep.ca/sites/cep.ca/files/docs/en/120724-Saskatchewan-LabourConsult.pdf

Grant, T. (2012, October 5). For laid-off Caterpillar employees, the fall continues. *Globe and Mail*. http://www.theglobeandmail.com/report-on-business/economy/manufacturing/for-laid-off-caterpillar-employees-the-fall- continues/article4593258/

Grant, T. and Keenan, G. (2012, February 23). Electro-Motive workers ratify closeout deal. *Globe and Mail.* http://www.theglobeandmail.com/report-on- business/economy/manufacturing/electro-motive-workers-ratify-closeout- deal/article548573/

Griffin, M. (2004, June 4-6). Caterpillar's Assault on the UAW. *Counterpunch.* http://www.counterpunch.org/2004/06/04/caterpillar-s-assault-on-the-uaw/ http://www.mining.com/rio-tinto-strikes-deal-with-canadian-locked-out-workers/

Jamasmie, C. (2012, June 6). Rio Tinto strikes deal with locked out workers in Canada. *Mining.com.*

Keenan, G. and T. Grant. (2012, October 11). In Ingersoll and Oshawa, Caterpillar's forgotten find new life. *Globe and Mail.* https://secure.globeadvisor.com/servlet/ArticleNews/story/gam/20121011/RBCAWJOBS1010ATL

Keenan, G., and McFarland, J. (2012, August 20). New battleground of wage freezes takes centre stage with CAW talks. *Globe and Mail.* http://www.theglobeandmail.com/report-on-business/new-battleground-of-wage- freezes-takes-centre-stage-with-caw-talks/article4490806/

La Botz, Dan. (2011, March 9). Ontario's 'Days of Action' – A Citywide Political Strike Offers A Potential Example for Madison." *Labor Notes.* http://labornotes.org/2005/01/ontario-days-action-citywide-political-strike

Moody, K. (1998, June). Despite Defeat, CAT Workers "Vote Solidarity." *Against The Current,* 74. http://www.solidarity-us.org/site/node/851

MacDowell, L. (2012, Jan-Feb) What's Wrong With Caterpillar?. *Our Times.* http://ourtimes.ca/Between_Times/article_188.php

Olive, D. (2012, January 3). Why Caterpillar has the upper hand in the London plant lockout. *Toronto Star.* http://www.thestar.com/business/article/1110094—olive- why-caterpillar-has-the-upper-hand-in-london-plant-lockout

Ontario PC Caucus White Paper. (2012, June). Paths to Prosperity: Flexible Labour Markets. http://www.ontariopc.com/paths-to-prosperity/flexible-labour-markets/

QMI Agency (2012, March 6). Revolutionary new contract could drive auto industry. *St. Thomas Journal.* http://www.stthomastimesjournal.com/2012/03/06/revolutionary-new-contract- could-drive-auto-industry

Rosenfeld, Herman (2009). The North American Auto Industry in Crisis. *Monthly Review,* 61(2, 18-36

——— (2012). CAW-CEP Merger: New Union in a Difficult World. *The Bullet,* 701. http://www.socialistproject.ca/bullet/701.php.

——— (2012b, October 1). Canadian Auto Workers Ratify 10 Year Two-Tier. *Labor Notes.* http://labornotes.org/2012/10/canadian-auto-workers-ratify-10-year-two-tier

Russell, J. (2011), *Our Union: UAW/CAW Local 27 from 1950 to 1990*. Edmonton, Alberta: Athabasca University Press.

Stanford, Jim. (2012, March 19). Buy Canadian' and upstream supply chain as sector development strategy. *Rabble.ca*. http://rabble.ca/columnists/2012/03/buy- canadian-and-upstream-supply-chain-sector-development-strategy.

Walkom, T. (2012a, February 3). Caterpillar Attack Part of coordinated attack to cripple unions. *Toronto Star*. http://www.thestar.com/news/canada/politics/article/1125920—walkom-caterpillar- closing-part-of-a-coordinated-attack-on-unions

——— (2012b, February 8). The real villain of Caterpillar shutdown? Mindless free trade", *Toronto Star*. http://www.thestar.com/news/canada/politics/article/1128113— walkom-the-real-villain-of-caterpillar-shutdown-mindless-free-trade

Wells, J. (2012, February 4). Caterpillar cunning yields London Shutdown. *Toronto Star*.

Yates, Charlotte, A. B. (2012b, January 30). High stakes in Caterpillar lockout. *Toronto Star*. http://www.thestar.com/opinion/editorialopinion/article/1123881—high- stakes-in-caterpillar-lockout

Yates, M. (2010). Editor's Introduction: Something is in the Air. In M. Yates (Ed.), *Wisconsin Uprising*, (pp.19-25). New York: Monthly Review Press.

Beyond the Economic Crisis: The Crisis In Trade Unionism

— Sam Gindin[1]

The earlier contributions to this collection might be summarized as warning us that that things are going to get a lot worse before they get... *worse*.[2] This is not just a matter of the sustained attacks on the labour movement but as much a reflection of the crisis within labour. For some three decades now, labour has been stumbling on, unable to organizationally or ideologically rebut the attacks summarized as 'neoliberalism'. Though the Great Financial Crisis held out the promise of finally exposing the right and its supporters and potentially opening the door to a union offensive and possible revival, the attacks on labour in actuality intensified and labour continues to have no coherent counter-response. As a prelude to directly addressing that impasse in labour, it is useful to begin with something that Greg Albo (2012) posed in his presentation to the conference forerunner to this collection: What is the larger historical significance of this particular crisis?

Though cyclical downturns are common in capitalism, structural crises are of relatively rare occurrence, generally separated by a generation or so (30 years or more).[3] Such crises reflect social and institutional barriers that block capitalism's normal continuation, and the question for capital and its governments then becomes what, if anything, might take capitalism to a new stage that allows for the resumption of its drive. For example, the outcome of the crisis that began at the end of the 1960s and ran through the

---

1   Sam Gindin retired from the Canadian Auto Workers' union in 2000 after 27 years on staff, the last 16 as assistant to the President. From 2001 through 2011 he was the Visiting Packer Chair in Social Justice at York University, Toronto.

2   See also the presentations from the conference: *The Global Economic Crisis and Canadian Austerity: Perception Versus Reality* available at http://www.alternateroutes.ca/index.php/ar/pages/view/Video

3   It is common to identify three structural crises in capitalism before the latest one: the first occurring in the last quarter of the 19th century, the second introduced by the 1929 stock market crash and lasting through the 1930s, the third breaking out in the late 1960s and running through the 1970s. See Panitch and Gindin, 2011.

1970's was first and foremost that the earlier strength of labour was broken. As well, finance was liberalized, globalization was accelerated, and the state was restructured – not weakened or withdrawn - to the end of establishing more autonomy from popular pressures and therefore actually emerging stronger in terms of supporting private accumulation. The resolution of that crisis, in short, set the conditions and contradictions that frame the crisis we face today (Panitch and Gindin, 2012).

Four aspects of this present crisis seem especially significant. First, in spite of the domestic and international turmoil there has been remarkably little challenge to globalization and free trade. Contrast this with the last time we had a crisis this deep, in the 1930's, when protectionist sentiments were strong and common, and capitalism as an international system seemed threatened. Yet today, no country has placed exiting global capitalism on the agenda.[4] The issue, rather, is that with globalization taken for granted, how can crises, particularly the financial crises linked to the expansion of global capitalism, be contained (i.e. managed).

This brings us to a second facet of the crisis. In spite of a general understanding that private bankers and other financial institutions were responsible for the crisis, the solution to the crisis is not to weaken but *strengthen* them and to develop the state capacities to contain – not end - future volatility. We need to understand this not as a matter of stupidity or corruption (though both play a role!), but as a reflection of the structural importance of finance to capitalism as a whole. We often separate finance from the rest of the system and describe it as a speculative parasite (Jim Stanford (2012, in an otherwise valuable presentation, tended to do this as well). But if that were the case, we should have expected divisions within the capitalist class with the rest of capital, suffering in terms of stagnating markets, ready to join the attack on finance. Instead, there has been remarkably little evidence of splits between financial capital and the rest.

This reflects the extent to which finance and industry are in fact tightly integrated. It is not so much that large industrial corporations need daily credit since they have more profits and cash than they know what to do with but rather the importance of credit to mergers and restructuring, the need on the part of global corporations for specialized financial services to ease trade and limit exchange rate risks and other uncertainties, the discipline financial markets impose on workers, states, and capital itself to be true to the priorities of profits and private

---

4   Even in Greece, Syriza (the leading left opposition group) has emphasized the need to modify, not transform, Greece's relationship to the international economy and has posed exit from the Euro not as a goal, but as a reluctant option if the counter-productive austerity pressures continue.

capital accumulation, and - in the case of the US - its special access to the world's savings. The contradiction lies in the fact that on the one hand all of capital would like finance to be less volatile and more orderly, but they don't want to see it regulated to the point that they lose the advantages that global finance has brought them.

A third aspect of the crisis is, as Greg Albo (2012) emphasized, the tendencies across countries towards a more authoritarian state. This has been most dramatic in Europe where external institutions have placed 'technical experts' at the head of government to carry out 'reforms' but is also seen in the legislation essentially trying to outlaw protest in the student strike in Quebec. This is part of a more general trend towards states gaining more autonomy from the electorate to do what's necessary for capital accumulation. And it has especially emerged in regard to the fourth aspect, downsizing social services and attacking public sector unions, generally the last standing bastion of trade unionism.

In this regard, the story of labour's defeat doesn't go back just to the 1970's but to the immediate postwar period when the left inside and outside the labour movement was marginalized. In spite of that defeat, trade unionism was able to make gains, real gains, for a while. But that defeat of the left came with a loss of capacities critical to understanding, strategizing, and mobilizing. And when capitalism changed and now identified past labour gains as a barrier to continued progress, labour no longer had the capacity to resist. So the second defeat of labour, taking place through the 1980's and 1990's, shifted from that of a small but influential left to trade unionism as a whole, especially the private sector. Today, capital is trying to consolidate and complete that defeat by going after the public sector and ensuring that it does not inspire any positive examples for private sector workers.

A central aspect of this three decades long assault on the labour movement has been a profound lowering of expectations. The intensification of competition from the Third World seems to have set boundaries on worker demands, even though most of our trade is still with the developed countries and most workers are now employed in private and public services, sectors not directly limited by trade. Greater globalization seemed to place possible government responses beyond the reach of domestic politics, even though it was states that endorsed globalization (and can potentially also check it). The state-endorsed defeats workers suffered left many of them angry but still redefining what might be considered 'success'. The world we criticized so strongly a short while ago was now looked back on with nostalgia.

Herman Rosenfeld (2012; this issue) captures this shift when he asks why responses that seemed so obvious in an earlier era are now so out of bounds (like rejecting a plant takeover at Caterpillar in contrast to the takeover, with less provocation, in the early 1990s). This shift in what is possible in terms of both goals and tactics highlights the cultural change in the labour movement. Talk to any worker and you don't have to convince them that capitalism doesn't work for them. They know that, but believe they just can't do anything about it. Confidence in resistance, let alone change, is at an all-time low. Fatalism is now the dominant mood and the main barrier to fighting back.

To some the stagnation of trade unions is often explained in terms of bureaucratization and the thin democracy characteristic of unions (even though relative to other institutions, unions democracy still compares very favorably). But as significant as such aspects are, they do not get to the core of the 'union problem'. As Steve Tufts and Mark Thomas (2012) noted in terms of their discussion of populism, you can have a very militant and democratic movement but it can also end up being very particularistic ('militant particularism', in the phrase used by Raymond Williams (1989) and elaborated by David Harvey (1996)). Workers can, for example, demand militancy but also insist that their union concentrate entirely and narrowly on defending the workers that finance its operations and not only ignore the plight of other workers such as the poor or new immigrants and even join in the attacks on them. Such sectionalism highlights the fact that though unions emerged out of the working class, they are not class organizations in the sense of representing the class as a whole.

That sectionalism is directly tied to the issue of bureaucratization and limited democracy. If members see their unions as insurance agencies – instrumental organizations paid for by dues – they won't be looking for more participation but only that they get the service 'contracted for'. Correspondingly, leaders don't see much priority in developing and mobilizing the capacities of workers – never mind raising expectations and putting more pressure on themselves – and so look to developing only that level of democracy, tempered by 'loyalty', to achieve a level of gains that doesn't undermine their leadership.

There was a time when that narrow solidarity of unions didn't hinder unions all that much; they made gains and those gains even spread to other workers and the community. But that era is over. The notion that workers can survive and defend past achievements, let alone make new gains, through just looking after their own with no larger understanding of the common attacks all workers face and their mutual dependence on the rest of the working class, is now daily exposed. Absent a class perspective unions can today neither defend their members nor come to grips with how to renew themselves.

Consider organizing. Only a broader sense of building the class will lead to the commitment of resources and voluntary energy to unionize in the present hostile climate. Moreover, making breakthroughs in the new sectors where the majority of workers are now employed is unlikely to occur without cooperation across unions. The present competition for union dues dollars blocks such cooperation and ends up undermining each union. It too can only come from recognizing that the issue isn't the growth of any particular institution – Canadian Auto Workers, United Steel Workers, Canadian Union of Public Employees or Ontario Public Service Employees Union – but that of building the working class as a social force. And it is only when we start from the class perspective that other creative approaches, like bringing individual workers into a union culture whether or not they have a bargaining unit. [5]

Or consider bargaining. In the 2012 round of the Canadian Union of Public Employees (CUPE) bargaining with the city of Toronto, individual CUPE locals bargained with the municipal state. It was obvious enough that the bargaining had ramifications for all CUPE members and of course workers beyond CUPE. Yet there was no explicit acknowledgment that individual locals can't win against the state and that coordination across the union – itself a step towards winning other workers and their communities over - was paramount. A coordinated strategy might have put the library workers, the workers with the greatest support, first out of the gate. It might have then contemplated selective tactical strikes, escalating to mass mobilizations and eventually bringing in the rest of the public sector while also mobilizing the community around the services provided.

The point is that the only way union renewal can happen in the public sector, is to recognize what workers are up against, the extent to which the state's focus is on isolating them, that it is the state itself and not 'an employer' the union is fighting, and *establish itself as the leader in the fight to defend and expand social services*. This is not easy; it requires a transformation of everything about public sector unions. It is not a matter of simply passing strong resolutions and putting up expensive billboards. The public is – understandably - too cynical to be moved by public relations alone.

---

5   The Canadian Auto Workers and Communications, Energy and Paperworkers Union, in preparation for their merger, recently announced their enthusiasm for such an approach. See CAW-CEP, 2012

Rather, it means rethinking union strategic priorities, rethinking the role of staff and their subsequent training, and coming to see union members as potential organizers for moving the public and shifting research and education to that end. It means not just defensively insisting that the public sector is 'good' but also being at the forefront of criticizing its bureaucratization and waste through acting as whistleblowers actively defending the public. And it even means moving to place the level, quality and administration of social services on the bargaining table (in the last municipal strike, for example, might not the municipal workers have emerged more successful, with greater protection for their members, if their primary bargaining demand – the one they might strike for – was keeping garbage services public rather than handing them over to profit-hungry and service-poor multinational corporations?). Finally, it means creatively addressing the contradiction that traditional strike tactics now isolate workers from the public while it is so crucial to win that public over: e.g. dumping garbage during strikes not in parks but on Bay street to make the connection between austerity and finance; continuing bus service but not collecting fares; delivering, as CUPW did in the 1990s, pension and welfare checks even though on strike.[6]

A class perspective is likewise central to union renewal in the private sector. Here the fundamental issue revolves around jobs. The function of unions is to negotiate the sale of labour power yet the greatest concern of workers is something unions have little or no input into – the existence of jobs in the first place. Unless unions can deal with workers' prime concern, union renewal can't happen and even the bargaining position of unions will be further eroded as workers, facing the alternative of indefinite unemployment or a very much inferior level of pay and benefits, end up vulnerable to making concessions in a vain attempt to protect their jobs.[7]

A number of things follow from any emphasis on seriously dealing with the jobs issue. Toby Sanger (2012; this issue) flagged one of them in noting that in not adequately reinvesting its profits in decent jobs, the private sector is openly admitting that it can't provide decent jobs

6   For a discussion of such an alternative strike tactics, which at least set the stage for when traditional strikes become necessary, see Hurley and Gindin, 2012.
7   One particular concession that reflects the logic of thinking instrumentally and undermines even the internal solidarity in unions is passing concessions on to future workers by agreeing to lower wages for new hires (as recently occurred at the Lear Siegler plant in Kitchener). This not only undercuts the union principle of equal pay for equal work but open the way for the next generation of workers using that 'lesson' to in turn betray retirees. And since the very first experience of the very workers on whom union revival will critically depend is to see unionism at its least solidaristic, it virtually guarantees its failure.

for everyone. Jobs must therefore depend on an expanded public sector, including into spaces that were formerly seen as inherently private. That is, it's not just a matter of keeping health care in the public domain and not outsourcing it, but also thinking in new ways about sectors like auto. For one thing, we can't build new alliances if we're calling for subsidies for GM and the rest of the industry while social services are being cut. Moreover, those subsidies won't, as we've seen deliver jobs because productivity in the auto industry keeps rising while the market is limited – and a push for far 'more cars' is also not a viable strategy given the already overwhelming traffic congestion and environmental concerns.

On the other hand there is enormous productive capacity in all of those facilities and worker skills; they can make the widest range of things that we do need. What needs to be placed on the agenda, by unions above all, is the waste of closing them when they could be converted to producing socially useful goods, starting with the environment. Taking the environmental crisis seriously means the entire material foundation of society will have to be changed: the transportation and communication infrastructure, the machinery and tools in every factory, the construction of homes and appliances, offices and equipment - everything.

This means explicitly talking about preserving our productive potential not GM and Ford, planning instead of competition, asking about social utility not profit. We obviously can't win this right now, but it poses the question of how we organize today so this becomes a real option down the road. As radical as this sounds it's worth remembering that in the Second World War, Canada and the US demonstrated a astonishing capacity to convert facilities in a remarkably short time and then reconvert them again after the war.

As fundamental as internal changes are to union renewal, this is only a step to changing the external environment facing workers. And in this regard, we can't just lament the power of the financial system over our lives and occasional shale our fists at them. We need to question why, in an allegedly democratic society, they stand above us – profiting enormously in good times, blackmailing us to bail them out in bad, and always insisting that what is good for banks should frame public policy. If they are in fact to be treated as having the weight of essentially being 'public utilities', they should be taken over and become *democratic* public utilities.

This is not just a matter of ideology; it is a practical issue. If we really want to convert industry, if we really want to defend the public sector, if we want to chart what kind of society we want to have, controlling finance is a precondition. Otherwise, we'll remain in the trap of catering to them and being disciplined by them whether it's in the workplace or in terms of government policy. Here again, taking on such a fundamental part of the Canadian power establishment is not something that will happen just because we assert its need. But unless we begin to talk about it now, educate around it and mobilize for it, it will always be out of reach.

In criticizing the labour movement for its failure to change, it is vital to understand this as being as much a failure of the left itself; the crisis of labour and that of the left go hand in hand. There's a strong case to be made that we will not see a renewal of the labour movement unless there's also simultaneously a renewal of the left. It seems clear enough that in spite of some positive developments, the leadership of the trade union movement has neither the inclination nor capacity to radically transform their organizations while the membership is too fragmented and too overwhelmed to sustain anything but the occasional sporadic rebellion. For rank and file workers to do more will require the resources and support from a left with feet both inside and outside unions that can link workers across workplaces, clarify what workers face and why a class response is critical to what workers now face. What, more specifically, might be done?

One initiative that came out of the crisis was the establishment of the *Greater Toronto Workers Assembly*. It was inspired by two realities. First, that the formation of a new socialist party was simply not on the agenda until a stronger labour base was laid. Second, the fact that, as noted earlier, out of the last comparable crisis – the Depression of the 1930s - a new form of working class organization was born and this pointed to the challenge today. The craft unionism that dominated working class organization at that time was inadequate to what workers faced and in a remarkable act of working class creativity, industrial unionism emerged as a dynamic alternative. Today we need to think just as honestly and creatively about whether unions in their present form are adequate.

It's not that unions are going to disappear; they will continue to soldier on and occasionally demonstrate their potential, but on their own unions are simply not enough to deal with what workers face. *The Greater Toronto Worker Assembly* was an attempt to think about a form of working class organization that could support union renewal but also act beyond unions.[8] It was anti-capitalist, not a coalition but organization of individuals looking for another kind of politics that was class based. It defined class very broadly to include not just the minority of

---

8   See www.workersassembly.ca

workers who are unionized, but the unemployed, the poor, and low-wage non-union workers. And it included all the dimensions of our lives that reflect class outside of the workplace.

One especially important goal of the Assembly in terms of union renewal – one it remains a long way from achieving – was to establish networks of activists across workplaces. This might take the form of fight back committees in every local that are focused on educating their own members, establishing links to the community, and engaging in joint solidarity actions.[9] The role of the Assembly would be to facilitate the formation of such committees, contribute to organizing the cross-workplace educationals and training, hold forums where experiences could be shared and generally support the development of groups of activists who, among other things, would also fight to inject a class perspective into their unions (Gindin, 2012).

Let me conclude with three observations. First, the argument that 'There Is No Alternative' (TINA) is actually true in the sense that moderate options simply can't stand up to what we today face in capitalism. Options have been radicalized and we need to recognize and confidently assert is that *the radical is now the only thing that's practical*. Directly related to this, we now have to *think bigger even to win small*. Even if we just hoped to defend what we have, the lesson of the past quarter century is clearly that tinkering around the edges or being modest will protect us. Either we think more radically and bigger or things will continue to get worse.

Finally, what we face is an *organizational* barrier. If we understand the inactivity of workers as reflecting their fatalism, their sense that nothing can be done, then this can only be addressed by concretely demonstrating the potentials of organized collective action. Workers aren't inherently radical and they're not inherently conservative; they adapt to the structured options they face. Once they are convinced that organizations exist that hold out some confidence that struggle can change things, even if that will take time, workers will be there. It's in this regard that the socialist Left has failed over the last quarter-century, and it is this organizational challenge that identifies the principal current challenge for the left.

---

9   A group of locals in the airline industry in Toronto (including locals from the International Association of Machinists and Aerospace Workers, the CAW and CUPE) have been working together with some other non-airline locals (particularly in the municipal sector) to support each other in conflicts, do joint educationals, and strategize.

REFERENCES

Albo, G. (2012, March 23). *The State and Exists From the Crisis*. Conference Presentation. The Global Economic Crisis and Canada Austerity, Alternate Routes, Ryerson University. http://www.alternateroutes.ca/index.php/ar/pages/view/Global%20Economic%20 Crisis%20%26%20 Canadian%20Austerity

CAW-CEP. (2012, August). *Towards a New Union: CAW-CEP Proposal Committee Final Report*. http://www.newunionproject.ca/wp- content/uploads/2012/08/Final.Report.pdf.

Gindin, S. (forthcoming, 2012). Rethinking Unions, Registering Socialism. *Socialist Register*, 2013. London: Merlin Press.

Harvey, D. (1996). *Justice, Nature and the Geography of Difference*. Oxford: Blackwell.

Hurley, M. and S. Gindin. (2011). The Assault on Public Services: Will Unions Lament the Attacks or Lead the Fightback? *The Bullet*. http://www.socialistproject.ca/bullet/516.php

Panitch, L. and S. Gindin. (2011). Capitalist Crises and the Crisis This Time. In Panitch, L., G. Albo and V. Chibber (Eds.), *The Crisis This Time, Socialist Register* (p.1- 20). London: Merlin.

Panitch, L. and S. Gindin. (2012). *The Making of Global Capitalism: The Political Economy of American Empire*. New York: Verso.

Rosenfeld, H. (2012, March 23). *CAT Closure: What Have We Lost? What Can We Learn?* Conference Presentation. The Global Economic Crisis and Canada Austerity, Alternate Routes, Ryerson University. http://www.alternateroutes.ca/index.php/ar/pages/view/Global%20Economic%20 Crisis%20%26%20Canadian%20Austerity

Sanger, T. (2012, March 23). *Public Finance, Pensions and P3's*. Conference Presentation. The Global Economic Crisis and Canada Austerity, Alternate Routes, Ryerson University. http://www.alternateroutes.ca/index.php/ar/pages/view/Global%20Economic%20 Crisis%20%26%20 Canadian%20Austerity

Stanford, J. (2012, March 23). *Canadian (Non)Exceptionalism: Crisis, Recovery, Austerity*. Conference Presentation. The Global Economic Crisis and Canada Austerity, Alternate Routes, Ryerson University. http://www.alternateroutes.ca/index.php/ar/pages/view/Global%20Economic%20 Crisis%20%26%20Canadian%20Austerity

Thomas, M.P. and S. Tufts. (2012, March 23). *Uneven Worker Power and the Populism-Austerity-Labour Nexus*. Conference Presentation. The Global Economic Crisis and Canada Austerity, Alternate Routes, Ryerson University. http://www.alternateroutes.ca/index.php/ar/pages/view/Global%20Economic%20 Crisis%20%26%20Canadian%20Austerity

Williams, R. (1989). *Resources of Hope*. New York: Verso.

Reviews

Book Review

Activism That Works

edited by Elizabeth Whitmore, Maureen G. Wilson, and Avery Calhoun. Halifax and Winnipeg: Fernwood Publishing, 2011. $19.95 CAN, paper. ISBN: 978-1-55266-411-7. Pages: 1-184.

Reviewed by Christine Pich[1]

Activism that Works provides an important empirical and collaborative contribution towards literature on action research and social justice activism. In raising the key question – "[h]ow do we know when we're making a difference?" (p.7) – the editors, through part of a larger collaborative project with nine social justice-oriented organizations, challenge us to think about what it means to be successful in activist work that contributes, in a broad sense, towards social change oriented by "social or environmental justice" (p.8). In partnering with a range of diverse organizations throughout Canada – such as *Oxfam Canada*, the *Calgary Raging Grannies*, and the *Social Justice Committee* – an aim of this book was to provide activists from these organizations the opportunity to reflect upon their work in terms of what factors they believe constitute effectiveness and success, and how they know that they are making a difference. It is in this regard that terms such as 'activism' and 'success' take on broad and encompassing conceptual meanings. For example, 'success' is understood as that which is "described by activists themselves reflecting on their own work" (p.8). This relates to the central theme of the book, that is, in attempting to understand what constitutes 'successful activism' in complex contexts, there is no 'right answer' or 'best practice' when undertaking social justice oriented work. It is in this regard that the editors challenge how success is commonly perceived in terms of linear and tangible outcomes. In contrast, the editors encourage us to think about success on a different scale through the everyday work and successes experienced by a wide range of people (paid workers, volunteers, members of the community) involved within these organizations.

The book is organized with the majority of the contents constituting stories from the organizations themselves (in no particular identified order), and with the editors writing the introductory and concluding

---

1   Christine Pich is a Ph.D. student in the Department of Sociology and Anthropology at Carleton University in Ottawa. Her research interests are in the areas of occupational health, work and labour.

chapters. It is within the chapters written by the editors that the theoretical and methodological focus is discussed. Within the introductory chapters they highlight the difficulties posed by neoliberal capitalism towards activist work. In this regard, they point to the potential of "emancipatory social inquiry" (p.20) in terms of collaborative work between researchers and social movements, and the knowledge co-produced from such efforts. To frame this discussion, they briefly draw upon the work of Antonio Gramsci (structural and conjunctural analysis; ideological hegemony), Paulo Friere (conscientization; praxis; participatory action research), and George Smith (political activist ethnography). In the concluding chapters, the editors elaborate upon complexity theory, with particular reference to the work of Brenda Zimmerman (2000). This theory is understood as "a loose network of ideas, a set of mental models" (p.155) which challenges "linear, mechanistic ways of thinking" (p.155) that are outcome-oriented. The theoretical works drawn upon, especially the introduction of complexity theory, provide an intriguing framework towards understanding the complexities of 'successful activism'. However, a tension in this regard was that they were only briefly drawn upon. It would have been interesting to delve into further discussion of, and identify any potential tensions between, the theoretical approaches.

Through the use of an Appreciative Inquiry (AI) lens emphasis is cast upon success and positive experiences, as well as the data sources generated, take a narrative form. This approach is well suited to frame the range of stories of what success means. For example, the *Disability Action Hall* considers successful features of their work to include building a "sense of community, sense of pride and culture" (p. 53), while the *Calgary Raging Grannies* highlight the ability to attain media coverage and energize themselves and others through humour and catchy songs.

The main contribution of this book is that it highlights how, even in a hostile neoliberal capitalist climate, successes of varying degrees are experienced within the *processes* of working on social justice issues and that important work is being done on a day-to-day basis in this regard. This is particularly important as it challenges the contemporary orientation of many funding sources in their measures of 'success' wherein focus tends to be on readily identifiable results and quantitative reporting mechanisms. In addition, through the involvement of various organizations, this book provides the space for activists to tell their own stories with through creative means, such as a comic book style format in the chapter by the *Youth Project*.

While providing important contributions, the main tension with the book stems from the framing of some key concepts – such as activists, social movements, and social justice – which could have benefited from a more elaborated conceptual analysis as they were quite broad and encompassing. While the intent may have been to provide generous conceptual framings, more discussion towards the potential benefits and limitations of this approach would have been useful. In addition, while the focus of the book is on 'success,' and the AI approach is suitable toward achieving this aim, the editors note the assumption "that something works in every organization" (p.24). It would have been useful to provide some discussion of what would be considered as falling outside of notions of success and positive work. Furthermore, while the editors introduce the organizations they have worked with within this project, what remained to be more clearly addressed is the methodological rationale for identifying and working with these particular organizations and not others.

Overall, Whitmore et. al.'s edited book provides an important collaborative space for multiple voices to creatively share and reflect upon what they understand as effectiveness and success and the importance of recognizing everyday successes that do not neatly fit into concrete outcomes. With its creative and accessible style and structure, this book will be of particular interest for researchers who work in researcher-community collaborative projects with the aim to co-produce knowledge, as well as a more general public and activist audience.

Book Review

Canada and Israel: Building Apartheid

by Yves Engler. Winnipeg: Fernwood Publishing, 2010. $15.95 CAN.
ISBN: 978-1-55266-355-4. Pages: 1-168.

Reviewed by Natalie Spagnuolo[1]

Canada's policy towards Israel constitutes a minefield of contentious issues which historians of Canadian foreign relations seldom directly address. Among the accounts that are most visible, few diverge from the nationalist narrative that represents Canada as historically favouring peace-keeping over militarism. This positive portrait of Canada, as suggested by Paul Heinbecker and Bessma Momani's, compliments a somewhat more critical stance that imagines Canada's role as a less consequential, neutral player in Middle East affairs.[2] In *Canada and Israel: Building Apartheid*, Engler problematizes the claims of current analysts, such the former Canadian Ambassador to Israel Michael Bell,[3] who would like to see greater Canadian involvement in the Middle East. Engler takes issue with the perception of Canada's suitability as an "honest-broker" in the Israel-Palestine conflict. He argues that a consistently pro-Israel attitude has characterized Canada's foreign policy towards the conflict from the nineteenth century onwards. Perhaps no other study makes as strong a claim as Engler does for historical consistency in terms of Canadian complicity in the Zionist expansion of Jewish settlements.

Building on the foundation of leftwing revisionist readings of Zionism as a form of colonialism, Engler implicates Canada in the controversial expansion of the state of Israel and the current Apartheid conditions by considering the domestic and international events that have supported these developments. Following a tradition that traces Canadian interest in the region back to the anti-Semitic Christian political

---

1   Natalie Spagnuolo completed an MA in History at Carleton University where her thesis examined literary processes that played a role in shaping the sociopolitical context that fostered the rise of Zionism. Currently a Ph.D. candidate at the Department of Comparative Literature at the University of Toronto, her research project is on the attempted desexualisation of developmental (dis)ability through literature and images.
2   Heinbecker, P. and B. Momani (Eds.). *Canada and the Middle East: In Theory and Practice.* Waterloo: Wilfred Laurier University.
3   Bell, M., M. Malloy, D. Sultan and S. Shaker. Practitioner' Perspectives on Canada-Middle East Relations. In Heinbecker, P. and B. Momani (Eds.). *Canada and the Middle East: In Theory and Practice* (pp.7-24). Waterloo: Wilfred Laurier University.

culture of the nineteenth century, the first chapter of this book attempts to develop a historical trend by assuming continuity between disparate time periods. Engler represents the general tone of entire decades with single statements that demonstrate a "fortuitous political climate" for the Federation of Zionist Societies of Canada (p.13). Considering the scope of the study, these leaps are likely made to allow Engler to address the present-day consequences of Canada's support for Israeli expansionism. Nevertheless, his less-than-precise treatment of Zionism conflates various versions of the movement and misleadingly overlooks participation by Canadians in anti-expansionist Zionist organizations, such as the Union of Progressive Zionists (UPZ).

Engler's larger point is that historically, Canadian society has facilitated Israel's expansion by conjuring its own justifications for sustaining nationalist aggression, and not by simply borrowing the arguments of political Zionists. Through salient case studies, he highlights some of the advantages that Canada has gained throughout various stages of its support for Israeli expansionism, including such economic benefits as might result from the sale of weapons by Canadian manufacturers to Israeli buyers (p.10). A more thorough exposition of this thesis occurs in chapters 2, 3 and 4, which focus on the ways in which Canadian policy has been influenced by broader international relations and a tendency to remain "preoccupied with the great powers," namely Britain and America (p.24). However, Engler derives this trend from a reading of various media sources without comparing coverage of events, and this, along with his reliance on secondary sources that are often considered polemical, detracts from the credibility of this section. His humanitarian convictions and his motivation to mould his argument along these lines leads to a somewhat univocal interpretation of events. By not considering the subjectivity of his own accounts, Engler consistently eschews the academic integrity necessary to persuade opponents of this perspective.

These early chapters are balanced with a final section that is derived from a leftist, politically-conscious reading of present-day Canada. More convincingly, chapters 5 and 6 document how Canada's supportive attitude for Israel has been consistent with the activities of intelligence agencies, lobby groups, and major Canadian corporations and charities. Engler exposes aspects of Canadian society that function to directly support Israel's expansion but which are, interestingly enough, unknown to most Canadians, supporting the idea that "Israel is highly dependent on North American financial, military, ideological and diplomatic support" (p.145). Key to Engler's claim is the connection he draws between the charitable status granted to Israeli expansionist organizations in Canada, such as the Jewish National Fund, and the support for Canadian industries active in Palestinian territory that falls beyond the Green Line.

Engler suggests the anti-Semitic nature of explanations exaggerate the role of Canada's Jewish communities. Carefully distinguishing between anti-Semitism and anti-Zionism in chapter 9, he highlights the extensive efforts of anti-Zionist Jewish organizations and warns against the use of anti-Semitism to discourage anti-Zionist values (p.146). Canadian complicity in Israel is, according to Engler, the outcome of a discourse that has developed while most Canadians have been "shut-out of the discussion" (p.147).

This political commentary is supplemented with Engler's own experience as a political activist. His skill in researching economic connections to foreign policy (see his *Black Book of Canadian Foreign Policy*) lends this book greater weight as a counter-narrative, despite his failure to follow academic conventions. Throughout *Canada and Israel*, Engler insists that the relevancy of the current conflict in Palestine and the suffering of Palestinians must be defended based on Canada's role in that conflict and "Canadian complicity with that suffering" (p.142). According to Engler, failure to adequately defend the prioritization of this issue to Canadians will not only sideline the problem but will risk insinuating anti-Semitism (p.142). Ingraining his argument in the thick fabric of controversy, Engler's book is a welcome contribution to the sparsely populated field of critical studies of Canadian-Israeli relations.

Book Review

Debt, the IMF, and the World Bank: Sixty Questions, Sixty Answers

by Eric Toussaint and Damien Millet. New York: Monthly Review Press, 2010. $17.95 US. ISBN: 978-1-58367-222-8. Pages: 1-361.

Reviewed by Jillian L. Curtin[1]

In their book, *Debt, the IMF, and the World Bank: Sixty Questions, Sixty Answers*, Eric Toussaint and Damien Millet provide an extensive overview of the impact that debt has on highly indebted poor countries (HIPCs). They show how debt inhibits HIPCs from investing in infrastructure, health, education, and other development-oriented social-policies. The problem, they argue, is not just debt itself, but the capitalist global economic system that fuels it. This process contributes to an endless cycle of poverty and human suffering.

The book is written for a general audience. It is organized in a way that showcases the causes of the cyclical debt crisis, the major actors involved, and ways of addressing the problems. It is especially proficient in outlining how private actors in the global financial system have had a negative impact on HIPCs. Throughout the book Toussaint and Millet display Marxists overtones. Their critique of the global financial system and the exploitive nature of the global trade system is accurate. They provide some "radical alternatives" to the current, broken system. However, many of their ideas are not overly radical. For example, their argument focusing on the elimination of structural adjustment programs (SAPs) is in line with many other experts in the field. In fact, this discussion on SAPs is the highlight of the book.

Toussaint and Millet give an in depth explanation of the role SAPs have played in this debt crisis. They describe them as entities geared toward developing institutions and policies to allow private foreign investment into countries. This process shapes the structure of the domestic political economic policy in debtor countries. It gives lenders

---

1   Jillian Curtin is currently completing her Ph.D. in Political Science at Carleton University, with a focus on political economy. She specializes in governance of the global economy and the politics of private enterprise. She is also the co-founder and content manager of *Discourse Magazine*.

the ability to control indebted countries through conditionality which has helped to create a system of dependence, exploitation, and indirect rule. The use of SAPs not only interferes with sovereignty but implies that some countries lack the ability to rule themselves. Toussaint and Millet argue that any lending should consist of a simple transaction in which the lender provides money solely on the condition that the debtor will pay it back. Conditions should not be applied. It is difficult to disagree with this position.

Interestingly, Toussaint and Millet do not call for the abolition of lending and debt all-together. However, they do argue against usury. They claim that private banks and investment houses in the global north have been making "easy money" off of the global south. These countries have paid back their debts – many times over – but the interest in some cases is so high that an endless cycles of debt ensues.

They also argue against certain foreign "investment" in HIPCs. They believe that often this "investment" is a cover which allows wealthier countries to take HIPCs' natural resources without sufficient financial compensation. This has had profound ecological and economic consequences for HIPCs and is why the shift toward Chinese investment – even though China infringes less on sovereignty – Is simply exchanging one resource exploiter for another. They articulate that the process of external loans in exchange for resources does not help a HIPC establish long-term human and/or economic development. It is the conditions under which lending and debt are currently conducted which is the crux of the problem.

One problem with this book is the way in which it answers its own questions. While they ask some great questions, often their answers could be further unpacked. For example, in addition to their argument on how debt has redistributed financial resources from important social policies like health and education they make some important points about the impact of debt on resources and food sovereignty. But, the analysis of these problems is somewhat shallow. More space could have been dedicated to explaining why these areas are essential to meaningful development. The analysis is also problematic when they discuss the significance of self-determination and the right to self-governance. Deeper, empirically grounded examples and a theoretical examination of the consequences of resources depletion and food sovereignty would have added more to their argument and allowed this book to make a deeper contribution to contemporary debates on development and debt.

A second problem is, at several points, the book borders on becoming a polemic. Often the author's choice of words is incendiary. They use loaded language to support their argument in areas where more empirically based explanations are desirable. This detracts from their overall argument. For example, they claim that the debt burden has "crushed all attempts" for HIPCs to develop. In addition to the implication of hopelessness, the tenor of the phrase externalizes the responsibility of development and ignores any complicity amongst the governments of the HIPCs. This is a problem found throughout the book.

Another issue with this work is that their solutions are only partly explained. They argue that much of the citizenry in HIPCs are too poor to formally participate in the market. As such, only governments are able to redistribute wealth and provide the programs necessary for human and economic development. However, they do not adequately address the potential problems of economic corruption associated with authoritarian regimes and shell governments. Their correlation between the elimination of debt and deterring the formation and maintenance of authoritarian regimes is weakly argued.

The rationale Toussaint and Millet do provide – that the immediate forgiveness of debt acquired under dictators would deter external lenders from providing credit to dictators – counters their own call for the abolition of the current risk and confidence-based financial system. This is a logical inconsistency in the book. Government control of economic assets often leads to dictatorships. Toussaint and Millet also fail to explain how wealth will be generated in these countries once debt is forgiven.

Aside from these problems Toussaint and Millet do provide a general overview of how the burden of debt is crippling development efforts in many countries. This is an ongoing crisis that has been overlooked in the wake of the current economic crisis that is preoccupying European and American politics. Their question and answer and answer format makes their work easy to understand. This book provides an enticing argument for interested readers with little to no background in economics, politics, or development studies.

Book Review

500 Years of Indigenous Resistance

by Gord Hill. Oakland, California: PM Press, 2009. $10.00 US, paper.
ISBN: 978-1-60486-106-8. Pages: 1- 72.

Reviewed by Kevin Partridge[1]

Gord Hill originally published this work as part of a revolutionary Indigenous newspaper in 1992 in order to provide a brief history of the colonization of the Americas from 1492. It is aimed at a broad audience of people who are interested in reading a historical narrative that is often suppressed and excluded from many discussions of the colonization of the Americas. It is well crafted for this purpose with its clear writing, brief length and interesting graphics by the author as well as the inclusion of some archival photographs. The arguments in the book are supported by a variety of citations and references that provide the reader with a good grasp of the field of research in which the author is locating his research. However, he does not reference many written sources and the book does not contain the sort of voluminous bibliographic information that is common to books aimed at a more academic audience.

The author claims that this book is just a plain historical chronology, yet it is clearly guided by a theoretical understanding of colonization and historical development that is well developed and considerably at odds with much of history that is written from a Eurocentric perspective. Hill seems apologetic when he writes about his own lack of knowledge of "authentic Indigenous philosophy" (p.5) but he provides a reflexive awareness of his own position as a member of the Kwakiutl (Kwakwaka'wakw) nation on the west coast, as well as his position as a political activist within a globalized system that continues to encroach upon indigenous lands. This is a book with a political purpose and it is useful for its qualities as a polemic and also for its straightforward explanation of the beliefs and motivations that lie behind the strong commitment shown by many people in Indigenous activist communities around the globe.

---

1   Kevin Partridge is a Ph.D. candidate in the Department of Sociology and Anthropology at Carleton University in Ottawa.

This book should not be seen as a corrective to the current mainstream construction of the history of the Americas - a sort of liberal attempt to provide a *balance* of viewpoints - but is instead an outline of a historical narrative that is created from the experiences of people who have often been eliminated from the historical record. The author is particularly interested in challenging the argument that colonization in the Americas is a process that will eventually be of benefit to the colonized as well as the colonizer. He bluntly states that the colonization process has been an "American Indian Holocaust" (p.6) that resulted in the deaths of millions of people and the destruction of entire nations and their respective cultures and histories. He then goes on to provide some of the stories and evidence both of this destruction and the resistance that has accompanied it from the time of the first contact with Europeans to current conflicts involving indigenous peoples. Since the book was originally written in the early 1990s, the conflicts he describes include the Oka confrontation in Quebec, the Lil'wat blockade in BC and an assault on logging operations on Lubicon Cree land in Alberta.

The book is composed of fifteen very short chapters that are organized in a broadly chronological order. They begin with a brief description of the multitude of peoples, nations and languages that were spread over the Americas before Columbus's ship, the Santa Maria, landed somewhere in the Caribbean region in 1492. The four pages allotted to this era is nowhere near enough space to do justice to the variety of histories that Hill is trying to cover but he does convey a sense of the cultural richness of the Americas. Unfortunately, as he points out, there was little understanding of this cultural wealth on the part of the Europeans who quickly grasped the material opportunities to finance their voyages by seizing goods and people using both deceit and superior weapons. This exploitation was rapidly formalized by the creation of colonial administrative structures guided by the expanding economic needs of European imperial countries.

Hill describes almost constant warfare and exploitation of labour, land and resources since European settlers first arrived. These struggles completely alter the social landscape of North America by bringing in people from many other places in the world as well as contributing to the deaths of many millions of Indigenous people, the profound alteration of social structures that survived, and the export of a huge amount and variety of resources. Hill provides a number of examples such as the brutal campaign to seize gold from the Americas for shipment to Spain (p.14). He also argues that there is a parallel history of resistance to these changes. He shifts his focus in the last two chapters to more specific struggles as he cites examples of confrontations at Oka, Oldman River and in the Lil'wat nation in British Columbia to show that Indigenous resistance is still an active and viable force within the political landscape of Canada in particular.

This book was originally written as a response to the 500th anniversary of the landing of the Santa Maria. Hill is presenting a history of resistance to this silencing of voices that is both still present and still relevant within our current political environment. He is successful in putting forward a narrative that illustrates both continuity and complexity. There is no attempt here to create a comprehensive story of the many nations that have been involved in this process and the focus of this book is primarily on Canadian history. Nor is he trying to argue the 'truth' behind the narratives. The length of the book does not allow for a great deal of discussion of the history that he presents. It appears that the point of the book, however, is not just to talk about history but to help change it. This book is successful in contributing to both the political dialogues and the struggles in which it is located. Despite Hill's own doubts about his place amongst an 'authentic' Indigenous philosophical tradition, this book shows that he has a definite and unique contribution to make to that history and this book is useful for those who are looking for alternative historical narratives and for people who may be trying to understand the motivations and understandings that lie behind apparently widely separated expressions of Indigenous resistance that repeatedly crop up in the mainstream news with little explanation. This work is a valuable contribution that could be very useful for teachers, activists and others who are interested in challenging the often complacent acceptance of the colonization of the Americas.

Book Review

Rosa Luxemburg: Ideas in Action

by Paul Frölich, translated by Johanna Hoornweg. Chicago, Illinois: Haymarket Books, 2010. $18 U.S., paper. ISBN 97-1-60846-074-8. Pages: 1-311.

Reviewed by Tiffany Hall[1]

Rosa Luxemburg: Ideas in Action is the intellectual biography of Rosa Luxemburg and her role in socialist party movements in Poland, Russia, and Germany at the turn of the 20th century. Author Paul Frolich sketches a portrait of a woman who greatly shaped the composition and direction of socialist ideology. The author was himself once a member of the German Socialist Democratic Party and, like Luxemburg, was a founding member of the German Communist Party. These positions allowed for an intimate relationship with Luxemburg, giving him access to her incredible character before she died. Frölich combines what few writings of Luxemburg still exist with other personal and political writings from other party members during that time. By doing so, he constructs a vivid account of Luxemburg's progression through the socialist party system up until her murder in January of 1919.

While reading Frölich's book it becomes questionable whether he should have created two separate pieces instead of one: only chapters one and ten speak specifically to Luxemburg's personality and life in a biographical manner. The other chapters, which make up a substantial part of the book, alternatively may have been presented as a history of the socialist party. Several chapters are more focused on the relationships between Luxemburg, Kautsky, Mehring, and Liebknecht, party members and writers who worked closely with Luxemburg and held key positions in the party, and many chapters describe the intricate details large events, such as the Russian Revolution and the First World War. Yet there are few mentions of Clara Zetkin, who was known to be Luxemburg's most intimate friend. Frölich's decision to create the book as it appears is a testament to the dedication of Luxemburg to the socialist cause; separating the two would be disingenuous. Thus, those looking specifically for information on Luxemburg the individual may be slightly disappointed; her life was too much a part of politics to ignore

---

1   Tiffany Hall is an MA candidate in Sociology and Anthropology at Carleton University, Ottawa.

any of her political endeavors in attempting to understand the person she was. For this reason, the book is a much more substantial contribution to understanding the creation and progression of the socialist party.

Due to her role in the changing nature of the party, Luxemburg could not help but have a heavy presence in the discussion of party politics. Frölich's strongest aspect is his detailing of the progression of socialist ideas and movement during the most intense times. For instance, the chapter on the outbreak of the First World War is a substantial contribution to the understanding of the socialist position in Germany and Prussia at the time. Frölich integrates aspects from Luxemburg's writing for pamphlets and articles to highlight the parallels and progression of her ideology. His discussion of her piece *The Accumulation of Capital* reveals Luxemburg's process in her own understanding of Marxism. He describes the effect it had on understanding imperialism and capitalism and how it changed the approach of the party toward policies for the working class.

Although the entirety of the book is informative and succinct, the real beauty of Frölich's writing as an author comes to fruition during the last two chapters of the book; the final two months of the German revolution leading up to Luxemburg's murder. Frölich describes the creation of the "Spartakusbund" and provides many excerpts from the *Rote Fahne*, the journal in which Luxemburg would write for the final time. Frölich points to this time period as the clearest indication of a direct extension of Karl Marx's ideas, particularly the *Communist Manifesto*. This adds greater emphasis on the importance of Luxemburg and her socialist advocacy within historical Marxism.

In final chapter, Frölich reveals the little known facts about Luxemburg's life and character, as well as provides his own opinion on the events leading to her death. The strength of the counter-revolution is seen by Frölich as a 'diabolical plan' in which Luxemburg and her Spartans were deliberately dismantled through political guises. Frölich's witness of the decline in mental health following her weakening physical state provides enough speculation for him to ask whether Luxemburg was the great leader they believed her to be:

> "...did her physical strength simply not suffice for the necessary tasks, or did this great leader, who as a theoretician and as a strategist of class struggle moved ahead with such unshakeable inner strength and tenacity, lack that crowning touch of the party leader who can make realistically sound judgments at critical moments irrespective of his mood

and who knows how to see to it that his decisions are carried out - that crowning touch which became Lenin's second nature. This question, of course, can never be answered" (p.293).

Frölich's question is somewhat sorrowful, as he acknowledges that the events led to the rise of the counter-revolution, and to the eventual rise to power of Hitler in 1933.

Overall, Frölich's piece allows for an extensive yet clear description of the creation of the socialist party in Prussia, Russia, and Germany at the turn of the 20th century. This newly translated edition provides greater detail of Luxemburg's life as well as excerpts from her most influential writings, particularly those that had great impact on the socialist party. Frölich's book provides a significant contribution to understanding the progression of the socialist party and, more importantly, to understanding the role Luxemburg had in advocating for socialism and the power of the working class. Frölich's book is an important historical contribution to Marxist literature and an important tool for understanding past socialist ideologies and the current political landscape.

Book Review

The Devil's Milk: A Social History of Rubber,

by John Tully. New York, NY: Monthly Review Press, 2011. $24.95 US.
ISBN: 987-1-58367-231-0. Pages: 1-480.

Reviewed by James Braun[1]

Drawing upon Marx's famous formulation of commodity fetishism, John Tully seeks to uncover "the whole buried world of social and ecological relations" that have historically constituted the production of rubber and its derivative products (p.359). Rubber, Tully argues, is an indispensable commodity for the industrial age, facilitating revolutions in transportation, sexuality and communications (p.41-45). Its myriad industrial applications and unique properties meant that government and industry were prepared to go to great lengths to secure a reliable supply, abusing workers and ecologies in their wake. From the Amazon rubber boom to the rise of synthetic rubber production in World War 2, Tully documents the history of rubber production and processing "inextricably bound up with the rise of capitalism, imperialism and modernity" (p.345)·

Although Tully presents his book as "a social history of rubber," his methodology focuses narrowly on labour history. From the subtitle, one might expect a comprehensive investigation of how rubber transformed everyday life from the viewpoint of "ordinary" people. The book hints at interesting directions such a history might proceed, but only ever briefly engages with them. The development of the rubber condom and its associated controversies suggests transformations in sexual and religious politics (p.44-45). Likewise, the pneumatic tire had crucial implications for the ascendancy of truck transport over rails, but the political and social contests that facilitated this change are glossed over (p.139-40). The subjects of Tully's history are primarily workers, and their lives away from the worksite are not given much consideration.

Most of the book documents in detail the brutal labour practices that characterized (and continue to characterize) the rubber industry. Wild rubber tapping in the Amazon and the Congo, driven by extortion and

1   James Braun is an M.A. candidate at the Institute of Political Economy, Carleton University. He can be reached at jbraun@connect.carleton.ca.

sadism, was supplanted by hevea plantations and indentured labour in Malaya, Liberia and Indochina, and ultimately synthetic production in World War 2 after Japan captured most of the world's natural rubber supply. His study of rubber production and processing begins with the early industrial revolution in Britain, but is primarily focused on the birth and growth of the pneumatic tire industry in Akron, Ohio. Despite rubber's many applications, this is a reasonable limit on scope; as Tully notes, by the end of World War 1, Akron tire plants processed roughly forty percent of the world's supply of raw rubber (p.138).

His discussion of worker resistance is somewhat uneven. Resistance tactics in Akron, Indochina and Auschwitz are discussed at length, whereas one is left with the unlikely impression that indigenous workers in the Congo and the Amazon hardly fought against their oppression. The methodological challenges of writing history from the perspective of rubber tappers or plantation labourers are obvious; nevertheless, a social history should seek to highlight the agency of its subjects and to make visible the world as they understood it, not to merely paint them as the passive victims of forces from above. Tully makes good use of Tran Tu Binh's memoir, a seminary-educated Communist organizer who worked as a coolie "in order to carry out Communist agitation among the Michelin estate laborers" in Indochina, but such first-hand accounts are exceedingly rare (p.239-40). Innovative readings of other types of sources would shed a much-needed light on these hidden histories, a task crucial to Tully's project.

Among Tully's admirable achievements is to bridge the histories of colonial rubber extraction and metropolitan rubber processing. Imperialism is a key theme of his work; at each stage in the rubber industry's development, political and economic power intertwines transnationally to secure the rubber supply so vital to industrial modernity. Among the more notable examples: British capital and Peruvian desperation to assert sovereignty in the Putomayo valley facilitated Julio César Arana's murderous rubber fiefdom (p.90-100). Leopold II of Belgium's instincts for political aggrandizement and financial enrichment coincide in his reign of terror in the Congo (p.102-103). Strikebreaking tactics developed by Firestone in Akron are used against plantation workers in Malaya (p.273). IG Farben's collusion with the Third Reich creates legal complications for US efforts to develop synthetic rubber during the Second World War, via Farben's agreements with Standard Oil (p.322-323). Throughout this history, capital operates both as a productive and constraining force, both feeding the ravenous resource appetites of metropolitan industry and frustrating the efforts of those who would put a more "human face" on the labour processes involved.

Given the importance of the colonized world in this book, there is space in his analysis to interrogate the coloniality of processes that brought rise to the rubber industry. The narrative he sketches in Chapter One, of rubber as a Mesoamerican article of ritual and curiosity transformed by European science and rationalism into a utilitarian commodity for industry, should be familiar to post-colonialists and other critics of modernity. The foundations of this rationalism have been thoroughly dissected, but Tully does not engage with those critiques. Rubber fetishism is described briefly as a cultural aberration on rubber's march to utilitarian respectability, but could be used as an avenue to explore ongoing affective relationships to rubber (p.45-46). Implicit in Tully's discussion of worker resistance in Malaya is an acceptance of a normative, Eurocentric conceptualization of economic organization. Tully describes how trade unions and strikes emerged from "primitive protests" such as assaults on overseers and desertion, but he misses how this tactical evolution normalizes the relations of the capitalist wage economy imposed by European imperialism (p.260-270).

In some respects, Tully has done for rubber much of what Sidney Mintz did for sugar. In highlighting "the social character of the commodity of rubber," (p.20) he demonstrates the crucial and brutal relationship between the metropolis and periphery that produces industrial capitalism. In other words, metropolitan machinery would not run without a steady stream of peripheral resources.

Book Review

Revolutionary Doctors: How Venezuela and Cuba are Changing the World's Conception of Health Care

by Steve Brouwer. New York: New York: Monthly Review Press, 2011. $18.95 U.S., paper. ISBN: 978-1-58367-239-6. Pages: 1-256.

Reviewed by Rebekah Wetmore[1]

Revolutionary Doctors explores the human needs based health care model developed in Cuba and how those involved are becoming protagonists of social change. Beginning with Cuba's original revolutionary doctor – Che Guevara – readers are guided through the origins of Cuban health care, how it spread to Venezuela and beyond, and the counter-revolutionary response.

Che Guevara's vision of "combining the humanitarian mission of medicine with the creation of a just society" (p.11) is being implemented in Cuba and Venezuela. Soon after the triumph of the Cuban Revolution, thousands of doctors and over a hundred medical professors left the country further weakening their inadequate medical system. The new Cuban government insisted on developing universal health care through adopting a preventative based system, opening a second medical school and creating positions for recent graduates of the University of Havana Medical School in rural areas. Health care continued to improve including through the creation of Basic Health Teams and *brigadistas sanitarias* or health brigades in the end of the 1980's. Every small neighborhood has a Basic Health Team, which includes one doctor and one nurse who live in the community. Not only did this increase community coverage to 99% by 2004 but it also gave residents more of an active role in their health care. Health brigades, made up of residents, assist doctors in prevention programs and public health campaigns. While Cuba created universal health care domestically, they continued their commitment to internationalism.

From Algeria to Angola and more recently Haiti, Cuba has sent health professionals on humanitarian missions for over five decades in response to emergencies and "long-term collaboration in developing

---

1   Rebekah Wetmore is an independent researcher and community organizer. She has an MA in Sociology from Acadia University in Wolfville, Nova Scotia.

another nation's system of primary health care" or the Comprehensive Health Plan (p.45). Along with humanitarian missions, the Latin American School of Medicine (ELAM) was founded in 1998 for students from around the World to study medicine for free. In return, students promise to serve the poor of their country through preventative community health care.

Venezuela's health care was in desperate need of an overhaul as "prior to 2003, there were just 1,500 doctors employed by the Venezuelan government to provide primary care in a public system that had 4,400 offices called *ambulatorios*" (p.85). As a means to improve health care the Cuba-Venezuela Comprehensive Cooperation Agreement, a precursor to the Bolivarian Alliance of the Peoples of Our Americas (ALBA), was signed on October 30, 2000. This agreement allowed for the exchange of goods, services and experts between the two countries with oil as the largest export from Venezuela and Cuba offering human capital through "thousands of teachers, agronomists, technicians and other experts" (p.81). After the failed economic coup in 2002, the government consolidated control of PDVSA, the state oil company, and its revenue, which was used to increase funding for social programs such as Barrio Adentro to address the inadequate public health system. Barrio Adentro has been expanded to include four different levels from preventative primary care, diagnostic centers, updating and modernizing the public health care system through increased community involvement, improved medical technology and the construction of new hospitals, and building new specialized research hospitals for specific areas like oncology, cardiology and nephrology.

Similar to the Cuban model, these missions mobilize community members to be active participants in their health care. If a community wants a Cuban doctor they are "expected to organize a committee of ten to twenty volunteers from the community who would commit themselves to finding office spaces, providing sleep quarters, collecting furniture and simple fixtures, and feeding the medical providers" (p.84). Though Brouwer singles out health professionals as protagonists of social change, community members who support the health programs are also shaping the socialist project. Integrating community members into the system empowers residents while giving them a direct role in shaping their health care and negating top down approaches. In terms of gender, women are becoming empowered through their involvement in health committees to increase their involvement in their communities. A main argument of *Revolutionary Doctors* – that those involved in health care are becoming protagonists for socialist change - can be extended to include all participants of missions or social programs in Venezuela. Not only are Venezuelans taking an active role in their health care but also other missions including education (Ribas, Robinson and Sucre) and local government through communal councils.

Both countries have made huge gains in traditional measures of health care and the social determinants of health but there are still problems internally and abroad. The United States attempts to undermine the new conception of health care through media, laws and aid to destabilizing groups. Domestically, problems include inconsistent coverage in the most disadvantaged communities and the inherited inefficient bureaucracy. Critics argue that Cuba's health care has suffered from a decrease in doctors as large numbers continue to go on humanitarian missions, which pays considerably more than practicing in Cuba. As is set out in the agreement between Cuba and Venezuela and all countries with humanitarian missions, Cuban doctors will leave and host countries must develop self-sufficient health care systems. A common critique is that an insufficient number of new doctors are trained and thus host countries continue to be dependent on Cuban doctors. As a response to potential dependency, Mission Sucre, the program for free university level education, in conjunction with Barrio Adentro, Medicinia Integral Communitaria, "university without walls" (p.15), and ELAM train new medical doctors.

In the end, Brouwer provides a compelling case for the needs based conception of health care, which has improved the lives of the poor around the World. His arguments are supported with the fascinating personal stories that are weaved throughout the book. From medical students studying in Medicinia Integral Comunitaria in the small village of Monte Carmelo to Cuban doctors' experiences in post-earthquake Haiti, there are numerous examples of seemingly ordinary people working to create a better health care system and society. These stories provide hope that there is an alternative to the profit-driven capitalist model of health care and capitalism in general.

Book Review

Mexico's Revolution Then and Now

by D. Cockcroft. New York: Monthly Review Press, 2010. $14.95 US, paper. ISBN-13: 978-1-58367-224-2. Pages: 1-160.

Reviewed by Naomi Alisa Calnitsky[1]

In *Mexico's Revolution Then and Now,* James Cockcroft interrogates the parallels between the Mexican Revolution of 1910-17 and current political conflicts in Mexico. He explores what persuasive ideas shaped and influenced revolutionary acts and the ways in which anarchist ideas and modes of thought were woven into revolutionary action. The author also attempts to provide a critical reassessment of continuities between early strands of revolutionary thought and those that persist, however embattled, in Mexico today.

In his first published book in 1968, *Intellectual precursors of the Mexican Revolution, 1900-1913,* Cockcroft explored the ideas which shaped revolution in Mexico. *Mexico's Revolution Then and Now* is a welcome addition to existing literature on Mexican revolutionary ideology, relevant for its assessment of the ways in which revolutionary ideas have shaped contemporary resistance movements. Cockcroft highlights *Magonistas'* influence upon the revolution, including their ideals of anarcho-communism and socialism. Scholars such as John Mason Hart have explored the critical role played by Ricardo Flores Magon as an organizer of a "pro-democracy movement" in Mexico from the 1890's through to 1910. Hart's emphasis upon the instrumental ideological work carried out by the Partido Liberal Mexicano (P.L.M.) mirrors Cockcroft's assessments of the movement. Cockcroft draws our attention to the "lessons and legacies" of the revolutionary period, illuminating present-day asymmetries and inequalities. In Mexico, for example, the minimum wage remains the "weakest" across Latin America.

Revolutionary struggles in contemporary Mexico enrich the narrative, which intertwines past and present. Cockcroft affords considerable attention the Oaxacan-born revolutionary, Ricardo Flores Magón,

---

1   Naomi Alisa Calnitsky is a Ph.D. candidate in the Department of History at Carleton University, Ottawa. She received an MA in History from Otago University in New Zealand, where she specialized in Pacific Island seasonal migration to New Zealand. Her doctoral thesis research seeks to enhance the voices of Mexican migrant workers in Canadian labour history narratives. She currently lives in Montreal, Quebec.

and the anti-imperialist Mexican Liberal Party. In 1906 the P.L.M. disseminated an agenda for radical agrarian reform for communities dispossessed of lands and set out clauses to protect indigenous peoples. Significantly, Cockcroft weaves in the revolutionary contributions and sufferings experienced by *Magonista* women (e.g. Margarita Ortega), redressing the paucity of historical attention devoted to Mexican women involved with the *Magonista* movement.

Cockcroft links revolutionary-era struggles to present-day labour conflict. The author emphasizes the *Magonistas'* goals of human emancipation and social justice and the role of the P.L.M. in co-ordinating a series of strikes prior to the Revolution and the repression faced by those who joined its ranks. Cockcroft flags persisting labour violations as key sites of contemporary struggle. Of note are conflicts between working people's rights and American, as well as transnational, companies based in Mexico from Anaconda Copper at Cananea to Continental Tire in El Salto. The current political scene in Mexico is assessed as wholly neoliberal and corrupt, poverty is viewed as generated (rather than worsened) by neoliberal policy, and mass emigrations and union-busting considered normalized features of Mexican life. The militarization of the Mexican border control, which increased under the Obama administration, and consolidation of contemporary imperialism, particularly in oil, feature in Cockcroft's intrepid work. Cultural items are treated in connection with the economy, including for instance, the dual monopoly over Mexican television which operates under the "iron control" of two Mexican billionaires.

Mexico's uneven economic development is counterbalanced with the Magonista era in which it was believed that the means of production were in need of a re-ordering. The Revolution and its aftermath are deconstructed to their very core through a wholly economic analysis rooted in a social history approach. The ascent of the Mexican bourgeoisie in the twentieth century is charted and the "institutional" revolution is exposed as counter-revolutionary, antagonistic to the interests of most Mexicans. Labour concerns remain at the heart of *Mexico's Revolution, Then and Now*, which unearths contemporary popular uprisings against neoliberalism in the face of state-led, patriotic pacification campaigns that emphasized the "glorious Revolution" and championed Mexican identity through the celebration of public art. While the study does not go to great lengths to enrich our understanding of the revolutionary period, it does a fair job at emphasizing the ideological contributions made by Magon and his followers.

Cockcroft assesses the Cárdenas administration as fraught with holes: during this time millions of hectares of land were transferred to peasants, yet best quality lands remained in the hands of twelve mostly foreign-owned corporations, enabling *neolatifundismo* to dominate Mexican agriculture in ensuing decades. The abandonment of revolutionary ideals and political corruption are key themes. His immiseration thesis identifies N.A.F.T.A. as responsible for Mexico's dramatic loss of self-sufficiency in agriculture. Neoliberal trading schemes are treated as naked imperialism. In spite of Mexico retaining state-owned resources such as oil, PEMEX profits have not trickled down to the population and this state-owned company continues to fuel American consumption. As in *Mexico's Hope* (1998), Cockcroft is tuned into Mexico's most recent social conflicts.

Cockcroft believes that, while population growth does not create immiseration, in reality it has more to do with how capitalism operates. Cockcroft credits injustices perpetuated upon the people to right-wing decision-making, and the book is concerned more with explaining current social ills facing the nation than with actually revisiting the revolutionary period. It emphasizes, for example, the high proportion of indigenous people and languages still present in Mexico and the spread of neo-Zapatismo from Chiapas to other indigenous communities. Resistance strategies are presented, for example the modern-day "sit-in" (*plantón*) of *Adelitos* and *Adelitas* advocating fair politics (actions taken by a female-led labour solidarity movement for *maquiladora* workers). Modern attempts to reinstate political democracy are emphasized, including the neo-Zapatistas who champion *Tierra y libertad* (a Magonista slogan) and continue to maintain autonomous "Good Government" municipalities. Women's issues are not ignored in this work. The author's critiques of transnational capitalism's inherently exploitative character refresh our understanding of current crises facing Mexico, offering a relevant and necessary contribution and critical manifesto for change. Perhaps lacking for not sufficiently engaging with the views of Mexicans on their own revolutionary past and current predicament, Cockcroft's diligent and methodical work remains radical in nature and should be considered required reading for all those interested in gaining a better understanding of Mexico today.

Book Review

The People's Lawyer

by Albert Ruben. New York: Monthly Review Press, 2011. $17.95 US
paper. ISBN: 978-1-58367-237-2. Pages: 1-200.

Reviewed by Rania Tfaily[1]

"My job is to defend the Constitution from its enemies. Its main en-
emies right now are the Justice Department and the White House."
(Bill Goodman, Legal Director of the Center for Constitutional
Rights, 2001)

For about five decades, the Center for Constitutional rights (CCR)
has waged significant legal, educational and public awareness battles to
defend marginalized communities and to uphold rights guaranteed by
the U.S. Constitution and the Universal Declaration of Human Rights.
Since its inception, it was dedicated to progressive politics, social justice
and social change. It branded itself as being in the service of the people's movements whether it is civil rights, women's rights, war against
Vietnam, and more recently campaigns against torture, renditions and
indefinite detention. The CCR cases often set legal precedents. However,
the impact of the CCR varied with times. During the 1990s, it suffered
from a financial crunch that intensified tensions between the board and
staff. These tensions which have been brewing for a number of years culminated in the staff's seven weeks long strike. After a period of decline,
the CCR saw its fortunes and profile increase following 9/11 and the
war on terror which resulted in human rights violations of thousands of
Arabs and Muslims.

The Center's decision to defend the right to *habeas corpus* of Guantanamo detainees was a turning point given that the CRC often focused
on civil cases, and it tended to represent people with whom it usually
shared a common (leftist) political vision. The CCR's decision to take on
the government of the U.S. during a time of high patriotic fever was not
without its risks, and a number of individuals and organizations with-
drew their financial support. After a definite defeat in two lower courts,
the Center's legal effort culminated in a surprising and significant win in

1   Rania Tfaily is an Assistant Professor of Sociology in the Department of Sociology and
Anthropology at Carleton University, Ottawa.

Rasul vs. Bush in which the U.S. Supreme Court ruled 6 to 3 that Guantanamo detainees have the right to access the Federal Courts. The CCR's budget rose from $1.2 million in 2001 to $5.5 million following this crucial victory.

Albert Ruben takes us through a condensed history of the CCR, from its humble beginnings to help lawyers in the South who were challenging racial segregation and the disenfranchisement of the voting rights of African Americans, to its involvement in women's rights movement, antiwar activism and more recently its defense of victims of the war on terror. Ruben shows how the CCR pioneered the creative use of the law by adopting novel and often untested arguments to launch legal battles along with educational campaigns with the purpose of facilitating social change. The CCR defined success not only in terms of winning cases and setting legal precedents but also in terms of its ability to raise public awareness and galvanize social movements.

Ruben provides us with detailed synopsis of the lives of the Center's four founding fathers – Arthur Kinoy, Morton Stavis, William Kunstler, and Benjamin Smith. He shows the significant impact that a handful of hardworking, motivated and committed professionals and activists can make. Ruben's book includes a detailed chapter about the CCR's most significant cases classified under "international human rights and solidarity", "government misconduct", and "attacks on dissent". It is obvious that Ruben highly values the CCR and the fighting spirits, motivation and dedication of its founding fathers and staff. Nevertheless, he exposes the struggles and the difficulties encountered in running the CCR. He does not shy away from including unflattering characteristics of the founding fathers.

"The People's Lawyer" is a valuable contribution detailing the history of one of the most progressive American organizations. It also depicts work-related challenges that face progressive organizations that do not wish to conform to the capitalist/ corporatist work model. These include monetary compensation, decision-making process, board-staff relations, and gender and generational tensions. The book raises the important question of how best to facilitate social change and whether channeling the struggle through the courts and its lengthy litigation defuses and sets back social movements. On this point, however, it fails to provide a clear assessment and position.

The book is written in a lively and engaging manner. It is definitely an interesting read for lawyers, activists and social scientists. However, the narrative of the book goes back and forth between different time periods and different issues. In addition, it does not adequately address the social, political and legal context that prevailed in the United States at various periods. I would have appreciated a more chronological history coupled with an analysis of whether the CCR's successes in the 1960s, 1970s and 1980s were byproduct of the social and political turmoil engulfing the United States at that time. This is relevant as one ponders the future of the CCR and the ability to challenge oppressive laws through the courts given the changing social and political environment.

The dramatic (and negative) changes in the U.S. justice system have included draconian sentencing, expansion of state surveillance, increased prosecutorial power and particularly diminished judicial authority and oversight. The increase in the power of prosecutors (often at the expense of judges) coupled with draconian sentencing means that the accused (often poor and marginalized) are almost always compelled to accept plea bargains even if they were innocent since the consequences of convictions are severe. About 90% of criminal cases end in plea bargains without trials. Recent journalistic articles in the New York Times and the Washington Post paint a very dim picture of the U.S. justice system which is characterized by concealing exculpatory evidence, framing and entrapment, evidence manipulation, incompetent and flawed forensic analysis, and prosecutorial misconduct. As we contemplate the future of progressive organizations such as the CCR, it is important to take into account that the U.S. Justice system is becoming increasingly repressive and that it is becoming harder to achieve significant social change through the courts.

Book Review

Broke but Unbroken: Grassroots Social Movements and Their Radical Solutions to Poverty

by Augusta Dwyer. Winnipeg: Fernwood Publishing, 2011. $19.95 CAD paperback. ISBN: 9781552664063. Pages: 1,169.

Reviewed by Sabrina Fernandes[1]

In *Broke but Unbroken*, Augusta Dwyer uses journalistic narratives to describe and examine stories of struggle, despair and success about four social movements: the Landless Rural Workers Movement (MST) in Brazil, the Peasant Union of Indonesia (SPI), the Indian Alliance, and Argentina's National Movement of Factories Recovered by Workers (MNFRT). The title term "broke but unbroken" provides the synthesis of what the book sets out to do: identify the intersections of hopelessness and hope where grassroots social movements concentrate their efforts on diminishing poverty in a more sustainable and effective way than governments or aid institutions. By collecting personal anecdotes and situating them in the broader social and political context of social movement struggle against capitalism and globalization within their countries, she connects the four movements as they work towards what Dwyer refers as imagining grassroots solutions to their daily struggle while promoting sustainable alternatives to problems created from local and global sources as a way to fight poverty rather than simply coping with it.

A major theme throughout the book is how the movements are reconfiguring the way poverty has been approached by policymakers and aid institutions. Dwyer emphasizes that the tactics of grassroots social movements are often misunderstood or misrepresented because of the way Western society has been shaped to think about poverty: as something so complex only elite experts from government or global institutions can manage it. In fact, grassroots tactics are perceived as out of the ordinary because they combine methods of protest and resistance with the search for and implementation of sustainable solutions. One of the

---

1   Sabrina Fernandes is currently a Ph.D. candidate in the Department of Sociology and Anthropology, Carleton Univeristy. Her research interests include Brazilian politics, development and underdevelopment, gender issues, and education.

ways this is done is through decentralized/horizontal decision-making, to which the author credits many of the success stories experienced by the movements. For the MST, decentralized decisions have been fundamental to the maintenance of such a diverse and widespread movement. The support for organic farming, for example, is a solution from below that has enabled MST farmers to keep afloat through small-scale organic production while avoiding the replication of the unsustainable industrial agricultural system they fight against. It is "production based on our values," one member says in reference to the rejection of chemical pesticides and fertilizers while ensuring that members can make a living from farming with fair prices and distribution of land and resources. This is also reflected in the relationship between forest dwellers and the forest in Indonesia.

Education is explored as another common element to grassroots movements' strategies. More often than not, research on grassroots movements highlights how "raising awareness" is a priority but only superficially explores how movements' organizational structure and their educational strategies are deeply entrenched. Dwyer corrects this gap by analysing education as a fundamental strategy of grassroots movements that truly believe in participatory democracy and autonomy. For the MST, education is such an important tool that it has established its own schools, training centres, and universities (p.18). For the SPI, the alliance between students and peasants strengthened their cause. In India, former slum dwellers take the role of educators in order to help others make a living and access secure housing (p. 89). For the MNFRT, education means access to training and information so that every worker has the knowledge to run the cooperatives (p.145).

The book's narratives are well analysed in a critique of capitalism and the impact of globalization on people's right to food, water, housing, and job security are also complemented with secondary literature. These include references made both by Dwyer and by the movement members themselves demonstrating how grassroots movements perceive the merging of theory and practice to be essential for the creation of alternatives. This shows how these movements' strengths go beyond organizational capacity; an argument she notes has been promoted in neoliberal thought to disconnect poverty alleviation from the need to actually transform political and economic systems. She challenges this view by proposing that, for example in the case of peasant movements in Brazil and Indonesia, "through direct action and the physical taking of land, their members are challenging the definition of empowerment that obscures the material basis of power" (p.78). Instead of promoting "empowerment" through aid, structural adjustments, and even some forms of microcredit, which the author argues do not always address the root of the problem and fail to take into account particular traits of each society and culture (p. 99), grassroots movements link it to changing mindsets, stronger class-consciousness, and the continuous flow of support that comes from community solidarity.

Although it is easy for the reader to get lost in the personal anecdotes of movement members, Dwyer's narrative style is effective because it brings a human face back to the understanding of social movements. By shifting power to those telling their own stories, she creates counter-frames to the ones promoted by opposing politicians and mainstream media. The book shows how it is in fact the innovation behind the movements' methods and the way they reflect the consciousness of the millions of people represented that make the movements capable of building resilience even when it is hard to develop solutions to crises. The author demonstrates this through examples of creativity, solidarity and strength when groups find themselves at a critical point; when it is *sí o sí* (yes or yes), as an Argentine factory worker put it. The combination of inventiveness, optimism, and altruism, which Dwyer successfully highlights, works because it is so novel and unusual to strategies inherent to capitalist dominance associated with conformism to systematic poverty and inequality that it shakes its structures and creates positive new ways of thinking and producing. These alternatives contrast with traditional policies and government initiatives that the movements claim have not provided a long-term solution but simply a way to "manage their poverty better" (p.99).

By presenting four grassroots movements from distinct parts of the world in a unifying way, Dwyer shows that, despite their many differences and peculiarities they share similar strategies, visions, and even transnational networks of support. That is mostly because they share a common enemy centered on capitalism and globalization, although it takes many shapes: agribusinesses, hydroelectric dams, mining, colonial states, corruption, perverse laws, and even conservationists. The portrayal of how movements have confronted these forces shows that, in addition to direct action and similar strategies, it may be necessary to negotiate and compromise in order to guarantee a reasonable outcome for the membership. While Dwyer shows some of these movements' successful stories, she poses the question of whether their methods can be replicated and bring about positive returns in places other than the countries she explores. By interweaving the stories of other, some smaller, movements, she shows that replication is possible though their success can only be sustainable when shaped towards the need of a wide membership, which emerges when the movement favours ideas from below through horizontal decision-making based on collective needs, autonomy, and the principle of solidarity within grassroots organizing (p.21). But the question remains on whether the changes are sustainable. The author argues that as long as the economic system persists in creating poverty, the poor will keep fighting. The analysis of the cooperatives in Argentina demonstrates the constant struggle with cycles of poverty and inequality and how crisis tends to return and create new vulnerabilities requiring movements to maintain their search for sustainable solutions to their problems in a way that prevents community gains from becoming losses.

www.ingramcontent.com/pod-product-compliance
Lightning Source LLC
Chambersburg PA
CBHW020606270326
41927CB00005B/194